THE
NEW
BABY
PLANNER

THE
NEW
BABY
PLANNER

WILLIAM SEARS, M.D.
MARTHA SEARS, R.N.

THOMAS NELSON PUBLISHERS
Nashville · Atlanta · London · Vancouver

Published in Nashville, Tennessee, by Thomas Nelson, Inc., Publishers, and distributed in Canada by Word Communications, Ltd., Richmond, British Columbia, and in the United Kingdom by Word (UK), Ltd., Milton Keynes, England.

Printed in the United States of America
94 95 96 97 98 — 5 4 3 2 1

Unless otherwise noted, all Scripture quotations are from the NEW KING JAMES VERSION of the Bible. Copyright © 1979, 1980, 1982, Thomas Nelson, Inc., Publishers.

Scripture quotations noted NIV are from The Holy Bible: NEW INTERNATIONAL VERSION. Copyright © 1978 by the New York International Bible Society. Used by permission of Zondervan Bible Publishers.

Scripture quotations noted NRSV are from the NEW REVISED STANDARD VERSION of the Bible. Copyright © 1946, 1952, 1971, 1973 by the Division of Christian Education of the National Council of the Churches of Christ in the U.S.A. Used by permission.

ISBN: 0-8407-3489-1

To Our Children
James
Robert
Peter
Hayden
Erin
Matthew
Stephen
Lauren

CONTENTS

PREFACE

Dear Christian parents, whether this is your first child or your sixth, each parenting experience is unique and requires special skills and tools to manage the demands and joys of childrearing. Throughout our twenty-seven years of experience in parenting our eight children, twenty years of experience in pediatric practice, and counseling thousands of parents in raising godly and giving children, we continue to grow in our belief that God has equipped each of us with the necessary love, intuition, and skills to meet our children's needs. Our goals are to help you identify and develop your God-given skills, teach you how to follow your own intuition and respond to your baby's communication cues, and to help you develop a parenting style that utilizes your unique skills and is based on God's plan for you as a parent.

In this book we will take you through the process of developing your own parenting style and then we will walk with you through the first year of your child's life—from pre-birth through the end of the twelfth month, addressing the major parenting decisions and childrearing issues with the goal of developing a loving, mutually beneficial attachment to your child. In growing as parents, you will also grow as Christians. In caring for your baby you will learn about yourself—a growth process that will help you and your baby bring out the best in each other. At the end of your child's first year of life you will have developed a God-intended bond with your child that will be the foundation for your child's development into a loving, mature, and giving child of God.

William and Martha Sears
San Clemente, California
1994

THE
NEW
BABY
PLANNER

CHAPTER ONE

DEVELOPING YOUR PERSONAL PARENTING STYLE

"Will I be a good mother?" "Will I be a good father?" "What type of baby will we have? Will we be able to meet our child's needs even if he or she has many special needs?" "How will our new baby fit into our present lifestyle, and what adjustments are we going to have to make?" "Will I be a godly parent and train up my child in the way he or she should go?"

Every day we talk to parents-to-be about the many questions and fears that accompany the joys and anticipation of childbirth. Each person we talk to wants to do her or his absolute best at raising children. These excited people, just like you, spend hours and hours researching the best parenting techniques, looking for that one method or theory that will make them an expert—the perfect parent.

We are here to tell you that there is no such thing as a perfect parent, just as there are no perfect babies. There are only parents who have studied babies and who have had more experience than you. As we go through this chapter we will discuss what we have found out about parenting in our own research and we will teach you how to evaluate all of the "advice" you will invariably hear about parenting from experts, from members of your church, and from family members and friends. After you have defined what you want your goals to be as a parent, we will help you develop your own parenting style based on your individual strengths and on God's plan for you as a parent.

Before you begin understanding who you are as a parent we want to share with you our favorite and most reliable parenting tip:

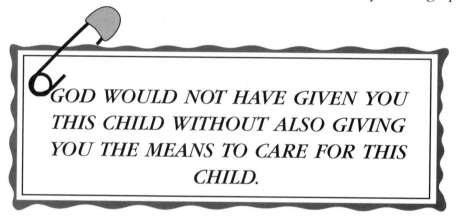

GOD WOULD NOT HAVE GIVEN YOU THIS CHILD WITHOUT ALSO GIVING YOU THE MEANS TO CARE FOR THIS CHILD.

We suggest that you write this tip on a large sheet of paper and tape it on your refrigerator. When parenting times get tough—and they will—keep this tip in mind. There will be times when you will doubt your abilities to be a mother or father and you will question whether the style of parenting you are using is the right one. Just remember that as you are able to give your child life, you will, given the appropriate advice and support, be able to develop a style of parenting that helps you care for your child.

WHY DO YOU NEED A PARENTING STYLE?

As with any task, say building a house or cooking a meal, you need a plan before you begin parenting—guiding principles that will influence every decision you make. If your goal is to build a Victorian home, your plan will include shopping for Victorian-style fixtures and paint colors that will suit your decor. If a low-cholesterol holiday dinner is your goal, your plan will include searching for low-fat recipes. If your parenting goal is to raise a loving, giving child, you will need a parenting style that will give you the best chance of instilling those qualities in your child. If a husband and wife take the time together to develop a parenting philosophy they will be able to address each decision and each developmental issue with unified goals and guiding principles. Their unity in this effort will strengthen their marriage bond, help them feel confident in the decisions they are making, and will in turn benefit their child by presenting a consistent parenting style.

Before we begin identifying your own parenting goals and developing your individual parenting style, let's briefly discuss two major types of parenting styles.

 ## PARENTING STYLES

While there are as many parenting styles as there are parents, we have observed two distinct guiding principles that affect the way most people parent. One we call "restraint parenting." People who are proponents of this style insist, "Don't let your baby run your life," or "Get that baby on a schedule." They issue dire warnings: "You're spoiling her"; "She's learning to manipulate you"; "If you let that baby into your bed, he'll never want to sleep anywhere else." These advisers feel that parents must let their babies "know who's boss" from day one. Many parents are still given this advice. It is important to note that this restrictive style of parenting is a product of early twentieth-century thinking, based in large part on trends in science in the early 1900s. "Modern" mothers tried to follow this advice, and babies were left to cry at night and were potty trained at nine months. Dr. Spock loosened the experts' grip in the 1950s by telling mothers, "You know more than you think you do," but our reliance on professionals continues.

Be wary of restraint parenting advocates, even if they seem to mean well. The advice that babies should be made to adhere to arbitrary rules prevents parents from getting to know their child as an individual. It creates a distance between parent and child and creates a lot of anxiety in parents (and in babies), since babies do not respond well to these kinds of conditions. They do not feel right, and parents and children are often in conflict. Restraint parenting disrespects the biological rules God has built into human fathers, mothers, and babies. Restraint parenting is *not* in accordance with God's design.

DANGERS OF "RESTRAINT PARENTING"

- Parents rely heavily on outside advice.
- Parents become anxious and worried trying to follow the "manual."
- Parents are less accepting of the child and miss out on enjoying his unique personality.
- The child doesn't learn to trust, and has a poor sense of self.
- The child is anxious and hesitant about learning independence.
- As an adult, the child's own parenting behaviors are handicapped.

The other major style of parenting is one that we have concluded is an ideal parenting style that works for most families most of the time, based on our experience of parenting our own eight children, our observations in caring for thousands of families over twenty years in pediatric practice, and our involvement in parenting organizations whose principles we respect. We call this style "attachment parenting." Attachment means that parent and baby are in harmony with each other. Baby gives a cue; Mother, because she is open to baby's cues, responds. Baby likes the response and is further motivated to give more cues (because he or she learns there will be a predictable response), and the parent-baby pair enjoys each other. They get used to each other. We have come to believe that attachment parenting agrees with God's design for parents and children. It is like God's on-the-job training program for new parents, since it uses the baby's inborn abilities—behaviors like crying —to teach mothers and fathers how to respond. Attachment parenting helps Christian parents accomplish what we believe should be the goals of Christian parenting:

1. To know your child
2. To help your child feel right
3. To enjoy your parenting
4. To lead your child to Christ

Notice that these four goals build on one another. Knowing your children will enable you to know how to help them feel right. This will lead them to trust and love you, and this trusting relationship will carry over into their relationship with God. Also, helping them feel right is another way of saying that you are forming their conscience in such a way that they know right from wrong and feel better when they do right. This is another way of leading your children to Christ.

"But," you say, "aren't we supposed to be talking about babies?" Yes, we are. Feelings of trust and rightness go all the way back to how newborn babies are cared for by their parents. The God who makes it easy for us to trust him is a loving God, and parents make it possible for children to trust God if the children have already learned as infants that they can depend on Mother and Father to help them feel secure.

Yes, attachment parenting sounds close and touchy. That's exactly what it is. Getting close to your baby, reading and responding to his or her cues, and growing together is attachment parenting in a nutshell. Ten characteristics of attachment parenting are emphasized during the baby's first year. (All of these ideas will be explored more fully in the chapters to come.) We have found that following these principles gets parents and babies off to a good start.

1. Prenatal bonding
2. A positive birth experience

3. Bonding from birth
4. Breastfeeding with infant-led weaning
5. Prompt responses to crying
6. Sharing sleep
7. Wearing your baby
8. Involvement of father
9. Discipline based on trust and harmony between parents and child
10. Christian commitment

This list of attachment parenting fundamentals, which we will elaborate on in the next chapter, is not given here to make you think that attachment parenting has a lot of rules. Actually, the absence of "rules" (external do's and don'ts) allows the style of attachment parenting to unfold naturally as you develop a relationship with your baby. The baby gives a cue and you respond. When your response seems to fill the baby's need, you both feel better. After many cues and responses, you find that you become very sensitive to your baby. Your intuition is well developed, and the two of you are in harmony. Mothers discover that they love breastfeeding because it has a calming effect on the baby. Fathers enjoy waking up next to a peaceful, well-rested baby every morning. Both parents feel confident, and the idea of letting the baby cry does not feel right to either one. As one father put it, "I'm hooked."

BENEFITS OF ATTACHMENT PARENTING

Baby:
- trusts parents
- trusts self, feels competent
- develops a healthy sense of self
- grows better
- cries less
- learns to give and receive love

Parents:
- become more confident in their God-given intuition
- know baby better
- find discipline easier
- can go with the flow and not worry

Parents and baby:
- experience mutual sensitivity, giving, and trust
- feel connected
- enjoy a flexible parenting style
- have lively fun together
- bring out the best in each other

 AVOIDING *THE SHEEP SYNDROME:*
EVALUATING PARENTING ADVICE

As you develop your parenting style, and throughout your entire parenting experience, it will be important for you to be discerning while listening to parenting advice. Love for your baby makes you vulnerable to any advice that promises to turn out a better baby. And the demand for parent education far exceeds the supply of parenting classes, a fact that opens up opportunities for false prophets of bad baby advice. If you blindly follow false teachings in the field of parenting, you run the risk of becoming a sheep and falling prey to a phenomenon we call "The Sheep Syndrome." When attending a parenting class or being on the receiving end of well-meaning advice, use discernment about whether the advice is accurate, biblical, and whether it fits your individual baby and your family situation. Try these exercises to improve your discernment:

1. Trust your intuition. Remember our first parenting tip: God would not have given you a child without also giving you the wisdom to care for her. All parents, especially mothers who practice attachment parenting, have built-in sensors to what is best for their baby. Before buying into a doctrine of parenting, run it through your internal sensor. You be the judge.

Write down the advice you hear: _____

_____

_____

_____

Does this advice sound right to you? Why? If not, why not? ___

_____

_____

_____

2. Beware of the authoritative approach. Be discerning in classes that offer quick fixes and boast that theirs is the only way or even, presumptuously, "God's way." Complex parenting problems do not have easy answers. Children have such unique temperaments and parents such diverse lifestyles that there is seldom one way to deal with parenting issues. Shun rigid classes; better to choose classes that give you the basic tools on which you can build a parenting style that works for you and your child.

3. Do the class teachings help you develop sensitivity? Our friend Susan was visiting a new mother who was fresh out of a parenting class taught at her local church. Her newborn began crying and exhibiting other hunger cues. The new mother continued her conversation, seemingly oblivious to her newborn's crying. Susan asked if the mother wouldn't rather attend to her newborn. The mother replied, "No, it's not yet time for his feeding." This well-meaning mother was following the dictates of the teacher's manual instead of her God-given maternal instincts. She had become desensitized to her baby's signals and to her own. She had become a sheep, following a blind guide.

4. Check out the teachings with wise parents. Surround yourself with wise and experienced parents. These persons will be your most credible advisers. List your concerns and run them by your advisers: _____

_____

_____

_____

Because parents are so vulnerable and babies are too valuable for you to get advice from only one person, we use this model in all of our teaching. Before our major writings go to press, we run them by wise parents and professionals whom we call our "board of directors."

5. If it isn't working, drop it. Do the teachings draw you closer to your child or create a distance between you and your child? _____

_____

_____

_____

Is your baby thriving physically and emotionally: for example, appropriate growth and development, emotional sparkles, adept at giving cues? _____

_____

_____

_____

Are you growing in your ability to read and respond to your baby's cues or are you becoming more confused? _____

_____

_____

_____

6. Watch for the biblical twist. Do the class teachings fit the Bible or does the teacher twist biblical teachings to fit his or her own preconceived biases? If the teachers are using scripture, do

DEVELOPING YOUR PERSONAL PARENTING STYLE **9**

they apply scripture correctly and in context? Do their teachings square up with the whole of scripture? This is especially true of heavy-handed, spank-controlled dogma that bases the entire parenting philosophy on the rod verses—those Old Testament proverbs that are prone to individual interpretation—or misinterpretation. We recently reviewed a parenting class manual that promotes "parent-controlled" feeding and claimed a biblical basis for this. Not only is there no scriptural basis for this feeding practice, but it is also scientifically unsound.

*7. **What are the credentials of the "shepherd(s)?"*** List them:

_____

_____

_____

Do the teachers have a lot of practical experience (i.e., cared for or parented lots of children)? Have the teachers studied children professionally for many years? Do they seem to be knowledgeable and sensitive? It's okay to be a sheep if you have a wise shepherd. Christ provided such a model—and he had credentials.

Before we take an in-depth look at attachment parenting, let's take a closer look at your own parenting goals.

WHAT ARE YOUR PARENTING GOALS?

When thinking about what they want to accomplish with their children, most people do not first think of what they want to do; rather, they think of what they don't want to do. These "don'ts" are usually negative memories from each individual's childhood. Abusive or unstable parents or uncomfortable worries such as fear of spoiling or fear of manipulation may interfere with your parenting.

List your particular concerns here: _____

_____

_____

_____

If you and your spouse feel that you need some more time to discuss the negatives from your own childhood, by all means do so. Airing all of your concerns with your spouse can empower him or her to encourage you to avoid negative patterns. Take some time to share your concerns with God and trust that God will help you overcome the negative patterns of your past. (Remember our first parenting tip!)

Think back to your earliest memories and what your mother and father have told you about your baby days. What were your parents' greatest gifts to you? _____

_____

_____

_____

What do you wish they had done differently? _____

_____

_____

_____

How was their life similar or different from yours? _____

_____

_____

_____

What stresses would have kept them from parenting as they might have wished? _____

_____

_____

_____

What resources did they have for learning about babies? _____

_____

_____

_____

DEVELOPING YOUR PERSONAL PARENTING STYLE

11

The time when you are pregnant and have young children is a wonderful opportunity to reconnect with your own parents. Talk about your early childhood days with them. Ask what sorts of problems your mother and father faced and what they did to solve them. Respect their decisions and actions, even as you expect them to honor your choices.

A free and open dialogue with your parents and your in-laws will help to prevent arguments and misunderstandings as you care for their grandchild. You may also learn a few valuable tricks of the trade.

After you have fully dealt with any negative patterns that you want to avoid from your childhood, list the positive things your parents did that you want to be sure to emulate. _____
_____
_____
_____

There may have been other people in your life who have made a positive impact on your thoughts about parenting. Take some time to think about these people and the things from their families that you want to incorporate into your parenting style. _____
_____
_____
_____

We all have mental images of what we want our children to become. Perhaps you see a doctor or an artist. We certainly can't control what professions our children choose, but we can influence what kind of character our children develop. In these troubled times, we Christians should be particularly concerned about raising children of character with a strong sense of right and wrong. Take some time to consider the character traits you want to instill in your child (for example: fairness, gentleness, conviction). _____

One aspect of parenting that we often overlook is what we as parents want to get out of the parenting relationship. You may have decided to have children because you wanted someone to play with or someone to nurture. These desires are good and should be considered as you develop your parenting goals. List your personal desires for your parenting experience. _____

_____

_____

_____

After we went through the above steps we outlined these four simple goals for our family:

1. To know our child
2. To help our child feel right
3. To enjoy our parenting
4. To raise a godly child

We wanted to raise trusting persons who had a healthy sense of who they were. We wanted our babies to learn that their small world is a warm and responsive place to be. We wanted our children to operate from an inner feeling of rightness, not from fear or mistrust. We wanted our children to be sensitive to the needs of other persons. From this inner sensitivity we wanted them to develop a spiritual and social conscience: to feel right when they act right, and feel wrong when they act wrong. We wanted our children to develop the quality of intimacy—to learn to bond to persons, not to things. We wanted them to become high-touch children in a high-tech world. We desired well-disciplined children, not children who operated out of a fear of an external force, but rather out of an inner motivation. We wanted our children to have a personal relationship with their Creator in a way that a trust in God became the building principle for their way of life. Finally, we wanted our children to grow and develop to their fullest potential. Whatever gifts God gave our children, we wanted to do our part to help our children develop these gifts.

Take some time to pray together about raising your child, acknowledging your fears and hopes before God. Then review your answers to all of the questions above and write out your parenting goals for your family and for your children. _____

_____

_____

_____

_____

_____

As we mentioned at the beginning of this chapter, we strongly believe that God would not have given you this child without also giving you the means to care for him or her. We also believe that attachment parenting is the best vehicle for accomplishing your parenting goals, utilizing your strengths as a parent, respecting God's design for parenting, and raising loving, giving children of God. Continue on with us to the next chapter as we further explore the fundamentals of attachment parenting and its benefits for you and to your child.

CHAPTER TWO

ATTACHMENT PARENTING

We cannot emphasize it enough: We believe that attachment parenting is the style that most closely follows God's design for parents. We believe that God gave cries to babies, enabling them to communicate with us, and God gave us parental intuition so that we would respond to our baby's cries and ultimately meet their needs.

Attachment parenting benefits both parents and babies. Children who are the products of attachment parenting are trusting. Because they feel secure inside, they are easy to discipline. They want to please their parents and are sensitive and loving toward others. When they grow up and become parents, they have good models to follow. With this style of parenting, mothers and fathers gain confidence in themselves. They know and enjoy their child and have realistic expectations for him or her. They do not have to go looking for advice and discipline methods because they are sensitive to their child's feelings. They even find it easier to share Christ with their children.

It is because of our confidence in attachment parenting that in this chapter we give you an in-depth understanding of this unique, yet natural, parenting style. While this chapter will focus on the general principles of attachment parenting, throughout the age-specific sections of our book we will give you some additional suggestions for applying the principles of attachment parenting to each of your child's developmental milestones. Before we examine the fundamentals of attachment parenting, we must have a better understanding of what it means to be "attached."

UNDERSTANDING ATTACHMENT

You will encounter the term *attachment* frequently throughout this book because, in a nutshell, it is perhaps the most important term in parenting. Write below what becoming "attached" to your child means to you. _____

_____

_____

_____

_____

Attachment is a special bond between parent and child; a feeling that draws you magnet-like to your baby; a relationship that when felt to its deepest degree causes the mother to feel that the baby is a part of her. This is a reflection of how the baby actually experiences existence as one with the mother. This feeling is so strong that, at least in the early months, the attached mother feels complete when she is with her baby and incomplete if they are apart. We will often use the term *mother-infant attachment,* not to exclude the father, but because, at least in the early months, in most families the mother-infant attachment is more obvious. This does not mean that fathers do not become deeply attached to the child, but it often seems to be a different type of attachment—not less or better than the mother's, just different.

Attachment means that a mother and baby are in *harmony* with each other. Being in harmony with your baby is one of the most fulfilling feelings a mother can ever hope to have. Watch a mother and baby who are attached (in harmony) with each other. When the baby gives a cue, such as crying or facial expressions, signifying a need, the mother, because she is open to the baby's cues, responds.

Initially, her responses may be a bit strained and not always what the baby needs. But as the mother-baby pair rehearse these cue-response interactions hundreds of times, after a few weeks or months into parenting this cue-response relationship becomes more natural and harmonious. The baby begins to anticipate the response that his mother will give and becomes further motivated to give more cues, because he learns that he will get a predictable response. Because the baby gives the mother the feedback that her mothering is appreciated, the mother-baby pair enjoy each other more. They get used to each other. One attached mother told us: "I feel absolutely addicted to her"—meaning that the mother feels right when she is together with her baby and not right when separated. This is the level of parenting that we believe God designed for the mother-baby relationship.

You will know when you get that attached feeling to your baby. When your baby cries and you respond from your heart with a natural and not a strained response, you are attached. When your baby gives you a cue and you respond with a feeling of rightness about your response, you are well on your way to becoming an attached parent. Periodically check your sensitivity index. If you are becoming increasingly sensitive to your baby:

- Your baby's cries bother you. You feel for your baby during colicky episodes. You are becoming attached.
- You are determined to work at developing comforting measures when your baby is fussy. You are becoming attached. (If your baby's cries cause a sense of panic or anger in you, you need someone to help you understand and manage your feelings.)
- You are learning to anticipate your baby's needs. A facial expression, such as a grimace, precedes a cry. You respond at the grimace stage before your baby needs to cry. You are becoming attached.
- Your responses are becoming more natural; they flow intuitively. Instead of making a science out of your baby's cries and going through mental gymnastics (Will I spoil her? Is she

manipulating me?), you naturally act and feel right about your response. You are becoming attached.

"It may help us to understand attachment if you tell us what it is not."

Attachment is not being detached or restrained: letting your baby cry it out, fear of manipulation, or lack of confidence in following your own intuition. This restraint approach is the opposite of attachment. Neither is attachment permissive, martyr-mothering, being a slave to your child or allowing the baby to drain and overtake the parents. The child is not in the "driver's seat"; the parents are, because they teach the baby to trust.

Attachment parenting is not rigid. On the contrary, it has options and is very flexible. Attachment mothers speak of a flow between themselves and their babies; a flow of thoughts and feelings that helps a mother pull from her many options the right choice at the right time when confronted with the daily "What do I do now?" baby-care decisions. The connected pair mirror each other's feelings. The baby perceives herself by how the mother reflects her value. This insight is most noticeable in a mother's ability to read her baby's feelings. As Martha observed: "One day I was scolding Matthew and expressing anger. I noticed the forlorn look on his face, and I perceived that he felt I was angry at him instead of at what he did. Whereupon I said, 'I am angry, but I still love you.' He said, 'Oh! really?' He had thought that my anger meant I didn't love him anymore."

Now that we have a greater understanding of what attachment is and what it isn't, let's look at the ten fundamentals of attachment parenting.

FUNDAMENTALS OF ATTACHMENT PARENTING

The following principles are the foundations of attachment parenting. While these principles will apply mainly to the relationship you have with your children while they are young, they will affect and guide your relationship with your children throughout their lives.

1. **Prenatal bonding.** Attached parents pray for and communicate with their unborn child during pregnancy. You might want to try a nightly ritual that we have followed in our own family during Martha's pregnancies. Before going to bed, as a couple, lay your hands on the pregnant bulge that is your baby and affirm your commitment to each other and to the tiny life inside as you ask God to bless baby's growth.

2. **A positive birth experience.** A healthy birth and good feelings about that birth carry over into parents' relationship with their baby. The tools needed for a good birth experience come from careful preparation. How the baby and the mother get started with each other often sets the tone of how this early attachment unfolds. A traumatic labor and delivery where fear and pain predominate or a caesarean birth resulting in the separation of the mother and the baby is not the ideal way to begin parenting. In this case, energy that should be directed toward a mother's getting to know her baby is temporarily diverted toward recuperating and healing.

3. **Bonding from birth.** Immediate physical contact with the baby at birth and continued contact in the first hours and days of life help parents get to know their baby right from the start. The early weeks and months are a sensitive period when mother, father, and baby need to be together. An early and continuous attachment allows the natural attachment-promoting behaviors of the baby and the intuitive care-giving qualities of the mother to unfold. Birth bonding gets the

new family off to the right start at a time when the baby is most needy and parents are the most eager to nurture.

"What if something happens to prevent our immediate bonding?"

Sometimes medical complications keep you and your baby apart for a while, but then catch-up bonding is what happens, starting as soon as possible. When the concept of bonding was first delivered onto the parenting scene twenty years ago, some people got it out of balance. The concept of human bonding being an absolute "critical period" or a "now-or-never" relationship was never intended. Bonding is a series of steps in your lifelong growing together with your child. Immediate bonding simply gives the parent-infant relationship a head start.

4. **Comprehensive breastfeeding with infant-led weaning.** Breastfeeding mothers and babies develop a wonderful harmony with each other, and their physical closeness carries over into the rest of their relationship. Breastfeeding works best when the mother follows the baby's cues and lets the child decide when he has been filled enough by this beautiful relationship and is ready to wean. At this point in our conversation, fathers often pipe up, "We're going to breastfeed!" Breastfeeding is a family affair. The most successful breastfeeding mothers we have seen are those who have a supportive spouse. The benefits of breastfeeding on enhancing a baby's health and development are enormous. But what is not fully appreciated are the magnificent effects of breastfeeding on the mother. Here's what's in it for you: Every time your baby breastfeeds, a fascinating hormone called prolactin enters your system. Dubbed "the mothering hormone," prolactin is the chemical basis of the term

THE NEW BABY PLANNER

mother's intuition. This special substance is a part of God's design as a biological boost to your nurturing.

5. **Prompt responses to crying.** Being sensitive to a baby's cries helps him feel secure because he learns that distress is followed by comfort. As his trust and his parents' understanding grow, he no longer has to cry every time to get his needs met by the people who love him. Reading and responding to your baby's cues is one of the most important right start tips in the overall attachment parenting style. One of your earliest frustrations will be decoding what your baby wants, intensified by the fear that you will misread cues. This is only one of the many "I'm not a good mother" attacks. Guess what? Your baby will help you learn how to be a good cue-reader. Infant-care teachers used to think that babies were only passive players in the parenting game. Now we know that babies actively shape their parents' responses. Here's how: Babies come wired with attachment promoting behaviors (APBs)—magnet-like qualities and behaviors so irresistible they draw the caregiver to the baby, in language so penetrating it must be heard. Some APBs are hard to miss—for example, your baby's cries, smiles, and clinging signals—others are subtle cues, like eye and body language.

Then comes your side of the mother-infant response equation. Every parent, especially the mother, has a built in, intuitive response system with which to listen and respond to the baby's cues. Like a transmitter-receiver network, the mother and the baby fine tune their communication until the reception is clear. How quickly this communication network develops varies among mother-baby pairs. Some babies give clearer cues; some parents are more intuitive cue readers. Good connections will happen, and here are two tips to make them happen: Be open; be responsive. Your baby gives a cue; because you are open and tuned into your baby, you respond from your heart. As all members of the family repeatedly rehearse this cue-response scene, the baby learns to cue better and you learn to respond better. In time you and your baby begin to flow together, developing a harmony between the cues the baby gives and the responses you give. You and your baby get "in sync," the first step toward learning to fit.

"So the advice we hear so often to let our baby cry it out is wrong?"

Absolutely. It's very easy for someone else to advise you to let your baby cry. Those persons are outside of the inner circle of the crying network. Unless they are extremely sensitive persons, nothing physical happens in their bodies when your baby cries. The more nurturing your response is to your baby's cry, the sooner your baby learns to cry better, meaning he or she develops a less disturbing cry, cries less, and gradually learns alternative language. As your baby learns to cry better and you learn to respond better, the whole communication network develops a more natural flow. By teaching your baby to cry better and yourself to respond better, you shape each other. The baby learns to "talk" better, and you learn to listen better. Be open to responding from your heart. When your newborn cries, respond to her! Don't ponder, should I pick her up? Will I spoil her? Is he manipulating me? Just pick the baby up! In time you will be better able to perceive why your baby is crying and how urgent your response should be. Also with time you can gradually delay your response, and your baby will learn to tolerate waiting a bit (when he's not in pain), just as he learns noncrying language and develops self-help mechanisms. One very sensitive and nurturing mother in my practice observed, "My baby seldom cries; she doesn't need to."

> *"How will my baby's cry affect me? I can't stand to even hear someone else's baby cry."*

Good! This means you are a sensitive person; and this quality of sensitivity will be your best friend in your parenting career. Let us get a bit technical for a minute. Your newborn's cry will bother you; it's supposed to. If we were to put you and your baby together in a laboratory and attach blood-flow measuring instruments to your breasts, here's what would happen: Upon hearing your baby cry, the blood flow to your breasts would increase, accompanied by the overwhelming urge to pick up and nurse your baby. Your baby's cry is powerful language designed for the survival of the baby and the development of the parents. Listen to it.

6. **Sharing sleep.** This may strike many new parents as a radical idea, but welcoming a baby into your bed helps him feel attached and comforted all night long. Sharing sleep has benefits for parents, too—including more rest.

   Very early in your parenting career you will learn that babies don't sleep through the night, except those in books or your friends' babies. There may be some nighttime juggling until you find where your baby and you sleep best. Some babies sleep best in their own room, some in the parents' room, and some sleep best snuggled next to Mommy. Wherever you and your baby sleep best is the right arrangement for you. Be open to trying various sleeping arrangements. We suggest you welcome your baby into your bed—a nighttime parenting style we call sharing sleep.

> *"Isn't sleeping with your baby in your bed kind of unusual?"*

Sharing sleep seems to invoke more controversy than any of the other attachment tips, and we don't understand why. We are amazed that such a beautiful worldwide custom is all of a sudden "wrong" for the Western world. Most babies the world over sleep with their parents. And even in our own culture more and more parents are enjoying this sleeping arrangement; they just don't tell their doctors or their relatives about it.

7. **Wear your baby.** Infants need the touching and stimulation that goes with being held. Attached parents use a sling or front carrier to soothe their babies, rather than parking them in swings or plastic seats or bassinets. This is the most exciting parenting concept to hit the Western world in years. As we were researching our top parenting styles of the world, we attended an international parenting conference, where we noticed that mothers from other cultures carry their babies in sling-like carriers that are fabricated as part of their native dress, as if they were wearing their babies. Impressed by how well-behaved these babies were and how attentive their mothers were, we inquired why these mothers wore their babies. They volunteered two simple but profound reasons: It's good for the baby, and it makes life easier for the mother. The light went on. That's it! That's what all parents want—to do something that is good for the baby and make life easier for themselves.

"Does babywearing mean I would carry my baby all the time?"

Not necessarily, but it does mean changing your mind-set on how you regard babies. You may imagine your baby lying quietly in a crib, gazing passively at dangling mobiles and being picked up only long enough to be fed, changed, and played with and then put down again—that holding periods are just dutiful intervals to calm

THE NEW BABY PLANNER

baby so you can put him down again. Babywearing reverses this view. Babies are carried, or worn, most of the time by parents or substitute attachment caregivers and are put down long enough to nap, sleep, and for caregivers to attend to their own needs.

Good things happen to carried babies and their parents. Most noticeably, babies cry less, as if they forget to fuss. Babies who fuss less are more fun to be with. Besides being happier, carried babies develop better, possibly because they divert the energy they would have wasted on crying into growth. Babywearing fits in nicely with busy lifestyles. Mastering the art of babywearing allows you to take your baby with you and not feel house bound. Home to your baby is where you are. Besides, a baby learns much in the arms of a busy parent. A babysling will be one of your most indispensable infant-care items. You won't want to be home or leave home without it.

8. **Father involvement.** Attachment parenting is a big commitment, one that should not be made by mothers only. Babies need loving responses from Dad, too, along with the special comfort and fun only a father can provide. Fathers also help to nurture their babies by loving and supporting their wives. The above attachment styles do not work as well without an involved and nurturing dad. While mother preference is natural to the baby in the early years, the father is not off the hook. The father creates a supportive environment that allows the mother to devote her energy to baby matters. Besides devoting energy to the incessant needs of a new baby, some mothers try to be all things to all people, carrying on busy lifestyles too soon after giving birth. Burnout is most likely to occur in the most committed mothers—you have to be on fire first in order to burn out.

Attachment mothers are prone to the "my-baby-needs-me-so-much-I-don't-have-time-to-take-a-shower" mind-set. A mother of a particularly energy-draining baby once confided to me, "I couldn't have survived without the help of my husband." Take breastfeeding, for example, which is the only infant-care practice fathers can't do. Yet the father indirectly feeds his baby by helping to care for the mother, who feeds his baby. As one involved husband boasted, "I can't breastfeed, but I can create an environment that helps my wife breastfeed better."

"Do you mean that fathers have only a supporting role in baby tending?"

No, although it will probably seem that way in the early months. Fathers are not just substitute mothers, pinch-hitting for the real mother while she is away. Dads make their own unique contribution to the development of their baby. Your baby will not love you more or less than his mother. Your baby will love you differently. Nothing matures a man like becoming an involved father.

9. **Discipline based on trust and harmony between parents and child.** Because attached parents know their child well, they can naturally and intuitively guide him in the way he should go. Punishment becomes less necessary because these children not only want to please their parents, but are emotionally better equipped to accept their parents' guidance as well. Distance between a parent and a child is an automatic stumbling block to discipline.

10. **Christian commitment.** Attachment parenting builds on the love and forgiveness that God has shown us in Christ. The parents' Christian living models this love for their children. As you will see throughout our book, attachment parenting presents a beautiful parallel between the child's relationship with his or her earthly parents and the child's relationship with his or her heavenly Father.

Ultimately, the most important principle is first to get connected with your baby. Take advantage of all the good things that attachment parenting does for parents and babies. Once connected, keep doing what is working and modify what is not. You will ultimately arrive at your own style. This is how you and your baby bring out the best in each other.

There are three major benefits of attachment parenting that we would like to mention: mutual giving, fostering independence, and mutual sensitivity. While we will address many benefits of this parenting style throughout this book, these three benefits are so outstanding they are essential to our understanding of attachment parenting.

PRIMARY BENEFITS OF ATTACHMENT PARENTING

Mutual Giving

"Attachment parenting sounds exhausting. It seems to be one big give-a-thon. What about my needs?"

At first glance attachment parenting may sound like the hardest parenting style, but, in the long run, it's actually the easiest. It is normal to initially feel that attachment parenting is all giving, giving, giving. To some extent that is true. Babies are takers and parents are givers. This is a fact of new parent life. But a concept we want you both to appreciate, and the one we will be emphasizing throughout the entire book, is mutual giving—the more you give to your baby the more baby gives back to you. There are small quiet moments of pure joy when your baby smiles at you or gazes seriously into your eyes. There is wonder in discovering the world anew through the eyes of a child seeing it for the first time. There is peace in knowing that all it takes is your presence, your arms to soothe and calm your baby's fears.

Remember one of the goals we want to shoot for is to enjoy our parenting. Mutual giving is where baby enjoyment begins. Remember, baby is not just a passive player in the parenting game. Your infant will take an active part in shaping your attitudes, helping you make wise decisions and helping you become an astute baby reader. For example, when you breastfeed you hold and caress your baby, you give your baby nourishment and comfort. Your baby, in turn, "gives" good things back to you. Your baby's sucking, together with caressing your baby, releases the hormone prolactin, which further enhances your mothering behavior. The hormones associated with breastfeeding help mothers to feel calm and loving. And parents find that all their giving to their baby matures them and helps them place the different parts of their lives in better perspective.

Here's another beautiful example of mutual giving. When you breastfeed your baby to sleep—a style we call "nursing down"—you give your baby your milk, which contains a recently discovered sleep-inducing substance. Meanwhile, as you suckle your baby, you produce more prolactin, which has a tranquilizing affect on you. It's as if the mommy puts the baby to sleep and the baby puts the mommy to sleep—a beautiful example of how each member of a biological pair helps the other by following a natural recipe in a way that was designed to work.

Another reason why attachment parenting is easier is the way it helps you read your baby. What is "hard" about parenting are the feelings, "I don't know what he wants," or "I just can't seem to get through to her." When you feel you really know your baby and have a handle on the relationship, then parenting is easier. There is great comfort in feeling connected to your baby.

Attachment parenting also leads to a deeper appreciation of how Christ gave himself for us. Christian living is not about serving the self, but about serving others. Having a baby is a crash course in learning to put someone else's needs ahead of your own, and the lessons learned carry over into the rest of your life.

Along with the benefit of mutual giving, we find that attach-

THE NEW BABY PLANNER

ment parenting also leads to a mutual shaping of behavior and personality. After becoming parents, you will never be the same—and you want the change to be for the better. Your baby can do something to you—or better, for you. An example of mutual shaping is well illustrated by how you and your baby learn to talk to each other. A baby's early communication is a language of needs. Crying and smiling are the earliest tools used by your baby to communicate and reinforce your responses to his needs. As you learn and respond to your baby's language, you may feel you are regressing to the level of your baby. You will act, talk, and even think at your baby's level. As you are mastering your baby's language, your baby learns to speak the language of the family. The baby then learns to act, talk, and think at the parents' level. All develop communication skills that none had before. Mutual giving and mutual shaping is what makes attachment parenting so special.

Fostering Independence

"How does attachment foster independence?"

Attachment and independence can be illustrated by what we call the deep groove theory. Think of your infant's mind as a record into which life's experiences and relationships cut deep grooves. Suppose the strength of parent-infant attachment is represented by the depth of the grooves in the baby's mental record. Between twelve and eighteen months, a baby can recall a mental image of the most familiar caregivers. This image helps to provide a secure base so the infant can begin to move more easily from the familiar to the unfamiliar. The mental presence of the mother allows the infant to, in effect, take mother with her as she moves further away from the mother to explore and learn about her environment. The most securely attached infants, the ones with the deepest grooves, show less anxiety when moving away from their mothers to explore toys. Periodically, these babies mentally and physically check in with mother for reassurance and a familiar "It's okay" to explore. The mother seems to add energy to the infant's explorations, since the infant does not need to waste energy worrying whether she is there.

When going from oneness to separateness (a process called "individuation"), the securely attached toddler establishes a balance between his desire to explore and encounter new situations and his continued need for the safety and contentment provided by mother. During an unfamiliar play situation, the mother gives a sort of "go ahead" message, providing the toddler with confidence to explore and handle the strange situation. The next time the toddler encounters a similar situation, he has confidence to handle it by himself without enlisting his mother. The consistent emotional availability of the mother provides trust, culminating in the child's developing a very important quality of independence: the capacity to be alone. (Some detached babies separate too "well", too early. This is different. Babies need to be dependent.) A toddler with shallower attachment grooves lacks confidence that his attachment figures will be accessible to him when he needs them. He may adopt a clinging strategy to ensure that they will be available. Because he is uncertain of his mother's availability, the poorly attached baby is always preoccupied with it or else spends tremendous energy "managing" without it. This preoccupation hinders individuation, exploration, and possibly learning. In essence, the attachment-parented baby learns to trust and develop a sense of self. These qualities foster appropriate independence. Studies have shown that infants who develop a secure attachment to their mothers are better able to tolerate separation from them when they are older. As one sensitive mother of a well-attached child said proudly, "He's not spoiled; he's perfectly fresh!"

Mutual Sensitivity

Another dividend to expect is mutual sensitivity. As you become more sensitive to your baby, your baby will become more sensitive to you. Here's an example of mutual sensitivity that Martha observed in our family:

> "Between eighteen months and two years, expect an attachment-parented baby to catch the emotional climate of the family and be sensitive to the needs of those who have been so sensitive to the baby. On a particularly busy day, my kitchen became overrun by ants. It was overload time for me, and I lost it, verbally and emotionally. As I continued to emote, I became aware of a sensitive flow between Stephen (then twenty-two months) and me. He watched me, sensing my needs. He connected with my eyes and embraced my knees, not in a frightened way, but as though to say, "It's okay. I love you. I would help you if I could." As Stephen got hold of me, I got hold of myself—a mother calmed by her baby's touch."

 ## SPOILING THE SPOILING THEORY

One of the most common concerns new parents have after learning about attachment parenting is that this style of parenting will spoil their child. They ask, "Won't holding our baby a lot, responding to cries, nursing our baby on cue, and even sleeping with our baby create an overly dependent manipulative child?" Our answer to them and our answer to you is an emphatic *no.* In fact, both experience and research have shown the opposite. As we have previously noted, attachment fosters independence. The spoiling theory began in the early part of this century when parents turned over their intuitive childrearing to "experts"; unfortunately, the child-care thinkers at the time advocated restraint and detachment, along with scientifically produced artificial baby milk—a "formula" for feeding babies that would be an improvement on God's design. They felt that if you held your baby a lot, fed on cue, and responded to cries, you would spoil and create a clingy, dependent baby. There was no scientific basis to this spoiling theory, just unwarranted fears and opinions. We would like to put the spoiling theory on the shelf—to spoil forever.

Research has finally proven what mothers have long suspected: You cannot spoil a baby by attachment. Spoiling means leaving something alone, such as putting food on the shelf to spoil. The attachment style of parenting does not mean overindulgence or inappropriate dependency. The possessive parent, or "hover mother," is one who keeps an infant from doing what he needs to do because of her own insecure needs. This has a detrimental effect on both the infant and the parents. Attachment differs from prolonged dependency. Attachment enhances development; prolonged dependency will hinder development.

Attachment studies have spoiled the spoiling theory. Researchers Drs. Bell and Ainsworth studied two sets of parents and their children. Group A were attachment-parented babies. These babies were securely attached, the products of responsive parenting. Group B babies were parented in a more restrained way, with a set schedule and given a less intuitive and nurturing response to their cues. All these babies were tracked for at least a year. Which group do you think eventually turned out to be the most independent? Group A, the securely attached babies. Researchers who have studied the affects of parenting styles on children's later outcome have concluded, to put it simply, that the spoiling theory is utter nonsense. Pick them up quickly and they'll get down quickly. A child must go through a stage of healthy dependence in order to later become securely independent. Spoiling does become an issue a few years from now, when overindulgence signals a parent's inability to set limits and boundaries. This happens most often in children who are materially bonded or whose parents are still trapped in dysfunctional patterns from their own childhood.

A PERSONAL COMMITMENT TO ATTACHMENT PARENTING

You now know the basics of attachment parenting, have learned some of the major benefits of attachment parenting, and have had some of your concerns about attachment parenting addressed. Spend some time evaluating your own feelings about attachment parenting.

What obstacles from your past life or present situation might hinder your practicing attachment parenting? List them here: _____

_____

_____

_____

Read the following questions and put a check mark next to those to which you would answer yes.

_____ Are there problems from the past in the way that you were parented?

_____ Do you have memories of how you were parented that need to be healed?

_____ Were you abused as a child?

_____ Are there current marital problems that may interfere with your becoming attached to your child?

_____ Are there financial problems that seem to necessitate full- or part-time work for your baby's primary caregiver?

_____ Do you have difficulty forming attachments in general?

_____ Do you have a problem with intimacy with your mate?

One of the benefits of attachment parenting is that it is in itself a healing process. In becoming attached to your baby, you increase your ability to form attachments. Attachment parenting, if practiced in the way God designed, becomes therapeutic for many families.

ATTACHMENT PARENTING   **33**

Can you see some ways that attachment parenting, by its very nature, could foster intimacy in your relationships and confidence in yourself? List them here: _____

_____

_____

_____

What principles of attachment parenting will be easy for you to follow? _____

_____

_____

_____

What principles will be difficult to follow? _____

_____

_____

_____

Refer to chapter 1 and the list of parenting goals that you made. How can attachment parenting assist you in meeting your parenting goals? _____

_____

_____

_____

After you have answered the above questions, spend some time with your mate discussing attachment parenting and the unique qualities you will use to create your own parenting style. Pray together for God's guidance as you forge ahead into parenthood.

CHAPTER THREE

THE ATTACHED CHILD

Train a child in the way he should go and when he is old he will not turn from it. (Prov. 22:6 NIV)

This is a proverb with a promise. Attachment parenting helps you know how to "train" and which way the child "should go"—the child's temperament. Practicing attachment parenting does not guarantee that your child will turn out right, but it greatly improves your chances, especially with a difficult or demanding baby. Many parenting advisers call these children fussy or strongwilled, words that have negative overtones. I prefer to describe them as high-need children. (You will meet this child in Chapter 9.)

"It's easy to see how the attachment styles help the parent-infant relationship, but what specifically does it do for the baby?"

Attachment parenting improves behavior. Attached babies cry less. They are less colicky, fussy, whining, and clingy. A very simple observation lies at the root of this observation: A baby who feels right acts right (operates from a sense of well-being). An in-arms baby whose cues are read and responded to feels connected, valued. Because of this inner feeling of rightness, the baby has less need to fuss.

"If attached babies cry less, what do they do with their free time?"

Attachment parenting improves development. They use it to grow and learn. During the last twenty-five years we have watched thousands of mother-infant pairs in action and interaction. We are constantly impressed by how content babies are who are worn in a carrier, breastfed on cue, slept with, and sensitively responded to. They just seem to feel better, behave better, and grow better. And here is why: Attachment parenting promotes the state of quiet alertness (also called attentive stillness). There seems to be some, as yet poorly understood, connection between a baby's behavioral state and the inner workings of his or her body. A baby in the quiet alert state is more receptive to interacting and learning from his or her environment. The state of quiet alertness promotes an inner organization that allows all the physiological systems of the body to work better. Babies divert the energy that they would have spent on fussing into growing, developing, and interacting with their environment.

The growth-promoting effects of attachment parenting can be summed up in one word: *organization*. An attached baby is organized. In their early months, babies spend a lot of energy trying to become organized—that is, adjusting to life outside the womb. For an attached baby, the womb lasts a while longer, birth having changed only the manner in which the attachment is presented.

Healthy, attached mothers and fathers act as behavioral, emotional, and physiological regulators for their baby. They act as conservators of their baby's energies, diverting them into growth and development, not into anxiety and fussing.

In essence, attached babies thrive. All babies grow, but not all babies thrive. Thriving means that your baby grows to his or her fullest potential. Attachment parenting and caregiving helps a baby be all that he can be. Researchers have long realized the association between good growth and good parenting.

---

*"If attachment parenting helps babies
act better and grow better, does it
make them smarter?"*

Yes! Attachment parenting is good brain food, and here's why. The human brain grows more during infancy than at any other time, doubling its volume and reaching approximately 60 percent of its adult size by one year. The infant brain consists of miles of tangled electrical "wires," called neurons. The infant is born with much of this wiring unconnected. During the first year, these neurons grow larger, begin to work better, and connect to each other to complete circuits that enable the baby to think and do more things. If nerve cells don't make connections, they die. The more connections they make, the better the brain develops. Brain researchers suggest it is these connections that we can influence to make a child smarter. Many studies now show that the most powerful enhancers of brain development are the quality of the parent-infant attachment (such as skin-to-skin contact) and the response of the caregiving environment to the infant's cues. I believe that attachment parenting promotes brain development by feeding the brain with the right kind of stimulation at a time in the child's life when the brain needs the most nourishment. Attachment parenting helps the developing brain make the right connections.

Many studies show that a secure mother-infant attachment and an environment responsive to the cues of the infant enhance brain development. Basically, these studies show that four relationships enhance a baby's intellectual and motor development:

1. Parent sensitivity and responsiveness to infant cues.
2. Reinforcement of infant's verbal cues and frequency of interchange during play.
3. Acceptance of and going with the flow of the baby's temperament.
4. Providing a stimulating environment with the primary caregiver and play activities that encourage decision making and problem solving.

A simple explanation of how this style of parenting contributes to early learning is that it creates conditions that allow learning to occur. Infants learn best in the behavior state of quiet alertness. Attachment parenting fosters quiet alertness, thus creating the conditions that help a baby learn.

 ## HOW DO ATTACHMENT-PARENTED CHILDREN TURN OUT?

"Do you notice any differences between how babies are parented in the early years and the type of children they become?"

Yes, but I offer a word of caution. Parents should not be too quick to take all the blame or all the credit for the person their child later becomes. Many factors contribute to the eventual person; attachment parenting during the early, formative years just increases the chances of a good outcome. Early in my career I studied the long-term effects of parenting styles. Parents who were into restraint parenting (scheduling, letting their baby cry it out, fear of spoiling, etc.—the crib and bottle set) got a red dot on their baby's chart. Parents who practiced attachment parenting, a blue dot. If the blue-dot parents practiced the big five of attachment parenting (wearing their baby, breastfeeding, sharing sleep, nurturing response to their baby's cries, and father involvement) they got an extra dot. This simple system was not meant to judge right or wrong parenting styles or the degree of "goodness" of the parents. I used this method simply to gather information from which I could draw conclusions. It was not very scientific, nor was there a perfect correlation between what parents did and what their children later became, but in general, here is what I observed.

Confident parents. The attachment parents developed confidence sooner. They used the basic tools of attachment parenting, but felt confident and free enough to branch out into their own style until they found what worked for them, their baby, and their lifestyle. In fact, during well-baby checkups I often asked, "Is it working?" I would advise parents to periodically take inventory of what worked and discard what didn't. What worked at one stage of development may not work in another. For example, some babies initially slept better with their parents, but became restless later on, necessitating a change in sleeping arrangements. Other babies slept better alone initially, but needed to share sleep with their parents in later months. These parents used themselves and their baby as the barometer of their parenting style, not the norms of the neighborhood.

Caring Children. As the months and years went on, I noticed one quality that distinguished attachment parents and their children: *sensitivity*. It is also noteworthy that this sensitivity carried over into other aspects of life: marriage, job, social relationships, and play. In my experience, sensitivity (in parents and child) is the most outstanding effect of attachment parenting.

As they grow older, connected children are deeply bothered by situations that aren't right. In fact, they seem to have an internal sensor that feels the rightness or wrongness of an action. They cry when other children cry and are quickly there to comfort. As teenagers, they are bothered by social injustices and do something to correct them. Because they are so firmly rooted in their inner-sensitivity, they swim upstream when others are following the wrong current. These are the movers and shakers and leaders and shapers of the future.

Please allow us to preach for a moment, because we care about the person your child will become. We are very concerned about a quality—or lack of it—developing in our youth, partly stemming from restraint parenting and partly from the entertainment industry. That "unquality" is insensitivity. Our youth are not bothered by anything. One night our family went to a movie that perhaps we shouldn't have (but, we thought, it was just a cartoon!). It was the old theme of one social group being insensitive to another, but the insensitive heroes were getting high marks in the movie. We watched the audience of parents and children. Some squirmed, some were visibly upset, a few left in disgust as did our family. Others had a ho-hum-that's-life-why-bother attitude. They had lost their sensitivity, and insensitivity is what gets most children, and adults, into trouble. The most frightening concern is that most who have lost their sensitivity do not realize they have lost it.

This sensitivity keeps you out of hassles with your child. You develop an awareness of a situation and intuitively get behind the eyes of your child and see situations from his or her viewpoint as well as your own. For example, one of the most common hassles that parents dread in the toddler years is the tantrums that develop when a child is asked to stop a play activity because "it's time to go." Many times I have heard parents say, "He just won't mind." I watched how Martha handled this problem with our toddlers. Because her sensitivity prompted her to get behind the eyes of her toddler and see things from his viewpoint, she understood why "stop play" hassles occur, and why a child throws a tantrum when he is asked to give up something before he is ready. She handled this with a routine she calls closure: part of leaving included Martha's getting down at our toddler's level and asking him to say "bye-bye" to each one of the toys and the children in the play group. This sensitive understanding gave him the ability to close out his own play activity. Attachment parenting makes life with a toddler easier.

Connected kids. Intimacy is the next quality I notice in attachment-parented children. These children learn to bond to people, not to things. They become high-touch persons in a high-tech world. The infant who grows up "in arms" is accustomed to relating to and being fulfilled from personal relationships. This infant is more likely to become a child who forms meaningful, healthy attachments with peers, and in adulthood would be more likely to develop deep intimacy with a mate. In contrast, the infant who is forced into self-soothing before it's time, accustomed to falling asleep clutching a synthetic bear, is likely to be more comfortable relating to things than to people. One of the main problems counselors and psychiatrists see in adults is the inability to form intimate ties. Attachment-parented children will not fill psychologists' waiting rooms. They are deep children, capable of deep relationships. That's what they grew up with. These children are capable of strong attachments because they use the mind-set they have learned from attachments to parents as a standard to measure all future relationships. The attached child has learned to give and receive love.

Attached kids come into their teen years with their emotional tanks full enough to have healthy expectations from peers when hormones surge. And with the foundation of attachment and a healthy sense of who they are as individuals, their transition into adult independence can be made relatively smoothly, the capacity for forming strong intimacy with a mate not far behind.

Competent kids. Attachment-parented babies become more competent. Every baby is endowed with abilities, primarily genetically determined. Competence is what the child does with these abilities. New and exciting research has proven what parents have long suspected: Nurturing and responsive parents are more likely to produce competent children. By watching a mother and infant play together, I have noticed how connected mothers foster competent babies, the mother providing a supportive presence. During block play, for example, the mother helps when needed, gives space when not; she knows just when to intervene and when not to. She shares the joy of success and minimizes frustration. She provides information to the baby in a way that he can process it and use it to focus on a task. Connected mothers use a lot of vivid language to interact with their baby, and the baby is receptive. There is mutual interaction between the pair. The end result is a better approach to problem solving. The baby learns how to learn. He develops competence.

Behaved children. Discipline—that magic word you've been waiting for—is easier for attachment children and their parents. The basic tools for Discipline 101 are to know your child and to help your child feel right. A child who feels right acts right. Because attachment parents know their child so well, the role of disciplinarian comes easier to them. Because attachment parented children grow up with an attitude of trust, they are easier to discipline. Trusting the authority figure is the basis of discipline. In my experience, one of the reasons many parents have difficulty disciplining their children is that they do not deeply know them. One of the reasons why some children are so difficult to discipline is that they operate from a basis of anger instead of trust.

Connected children tend to be more cooperative; they operate from internal controls, rather than from external force. This is the basis of sound discipline. The desire to be in harmony with the parents, the desire to please, motivates these children toward desirable behavior. Attachment parents are better able to convey what behavior they expect of their children, and their children are better able to perceive what behavior is expected of them.

One day in my office I was watching a mother care for her baby. She nursed her baby on cue, comforted him when upset, played with him when she read his playful moods and sensitively nurtured her baby. Mother and baby seemed to be in harmony. I couldn't resist saying to her, "You're a good disciplinarian."

Restraint parents do not seem to know their children so deeply, and they misread cues and behavior because of the fear of manipulation. They always seem to be playing catch-up instead of leading the child. Ultimately, they are the ones whom I see later for discipline counseling. If I see parents who boast about their rigid scheduling, letting their baby cry to train him and not letting their baby get too close for fear of dependency, I red tag their chart and begin counseling early, otherwise I'll be counseling these parents down the road when they come in complaining, "Doctor, I just can't seem to discipline my child!" These parents become what we call in the trade Dr.-tell-me-what-to-do's—and let me confess, the doctor often doesn't know what to do.

High-need children. The real payoff occurs with the high-need baby, the one who at birth says, "Hi, Mom and Dad, you've been blessed with an above average baby, and I need above average parenting. If you give it to me, we're going to get along; if not, we're going to have a bit of trouble down the road." This style of parenting helps you match the giving level of the parent with the need level of the baby. The result is that you bring out the best in each other. Matching a high-need child with unconnected parents often brings out the worst in each.

LONG-TERM INVESTMENT

Yes! This brings up one of the most important long-term effects—the concept of modeling. Keep in mind that you are bringing up someone else's future husband or wife, father or mother. The parenting style that your child learns from you is the one he or she is most likely to follow as a parent. To illustrate how children pick up nurturing attitudes at a young age, let me share two personal situations that occurred in my practice and in our family. One day a mother brought in a newborn, Susan, for a check-up, accompanied by her three-year-old daughter, Tiffany, the product of attachment

THE ATTACHED CHILD 43

parenting. As soon as Susan started to fuss, Tiffany pulled at her mother's skirt saying with much emotion, "Mommy, Susie's crying. Pick up, rock, rock, nurse!" What do you imagine Tiffany will do when she becomes a parent and her own baby cries? She won't call her doctor; she won't look it up in a book. She will intuitively pick up, rock, and nurse.

Even teenagers pick up on your parenting styles. One day Martha and I were sitting in our family room when we heard our nine-month-old daughter, Erin, begin to cry in our bedroom where she was napping. As we approached the door, the cries stopped. Curious, we looked in to see why Erin had stopped crying, and what we saw left a warm feeling in our hearts. Jim, our sixteen-year-old son, was lying next to Erin, stroking her and gentling her. Why did Jim do this? Because he was following our modeling that when babies cry, adults listen. Parenting is a long-term investment.

CHAPTER FOUR

THE ATTACHED PARENT

Just like the child, parents receive enormous benefits from attachment parenting. Most notably, attachment parents seem to enjoy parenting more. They get closer to their babies sooner, feel more confident about their parenting abilities and decisions, and even feel better about their marital relationships because of the teamwork and unity developed through the parenting process. In this chapter, we explore some of the unique aspects of parenting the attachment way.

 ## BIOLOGICAL BASIS OF MOTHERING

"It seems that a mother doesn't have to be rich or smart to help her baby develop; she just has to be there. Why is it so important that a mother and baby be together a lot?"

Let's get into the biological workings of a mother and infant and see what happens when they're connected. When we were trying to decide what would be the best parenting style for our family and the one we wanted to teach, we consulted anthropological writings. Anthropology is the science of how human relationships are supposed to work, not how social and economic pressures have forced them to operate. The evidence was overwhelmingly in favor of the mother and baby being together a lot.

Studying the characteristics of the milk of various species gives us a clue to the parenting style expected. Some mother animals are away from their young for many hours at a time to forage. These mothers produce a milk very high in fat and protein so that feedings can be few and widely spaced. These animals are called intermittent contact species. Human milk, on the contrary, is relatively low in fat and proteins, showing that human infants need frequent feedings and extensive maternal contact. This is why we are called a continuous contact species.

Another clue that good things happen when baby and mother are together is the effect that frequent interactions have on a mother's hormones. Biological substances don't hang around long in the body; they get used up fast. Like medicines, some exert a quick but short effect, others are like time-release capsules. The biological term for how long a substance lasts is *half-life,* meaning the time it takes for one half of the substance to dissipate from the body. The mothering hormone, prolactin, has a short half life, less than an hour.

"So if I want to keep my prolactin high, I have to do these hormone-stimulating things more often?"

Exactly. Frequent nursing, holding, and caressing your baby stimulate your mothering hormones. We've all heard about the importance of a harmonious relationship with your baby. We call this frequency of interaction a "hormoneous" relationship. So, when your baby has one of those days when she wants to nurse and be held a lot, remember the biological reason why the relationship is designed that way. One time we did a computer search on the relationship between parenting styles and the biological effects on mother and baby. The term *frequency* kept coming up: frequency of sucking, frequency of caressing, frequency of holding—all enhancing a baby's behavior and development.

Studies on other animals in a continuous contact species showed fascinating physiologic benefits of mother-infant attachment. Infant animals who stayed closer to their mothers had a higher level of growth hormones and enzymes essential for brain growth. Separating from or not interacting with their mothers caused the levels of these growth-promoting substances to fall. Attachment researchers summarize all this rather sophisticated research with the simple statement: "Mother acts as an organizer for her baby's systems. The continued presence of the mother is necessary for the optimal functioning of the baby's physiological systems."

"It sounds like the old 'schedule your baby" theory is going the way of the spoiling theory. Is that right?"

Yes! We would like you to replace the rigid term *schedule* with the more flexible concept of routine, or even better with a more flowing expression, *harmony*.

"The evidence is convincing, but couldn't a mother feel tied down by constant baby tending?"

THE ATTACHED PARENT   47

Yes, mothers need baby breaks. This is why shared parenting by the father and other trusted caregivers is sometimes useful. Instead of feeling "tied down," a healthy mother-infant attachment leads to feeling "tied together." Once you form a healthy attachment you will want to be with your baby, not as a duty, but as a desire. Attachment mothers we interviewed described their feelings:

- "I feel so connected with my baby."
- "I feel right when with her, not right when we're apart."
- "I feel fulfilled."

If we could interview babies, they would tell us that their very lives as well as their personality development depend on having a connection: in arms, at breast, and in touch. Want to learn about mother-infant attachment? Ask attached young children to draw a mother and a baby. They draw them as one unit. Their idealistic minds have not yet been influenced by life's unfortunate mother-baby separating practices.

 MESSING UP!

"With attachment parenting you set high standards for parents. Could a mother feel guilty if she couldn't or didn't want to do this whole attachment style? And what if I mess up?"

We all mess up, but attachment parents mess up less often. Also, secure children have one big quality that helps take the pressure off parents: resiliency. They can bounce back like a forgiving friend. Children tolerate a wider range of parenting styles than we tolerate children's mood swings. Try not to think of the attachment style as a list of things you must do to have a bright and behaved child. The attachment concepts are like starter blocks, first steps in building your own parenting style. They are very basic, intuitive, commonsense ways of caring for a baby. Upon this foundation you then build your own parenting style according to your own individual lifestyles and the temperament of your baby. You may not be able to practice this whole style at any one time with each child.

Yes, you will at times feel guilty. Parenting is a guilt-laden profession. Love for your baby makes you vulnerable to feeling you're not doing enough. I feel guilty every time I write a book, realizing I cannot do all the right things all the time. But it does not mean that I should not be aware of what the ideal is and reach for that ideal. As long as we don't let guilt overrun us, the feeling of guilt can be healthy; guilt is our inner warning system, a sort of inner alarm that goes off when we behave the way we are not supposed to. Part of maturing as a person and as a parent is recognizing healthy guilt and channeling these motivating feelings toward which decision to make and which path to take. Attachment parenting helps you develop a sensitivity, an inner signal that helps you make important baby-care decisions.

 ## HANDLING CRITICISM

---

*"I believe that attachment parenting
will be the right style for our family,
but my confidence is a bit shaky when
I read books that advise the opposite.
And what do I say to people who
believe otherwise?"*

As an attachment parent, your most important reading assignment is to read your child. As a Christian, measure everything you read against scripture. One of the fringe benefits of attachment parenting is that you will become more discerning about advice. As new parents you will be bombarded with advice, everyone offering personal "how to's". This style of parenting is a real confidence builder, enabling you to listen to some advice and learn from it, and discount the rest. You will not put blind faith in the "experts"—you will check what they have to say against your own instincts and wisdom. Nothing divides friends like different opinions about child-rearing, so you will naturally gravitate toward like-minded parents (and their ways are contagious!). Also, you don't have to defend your style. Just say, "It works for us."

 ## WORKING AND CARING

"Does attachment parenting require a full-time at-home mother? What about the mother who chooses to or has to return to work?"

Attachment parenting is easier for a full-time mother, but that diminishing luxury is not absolutely required. In fact, this style of parenting would be even more beneficial for employed mothers and their babies. In our prenatal counseling we have a session geared for mothers who need to juggle working and caring. Here are the steps to consider:

- During your early weeks of full-time mothering, make the most of your maternity leave. Don't be preoccupied with W-day, the day you return to work. Don't let it, even subconsciously, keep you from getting close to your baby for fear it will be more difficult to leave him.

- Enjoy your full-time mothering to the fullest and extend it as long as possible. Practice as much of the attachment style of parenting as you can. Get attached early on, as this will improve your skills as a part-time mother.
- Seek a like-minded caregiver as a substitute mother, a nurturing person who sensitively responds to your baby and who basically believes in and is experienced at in-arms mothering. Make it a priority to keep this same caregiver at least two years. If possible, involve the father in child care.
- After returning to work, continue the attachment style of parenting. Continue breastfeeding; wear your baby when you are with him; consider sleeping with your baby at night. These attachment tips help you to reconnect to your previous attachment, preventing a distance from developing between you and your baby as you learn to combine working and mothering. (See chapter 8 for an in-depth discussion of how to keep the attachment while working.)

SPECIAL CIRCUMSTANCES

"Which style of parenting would you recommend for adopting parents?"

Most adopting parents naturally select attachment parenting. Their intense longing to nurture an infant prompts them to thoroughly research baby-care options, and they nearly always become attachment parents. In fact, this style especially fits adopting parents by giving the mother the hormonal boost that biological mothers have.

"What's in it for single parents?"

Any special circumstance that lessens a parent's support base is helped by attachment parenting. The added stresses to a single-parent family makes attractive any style of parenting that improves the behavior of the baby and the sensitivity of the parent. Attachment parenting adds an extra support resource to any less than ideal situation. A single mother will learn that she must find support in her parenting from family, friends, and groups.

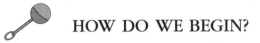 ## HOW DO WE BEGIN?

At this point we hope you have developed at least a starting point for your parenting philosophy. We hope that after reading these introductory chapters you feel confident in your instincts and God-given parenting abilities and are eagerly anticipating all of the joys and challenges of parenting. In the remainder of the book, we will deal with specific parenting issues, utilizing the principles of attachment parenting. But always feel free to refer to these early chapters for a refresher or for encouragement. And when your parenting adventures are really tough, remember our first tip:

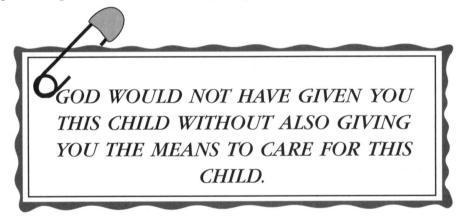

GOD WOULD NOT HAVE GIVEN YOU THIS CHILD WITHOUT ALSO GIVING YOU THE MEANS TO CARE FOR THIS CHILD.

CHAPTER FIVE

BIRTH IN THE CHRISTIAN FAMILY

Pregnancy and childbirth are mind-boggling, emotion-scrambling experiences. The tender, but sometimes confused, feelings of pregnancy and the intense demands of labor are part of God's plan for preparing you for parenthood. These challenges are actually opportunities for growth as new parents, in your marriage, and in your faith in God.

 ## BECOMING ATTACHED TO YOUR UNBORN CHILD

Your bond with your child begins from the moment you first suspect that you are expecting a baby. Your mind races ahead, trying to envision this new person, trying to imagine yourself as a mother or father. If this is a planned pregnancy, you may feel happy and excited right from the start. If this pregnancy is a surprise, other feelings may cause a struggle as you work to accept the will of God for your life. In either case, pray for the Lord's help in caring for this new life, even before it is born. Both parents' feelings about the baby during pregnancy affect the bond that is formed with the child, and will carry over into caring for the baby after birth.

What were your first feelings upon learning that you (your wife) were pregnant? _____
_____
_____
_____

Describe any worries or negative feelings you had or may have still. What have you done to resolve them? _____
_____
_____
_____

What were *your* parents' thoughts and feelings when they were expecting you? _____
_____
_____
_____

What does your baby look like in your mind? _____
_____
_____
_____

What are your hopes and dreams for him or her? _____
_____
_____
_____

Ideally, what kind of a parent will you be? _____
_____
_____
_____

What mistakes do you wish to avoid? _____
_____

PREGNANT FEELINGS: THE FIRST TRIMESTER

The reality of the pregnancy hits home first with the mother, who does not exactly feel or look pregnant, but who suddenly finds herself coping with nausea and fatigue. She wakes up in the morning feeling lousy, finds her usual morning coffee revolting, and falls asleep soon after supper—despite the nap she had. Even before they know for certain that they are pregnant, some women find themselves "sleeping for two."

Not every woman has these symptoms during the first three months of pregnancy, but they are very common. Mix them with a normal amount of ambivalence about the changes ahead and a few fears about miscarrying or not having a healthy baby, and you can see why the first trimester presents real challenges in adjusting to the idea of being pregnant.

The pregnancy is not nearly so obvious or real to husbands at this point, and they may need to keep in mind that their wives' emotional mood swings are caused in part by the very real physical changes of pregnancy. Many of the emotional changes are related to hormone levels that make it possible for the woman's body to grow and nourish another human being, and these hormonal changes are most dramatic even before the pregnancy begins to show. The highs and lows are also related to the fact that this is a time when a woman's life is changing and she is learning a new role and developing greater maturity. Dealing with the worries and experiencing the joys actually help her begin to form her new identity as a mother.

PRAYING FOR YOUR CHILD

It's important for Christian couples to pray for their unborn baby. Doing this early in pregnancy sets the stage for the growth and adjustment ahead. Together, laying your hands on the wife's soon-to-bulge abdomen as you pray reminds you of the reality of the life within. With our own pregnancies, this nightly ritual became such a habit that after the baby was born I couldn't go to sleep without laying my hand on our newborn's warm fuzzy head and praying for her.

Write a blessing for your unborn child. _____

_____

_____

_____

 ## PREGNANT FEELINGS: THE SECOND TRIMESTER

The middle three months of pregnancy are much easier for mothers than is early pregnancy, but they may be more difficult emotionally for dads. The mother begins to feel better, as nausea and fatigue lift. She begins to take a certain pride in her changing figure and goes shopping for maternity clothes. The highlight of this period is feeling your baby move. The mother first notices these flutterings around sixteen to eighteen weeks, and the father will be able to detect them a few weeks later. This, combined with his wife's changing shape, confirms that there really is a baby in there! And suddenly Dad's concerns about being a good provider and about sharing his wife with a child are off and running.

Having a child matures a man like nothing else. Already during pregnancy it calls on him to put someone else ahead of his own needs and to evaluate the roles of career and family in his life. Fathers tend to worry a lot about money during pregnancy, and they may exaggerate fears about being a good provider way out of proportion. This can lead to more time spent at the office or the work site, and soon the job takes priority over the marriage. Now is the time to get these priorities in order and to become more involved in the life of the family. This will help you to put fathering

 56 **THE NEW BABY PLANNER**

first after the baby is born. Ask God for the wisdom and maturity you need to be a good father and husband and place your worries in God's hands as well.

Pregnancy calls for mutual sensitivity in a marriage. At a time when a woman is feeling especially vulnerable and in need of protection, her husband may worry about his ability to take care of her. Listen to each other carefully during these months and accept each other's feelings. You each may be feeling very anxious and will be looking to the other for support. Pray for each other and for your marriage, and continue to pray over your baby's development and security. Now is the time to practice working together intellectually, emotionally, and spiritually. These skills are the foundation of a Christian home and of attachment parenting.

The thing I don't understand about my husband at this point is _____
_____
_____
_____

The thing that puzzles me most about my pregnant wife is ___
_____
_____
_____

I wish my spouse would understand that _____
_____
_____
_____

What I wish my spouse would do for me is _____
_____
_____
_____

Share your answers with your husband or wife.

 THE FINAL MONTHS

In the last three months, excitement and anticipation increase as the baby's due date grows near. The wife's body grows fuller, and she glows with pride and the special status granted her as a pregnant woman. She may also begin to feel awkward and tired, so she needs regular reassurances of her husband's love for her in this new shape. Toward the end of the pregnancy her interest in sex decreases, not because she loves her husband less, but because she feels big and uncomfortable and because her hormones are now focusing her attention on the mothering tasks ahead.

Wives, keep in mind that your husband's hormonal system does not change during pregnancy. Now may be the time to be especially inventive during sex, so that the needs of both can be satisfied. You may want to try different positions and different ways of stimulating each other and enjoying your closeness. Sexual intercourse will not harm a normal, healthy pregnancy, so there is no reason to be afraid of hurting the baby. For many couples, that feeling of a new life within adds a special tenderness to their sexual relationship during pregnancy.

During the last weeks before the baby's birth, the mother's nesting instinct may appear, threatening to impose order and cleanliness on every corner of the couple's abode. Sudden bursts of energy do help to get the house clean and loose ends tied up, but be careful not to exhaust yourself. Labor requires lots of energy, which you won't have if you've just finished shampooing all the carpets, cleaning the kitchen cabinets, wallpapering the nursery, and sweeping out the garage single-handedly.

In these last weeks, the mother's feelings may turn inward, tuning in to the child inside her and preparing her mind and body for the work of childbirth. It is a quiet period, a season to relax and purposefully slow down. It is not a good time to add a room onto the house or move to a larger one, or even a new city. Anticipate as much as possible so the nest is settled and the feathers all in place.

God provides this time for the husband and wife to enjoy the peace and quiet and savor these final moments together.

Make a *short* list of tasks to complete before your baby's arrival. Be realistic. _____

_____

_____

_____

_____ Did you include time to relax?

CARING FOR YOUR UNBORN BABY

How do you care for your unborn baby? By caring for the woman who is that baby's whole world. The child in the womb is affected by what the mother eats, what other substances she puts into her body, and how she lives day to day.

NUTRITION FOR EXPECTANT MOTHERS

Pregnant women need to eat a high-quality diet. This means emphasizing appropriate quantities of nutritious foods and avoiding empty calories. Normal weight gain during pregnancy is about twenty-five to thirty pounds (or more if you started out under-weight), but each woman is unique. Weight gain should not be governed by strict limits or fearmongering by doctors and nurses whose eyes are focused only on the scale.

If you are eating the right foods, limits on weight gain are not necessary. Excessive weight gain—the kind that doesn't come off easily during the first six months of breastfeeding—is usually caused by eating foods that are high in fat and sugar—that is, junk food. Eating lots of the right kinds of food will assure that your baby gets everything she needs to grow, and that the weight you gain is right for you.

Protein is a particularly important nutrient for pregnant women. You should get at least seventy-five grams per day, which you can do by following the dietary suggestions in the box on page 61. Books on nutrition and some books on pregnancy contain charts with the amount of protein in various foods, and good childbirth classes will emphasize this. Keeping track of what you eat for two or three days and adding up the total daily protein can help you pinpoint areas in which you may need to improve your diet. Snacks can help you upgrade your eating habits. Choose snack foods that are high in nutritious protein, such as yogurt, cheese, nuts, and seeds.

Pregnant women should also be certain to eat generous amounts of fruits and vegetables, along with whole grain bread and cereal. Constipation is a common problem during pregnancy, and these kinds of foods, which are high in dietary fiber, help to prevent it. Drinking lots of water throughout the day will also help you minimize problems with constipation.

Eat a good breakfast, and don't skip meals. You wouldn't let a tiny baby go eight or ten hours without eating, would you? Babies in utero are affected by the fluctuations in blood sugar and other body chemicals that accompany periods of hunger.

Write down everything you've eaten in the last twenty-four hours. _____
_____
_____
_____
_____

Was this a typical eating day for you? _____

Take a critical look at your list and compare it to the list of what a pregnant woman needs every day.

Here's what's good about my diet: _____
_____

Here's what I'd like to improve: _____

_____

_____

NUTRITION GUIDELINES FOR PREGNANT WOMEN

Each day you should eat the equivalent of the following:

Two eggs

One or two servings of fish or lean beef or chicken (and liver one or two times a week)

A large salad of leafy green vegetables

One quart or more of milk (whole or skim)

One serving of cheese or yogurt (more if you can't drink milk)

Two to three slices of whole grain bread

Two servings of whole grain cereal or other grains

One serving of yellow vegetables (rice, corn, pasta)

One whole baked potato three times a week

Two servings of fruit or fruit juice (one citrus)

 ## HARMFUL SUBSTANCES TO AVOID

Scientists and physicians used to think of the placenta as a barrier that protected the fetus from substances ingested by the mother. Experience has unfortunately proven otherwise, and we know now that much of what a mother puts in her body will reach her unborn child. We don't know very much about the effects of

BIRTH IN THE CHRISTIAN FAMILY 61

each and every kind of drug on the fetus, since it would be unthinkable to experiment on pregnant women. We must depend on animal experiments and studies that are essentially hindsight in order to arrive at advice for human mothers.

Medications. Keep in mind, then, that there must be a good reason for taking any kind of medication or using any sort of drug during pregnancy. For some women with chronic conditions that are controlled by medication, taking drugs is necessary even during pregnancy, since not taking the medicine may present greater risks to the mother and baby. But in other cases, where using the drug is optional, it may be best to avoid it altogether. Seek advice from your doctor or midwife before taking any medication during pregnancy —or even if you think you might be pregnant. This includes over-the-counter medications for colds or minor aches and pains.

Pregnant women should definitely not use illicit drugs, such as marijuana or cocaine. There is no justification for using these substances, and the risks to the baby, especially from cocaine, are high.

Alcohol also presents dangers to unborn babies. The problem of increasing numbers of "cocaine babies" gets a lot of attention from the media, but many experts feel that alcohol is responsible for many more problems in children, sometimes very noticeable, sometimes more subtle. Because alcohol is legal, we tend to forget its potential for harm, and it is only within the last decade that pregnant women have been warned against drinking. How much alcohol can you drink without causing damage to your baby? No one knows just what the threshold is. Five or more drinks at one time or an average of two drinks per day throughout pregnancy is known to cause harm, but lesser amounts may also be harmful. (The term *drink* here is defined as one ounce of hard liquor [i.e., whiskey], one twelve-ounce glass of beer, or one eight-ounce glass of wine.) The wise course is to avoid alcohol altogether.

If you enjoy a glass of wine or a drink with meals or when you go out, you may find yourself missing it during pregnancy. Here are some healthful alternatives: orange and other fruit juices, straight up or mixed with club soda; tomato juice; club soda with a twist of lime or lemon; iced herbal tea; mineral water. Avoid soda pop—it's nothing but empty, nonnourishing calories.

Smoking. Studies have shown that babies born to mothers who smoke weigh less, are more likely to be premature, and may have diminished brain growth. Nicotine decreases the blood supply to the placenta, hence it decreases the nourishment going to the baby. Being pregnant provides good motivation to quit smoking, or if quitting proves impossible, to at least cut down. The risks increase in proportion to the number of cigarettes smoked each day.

Both fathers and mothers who smoke should be aware of the dangers of secondhand smoke to infants and children. Studies have shown that children who live with a smoker have more colds and other respiratory problems. Secondhand smoke also poses cancer risks. Smoking is a difficult habit to kick, but the rewards of stopping include better health for the whole family. Pray for God's help and guidance in your efforts to quit.

Brainstorm. Think of ways to motivate yourself to quit smoking. _____
_____
_____
_____

Now, think of ways to avoid or cope with situations in which you usually smoke. _____
_____
_____
_____

Stress. New research is showing that the womb environment affects infant temperament and behavior after birth. Anxiety and stress are not just abstract emotions; they have physical manifestations, including increased levels of certain hormones that pass through the placenta to the baby. Chronic, steady exposure to these body chemicals may affect the baby's nervous system, producing a physical basis for a difficult or fussy temperament.

This does not mean that each time the pregnant woman gets upset about something or she and her husband have an argument she risks messing up her baby's personality. Researchers in fetal awareness believe that temporary stresses do not have any lasting ill effect on the baby. But be aware that constant anxiety and worry, the sort of emotional state that can accompany intense, unresolved conflicts, may affect your infant. Husbands can be especially helpful in protecting their wives from anxiety during pregnancy. Here is another reason for prayer and truthful, loving communication during the months before the baby is born.

What are the sources of stress in your life? Job? Family? Self? Busyness? _____

_____

_____

_____

How do you keep stress from building up? _____

_____

_____

_____

Are there major problems in your life that need some attention during pregnancy? _____

_____

_____

_____

Pregnancy has a way of causing unresolved (even unremembered) conflicts to surface. Professional counseling is often needed when this happens.

TEN TIPS FOR A SAFE AND SATISFYING BIRTH

Besides growing a baby, pregnancy is a time when you grow as a person, working out a birthing philosophy, managing fears about birth, assembling the right birth team, and selecting the right place for the birth. Women enjoy more birthing options today than at any time in history. In this section, we want to help you work out your own birthing philosophy to increase your chances of having the birth you want.

God has blessed us with eight beautiful children. We have been around the birth scene for a long time, Martha as a childbirth educator and labor support person, and Bill as a pediatrician. We have grown to appreciate how beautifully God designed the birth process. But we also realize that for some mothers birth is a less than satisfying experience, sometimes due to medical complications, but most often because someone interferes with the natural process of labor and birthing. We want parents to take *responsibility* for their birthing decisions, and we will give you the tools to do so. Our goal is to help you make the best birth choices and equip you to enter labor and birth knowing and trusting in your body. Here are ten tips to increase your chances of having a safe and satisfying birth experience.

1. Trust Your Body

The call comes from your doctor's office and the answer is "Yes —you are pregnant!" Or the color change on a home pregnancy test affirms what your body is telling you—you're going to have a baby. If this is your first baby, your first impulse may be, "Gosh, I'm pregnant. I'd better set up an appointment with my doctor!" But you're not sick; you're pregnant. The common reaction that pregnancy is a potential illness rather than a normal bodily function underlies the fact that many women distrust their bodies during birth. Also realize that the medicalization of birth sets you up to distrust your body. You choose a doctor *in case* something goes wrong; you choose a hospital in case an emergency happens; you submit to a battery of prenatal tests in case something is going wrong in your body or in your baby. But for 90 percent of women, birth can go *right*. Around 10 percent of women need special medical help to deliver healthy babies.

Be confident in your body's ability to deliver a baby. Reflect on the concept of *Creator*. God designed all the organs in the human body to work well—and most of the time they do. The birthing organs also work well. For the majority of mothers, birth is a normal physiological process, and the system works well as long as the mother takes care of it and no one interferes with it. Professional help from a midwife and/or obstetrician and childbirth classes teach you how wonderfully your body is made to give birth and all the things you can do to work with your body instead of against it to increase your chances of having a satisfying birth experience and delivering a healthy baby. Be confident in your body. Trust that your body is built to give birth. How is your confidence level in general? Is your self-image high? Low? If you are generally a confident person, you are more likely to take responsibility for your birthing decisions. The more confident you are that the birth will go right, the more likely it will. On the other hand, is your self-image under attack and your overall confidence level low? If so, pregnancy is a time for boosting your self-image.

Identify what pulls you down: _____
_____
_____
_____
_____

Which of these counterproductive items can you correct? Is there one you struggle with over and over? Seek professional help. Is there marital stress? Don't expect a baby to heal your marriage. Seek professional marriage counseling during your pregnancy, as the added stress of a baby is more likely to weaken an already stressful marriage.

Women who lack confidence in their bodies are more at risk of having a less than satisfying birth experience. They are more likely to hand over responsibility for the birthing decisions to someone else. Women who have low self-image are more likely to have a medically managed birth rather than a self-directed birth. This is a set-up for a medical and technological childbirth and often a cesarean section. This type of birth further weakens an already shaky self-image. A woman with this experience is often left with the feeling "My body couldn't do it," which translates into *"I couldn't do it."*

In contrast, a woman with confidence takes primary responsibility for her birthing decisions and directs the birth she wants—and is more likely to get it. For many women, birth is the high point of their sexuality and femininity, an incredible boost to their self-esteem. Many times after the mastery of birth a woman shouts "I did it!" A positive birth experience can be therapeutic to a woman's self-worth. "I can do all things through Christ who strengthens me" (Phil. 4:13).

2. Overcome Your Fears

We want to take the fear out of childbirth. While it's normal to be apprehensive about labor, especially if this is your first baby or you have had previous unsatisfying birth experiences, prolonged unresolved fear sets you up for a less than satisfying birth. And no wonder women fear birth. Instead of viewing birth as a high point of their sexuality, young women hear war stories about how awful birth is. Movies portray the pain of birth, but seldom its pleasure. And the current medical system contributes to childbirth fear. Much of a woman's prenatal care is geared toward the *for fear that* mind-set. A woman is electronically monitored during her labor *for fear that* something will go wrong. A mother employs a doctor to deliver her baby *for fear that* the birth may go wrong. Both the doctor's and the mother's feelings toward birth are the *for fear that* mind-set. And hospitals contribute to this by surrounding a woman with technology *for fear that* something may happen. There is a mystery to birth, especially for a woman who's unprepared for the normal

BIRTH IN THE CHRISTIAN FAMILY **67**

functioning of her body in labor. People fear what they don't understand.

Misinterpretation of scripture has also contributed to the fear of childbirth. Male biblical scholars—who will never experience childbirth—nevertheless have promoted the *curse of Eve* myth. The early church taught that women must endure suffering in childbirth as a consequence of original sin. In her book *Natural Childbirth and the Christian Family,* Helen Wessel researched the original Hebrew meaning of certain terms related to childbirth and exposed the curse of Eve as a myth of mistranslation. She showed how modern translators have done childbearing women a disservice. For example, in Genesis 3:16 the translation reads, "To the woman he said, 'I will greatly increase your pains in childbearing; with pain you will give birth to children'" (NIV). But in Genesis 3:17, God said to Adam, "Cursed is the ground because of you; through painful toil you will eat of it all the days of your life" (NIV). In both of these verses the Hebrew word *etseu* was used, but it was translated as "pain" for Eve and "toil" for Adam. Why should the same word be translated one way for Eve, but another for Adam? More correctly, this scripture states that childbirth is to be *hard work* for women, and few mothers would argue with that. And most farmers toiling in the field would agree that there could be some aching, even painful, moments in their work. Of course, hard work has its benefits.

> Now the time came for Elizabeth to give birth, and she bore a son. Her neighbors and relatives heard that the Lord had shown his great mercy to her, and they rejoiced with her. (Luke 1:57–58 NRSV)

The intense, hard toil of birthing ends in rejoicing as the mother finally holds her infant in her arms. Some studies suggest that the way the mother experiences childbirth may affect the rejoicing that follows. Seeing and feeling and fully experiencing birth helps women bond with their newborns and feel more positive in the postpartum period. A negative birth experience, where fear and pain predominate and the woman feels like a helpless victim, can contribute to problems in postpartum adjustment. Mothers and fathers need to start their parenting careers on a positive note.

What images do you hold in your mind about childbirth? Where do they come from? _____
_____
_____
_____
_____

Imagine Elizabeth's labor and the rejoicing that followed. Read the story of the naming of her son, John, and pray the song of his father, Zechariah, in Luke 1:57–80. What are God's promises for your child? _____
_____
_____
_____

Why is fear labor's foe? Obstetrician Grantly Dick-Read has observed the relationship between fear and pain in childbirth. The natural process that God designed is a marvelous interaction between muscles, nerves, movement of bones, and relaxing of tissues —the normal workings of which are intricately tied to a woman's emotions. Simply put, if a woman feels right during labor, her birthing system is more likely to work right. Fear frightens the uterus. The workings of this magnificent muscle are affected, for better or for worse, by a neuro-hormonal pathway that connects a mother's brain, circulatory system, and uterus. Fear reduces the blood and oxygen flow to the uterus, increasing pain and slowing the progress of labor. Fear causes the cervix and the muscles in the lower part of the uterus to tighten instead of relax, while the muscles in the upper part of the uterus (those not so much affected by the fear pathway) automatically keep on contracting, in effect pushing the baby against resistance.

Fear, tension, and pain. Many Christian childbirth educators believe that women should not expect severe pain and suffering during childbirth, but they should expect to experience intense physical and emotional sensations. God has designed women's bodies for giving birth, and the great majority of women should be able to birth their babies with only patient, watchful medical attendance, and not a great deal of technological assistance. However, actual statistics don't bear this out. The cesarean rate in the United States is 25–30 percent, and the use of medication and various technologies during labor is very high. Something is wrong here. Why does the birth process go astray this way, and why do so many women suffer and get medication during labor?

Fear is the main culprit. As Dr. Grantly Dick-Read wrote in his book, *Childbirth Without Fear,* first published in the 1940s and still available today, fear produces tension and tension produces pain. During labor, the muscles of the uterus, the cervix, and the birth passage work hard, pressing forward, stretching, opening, and pushing the baby out. This effort produces intense sensations that can, quite honestly, be interpreted as painful, especially if things are already tense. If the laboring woman reacts to these sensations with fear, her body will become more tense, and this tension makes it more difficult for her birthing muscles to do their job. As the uterus works to push the baby out against muscles tight with fear, sensations of pain intensify, and the woman becomes even more fearful and panicky. A cycle of fear, tension, and pain is established, which can impede the progress of labor and cause fetal distress, making medical or surgical intervention necessary.

To give birth the way God intended the system to work, you must break the fear-tension-pain cycle or prevent it from ever taking hold. Yes, drugs can be used to take away the pain as labor progresses, but no drug is risk-free and doing away with the sensations of labor robs women of some of the rejoicing as well. Better to interrupt the cycle earlier by reducing fear and to find natural ways of coping with tension and pain.

Just as there is a right chemistry for life, so also there is a right one for birth. Normal birth is a balancing act of hormones, chemical messengers that travel throughout a mother's laboring system helping labor to progress more efficiently and comfortably. There is a balancing act of nearly ten different birth hormones. Some of these hormones relieve discomfort (e.g., endorphins, the body's natural narcotics) and enhance progress; others, namely stress hormones, can, if excessive, hinder labor. Fear upsets the balance of these birth hormones, allowing the labor inhibiting hormones to overtake the labor enhancing hormones, resulting in increased pain and length of labor.

What you can do. Identify your fears. List all the parts of labor and birth you are afraid of. _____

_____

_____

_____

_____

_____

_____

One by one, check off what you can do to overcome these fears *before* labor begins. If your main fear is how much childbirth will hurt, you can lessen pain by following the suggestions listed in tip number 8, page 92. If you fear having a surgical birth, the good news is that you can lower your chances of a cesarean section by following the suggestions given in tip number 10, page 98.

Pick out the fear that binds you and work through it. Seek help from professionals who are knowledgeable and experienced in dealing with childbirth fears. Your obstetrician, midwife, childbirth educator, or friends who have successfully overcome their fears are trusted referral sources. Exercises in fearbusting help to tackle new fears that may unexpectedly crop up during pregnancy or labor. As we will later discuss, giving birth is as much a mental process as a physical one. Using your mind to control emotions that interfere with labor is a valuable helper to bring to your birth.

Fighting back fear. Fear can be overcome by learning about birth and having some idea of what to expect. If you know why your body is doing what it is doing, understand the awesome sensations this is causing, and have faith that this is what God intended; you need not be afraid or panic when confronted with the growing intensity of labor contractions. You will know that your body is doing its job and that the increased feelings of pressure and your own total absorption in your work are bringing you closer to seeing your baby. A good childbirth class can help you learn about birth, as can reading and studying on your own. (See suggestions for further reading on page 79.)

You also need to take a close look at your past experience with labor, if you have given birth before, and at your beliefs about childbirth and where they come from. Identify your fears and talk about them with your spouse, with your childbirth educator, and with another sympathetic, experienced parent. Then trust them to God and replace them with more positive messages.

Episodes from past labors that I don't wish to repeat: _____
_____
_____
_____

The thing I fear most about childbirth is: _____
_____
_____

What information do I need to address this fear? _____
_____
_____
_____

Write a prayer that places this fear in God's hands. _____
_____
_____

You can also overcome fear by planning your birth, thoughtfully and prayerfully choosing a place of birth and people who will attend you who share your birthing philosophy. Writing a birth plan will help you think through what you want in a birth experience. Sharing the plan with your physician and others who will be with you at the birth will help you to feel safe.

Fearless company. During pregnancy and labor, surround yourself with people who do not project fear. You don't need friends and relatives telling you how awful birth can be. If you sense that someone whom you've invited to your birth has a fearful mind-set, remember, fear is contagious—you don't want this person to infect the birth event with her or his fears.

Knowledge reduces fear. The more truth parents know about birth, the less they have to fear. Take responsibility for learning the normal workings of your body during labor and delivery, what your birth signals mean, and especially why not to be afraid of them. Also, learn about abnormal signals. Part of a good childbirth class is to teach you to respond to your body signals not with fear, which is counterproductive, but with various comfort measures, such as a change in position.

Heal past memories. Traumatic memories can create tension that will interfere with the progress of birth and increase pain. Unpleasant memories from past births (sometimes experienced as having one's body violated) often resurface to infect your next birth. If you have an actual history of sexual molestation, be aware that pregnancy can push buttons from this past. Labor can cause a mother to have flashbacks of molestation memories, resulting in her clicking into a "tense-up" mode rather than the release mode. The secret of helping your labor progress more efficiently and more comfortably is *relaxing and releasing,* opening up your body to give birth. For labor to progress more efficiently and comfortably, a mother must yield to the workings of her body and not try to control them. A woman with a history of sexual abuse may overreact during labor and try to control her bodily actions as much as possible. The prospect of losing control over her body pushes these buttons from the past when she had been vulnerable or out of control. Also, a mother who has memories of abuse may find it hard to trust helpful birth assistants—even relaxing may cause her to feel vulnerable. Tense muscles tire more easily and become painful. Relaxed muscles work better and more comfortably. A history of sexual molestation is definitely one fear that you must come to terms with before birth. Not all sexually abused women replay flashbacks from their past. But if these memories have frequently resurfaced, birth is likely to bring them out even more vividly, and their effects more dramatically. Seek counseling from a professional experienced in this area.

As you can see, the fear-tension-pain cycle is under your control during labor. By identifying present fears and healing past memories you open yourself up for a more satisfying birth.

Letting go of tension. Tension can be decreased by using relaxation techniques to let go of the tension in your muscles. It is important to "let go" with the mind as well. For the Christian, this means trusting God, letting him take care of your worries and your pain. "Commit your way to the Lord; trust also in Him, and He shall bring it to pass" (Ps. 37:5). You can prepare for both physical and mental relaxation during pregnancy by practicing the techniques you will learn in class and by deciding to make trust in God a habit in all the areas of your life.

Think of a place you love to be—the ocean shore, the woods, your favorite corner at home. Imagine all the details—sights, sounds, smells, colors, the feel of the air on your skin. Hold this picture in your mind and use it to help relax your breathing, your body, your thoughts. Use this picture and all the sensations that are a part of it daily to help you relax. With practice, it will be ready for you to summon up in labor as a way of easing tension.

Is there some person or some little worry that bothers you daily? _____

_____

_____

Make it your goal during pregnancy to stop fussing about it and leave it up to God. Pray for his help. _____

_____

_____

_____

3. Take Responsibility for Your Birth Choices

If you don't, someone else will. You may think that as soon as you find out you're pregnant you simply show up for your prenatal checkups and your doctor will tell you what to do. Leaving the responsibility to your birth attendants to make decisions for you sets you up for a less than satisfying birth. The reason why we strongly encourage parents to be in charge of the birth is that over the years of attending births and counseling women after birth we have grown to appreciate that the way a woman gives birth is related, for better or for worse, to her overall self-image and confidence and to how she is able to mother her baby. Consider that giving birth is the most powerful act you will ever perform and that it should leave you feeling good about yourself. Come to birth empowered to make choices that will give you the birth you want. Here's how:

Take a childbirth class. Perhaps God meant pregnancy to take nine months to give you time to prepare. And preparing does not mean simply clutching your pillows and following the crowd in and out of the six-week hospital childbirth class. Find out what other childbirth classes are available in your community and select the one that best fits your birth-experience goal and your individual obstetrical situation. You may find some Christian childbirth classes in your community (see resources, page 79) which adds an extra dimension to your childbirth preparation. When Martha was teaching childbirth classes, she gave her students a list of scriptures to study during pregnancy and then to bring the comfort and power of these scriptures to birth. Here are some examples:

Scripture verses about how faith overcomes fear:

- Isaiah 41:10, "So do not fear, for I am with you . . . I will strengthen you." (NIV)
- 1 Peter 5:7, "Cast all your anxiety on him, because he cares for you." (NIV)
- Isaiah 43:1, "Fear not, for I have redeemed you." (NIV)
- 1 John 4:18, "There is no fear in love. But perfect love drives out fear." (NIV)
- John 14:27, "Peace I leave with you; my peace I give you. . . . Do not let your hearts be troubled and do not be afraid." (NIV)
- 1 Timothy 2:15, "But women will be saved through childbearing—if they continue in faith, love and holiness with propriety." (NIV)
- 2 Timothy 1:7, "God has not given us a spirit of fear."

For relaxation, try these verses:

- Isaiah 26:3, "You will keep him in perfect peace,/Whose mind is stayed on You,/Because he trusts in You."
- Matthew 11:28, 30, "Come to me, all you who are weary and burdened, and I will give you rest. . . . For my yoke is easy and my burden is light." (NIV)
- Psalm 37:7, "Be still before the LORD, and wait patiently for him." (NIV)
- Psalm 55:22, "Cast your cares on the LORD/and he will sustain you." (NIV)

For trust in your ability to give birth:

- Psalm 22:9–10, "Yet you brought me out of the womb;/you made me trust in you/even at my mother's breast./From birth I was cast upon you;/from my mother's womb you have been my God." (NIV)
- Psalm 71:6, "From birth I have relied on you;/you brought me forth from my mother's womb./I will ever praise you." (NIV)
- Proverbs 31:17, "She sets about her work vigorously;/her arms are strong for her tasks." (NIV) (This verse reinforces the importance of physical conditioning for birth.)

Childbirth classes. A Christian childbirth class led by a qualified childbirth educator is an important part of your preparation. In these small, intimate support groups, couples learn and pray together. This support group can become a valuable resource both during pregnancy and after birth. In addition to Christian principles, childbirth classes teach you prenatal exercises, breathing and relaxation techniques, a knowledge of what's happening in your body during pregnancy and in birth, self-help techniques to relieve pain and enhance the progress of labor, what you should know about various procedures and medications, and how to make informed choices through knowledge of all the alternatives. Upon graduation, you should be able to come to birth equipped with a plan for the birth you want, knowledge and techniques on how to get it, and the wisdom to be flexible if, due to circumstances beyond your control, the birth does not go according to plan. One of the most valuable parts of exploring all the birth choices in these classes is that the very process of exploring birth choices can be therapeutic. Understanding and making choices compels you to examine yourself, to know your strengths, your weaknesses, and your fears.

Perhaps the best part of taking a childbirth class is that it creates an environment to help you formulate your own birth philosophy. As you are making your birth choices (birth attendants, birth place, use of medical pain relief if necessary, etc.) you are forming a birth philosophy. And you will find the exercise of formulating your own birth philosophy both therapeutic and strengthening. How a woman approaches birth is intimately connected with how she approaches life. Formulating your own birth philosophy helps you to actively participate in important birthing decisions. Taking responsibility for your birth choices is important to have positive birth memories. If you need certain tests, technology, or a surgical birth, you are most likely to have no regrets if you have actively participated in these decisions. However, a woman who does not participate in her birthing decisions is often left with a "regret" birth, wondering what she could have done differently, and is likely to have less than satisfying birth memories.

Finding good childbirth education is an important way to equip yourself for a healthy pregnancy and a satisfying birth experience. There is much out there from which to choose. Childbirth classes are not all created equal, so don't just select the one that falls on a convenient night of the week.

While most hospitals offer childbirth education, they may not be the best place to learn about natural birth. The instructor may be more interested in teaching you how to be a "good"—that is to say, compliant—patient. She may herself be an obstetrical nurse at the hospital, and while she knows a lot about how things are done there, this may not be the way you wish to give birth.

Independent childbirth educators have a greater commitment to preparing couples to give birth as naturally as possible. Your doctor or midwife may be able to recommend someone, or ask around at places where new parents gather in your community. La Leche League or the local I/CAN (International Cesarean Awareness Network) group may be able to offer suggestions. You might want to look for a class that includes couples who are planning home births; this is a good sign that the instructor values intervention-free childbirth and will give you the tools you need. The class should cover the process of labor and delivery; techniques for dealing with pain, including relaxation and breathing; medical technology surrounding childbirth; how the husband and wife can work together; and breastfeeding and postpartum adjustments.

We urge you to look for a Christian childbirth class, if at all possible. You can benefit greatly from being around other Christian expectant parents, as all of you share your experiences, lift each other up, and grow together while awaiting the births of your babies. These classes are led by a qualified childbirth educator and use scripture references to study ways of dealing with fear and pain. Faith is the antidote to pain, and studying and praying together with others will build up your faith. You'll also learn the things included in any good childbirth class. To find a Christian childbirth class see the resources listed on page 79. If there are none, or if the class doesn't teach what you need, choose the best class for you and supplement this learning with one of the excellent books on Christian childbirth.

Some childbirth classes may use New Age ideas that are not acceptable to Christians, so be wary. These techniques may include hypnotic focusing of the eyes, transcendental meditation, and yoga. This vague kind of "spirituality" is definitely not of God.

If there are no Christian childbirth classes in your area, don't abandon the concept of having a spiritual emphasis for your birth. Choose a book on Christian childbirth, read it and pray through it thoroughly—use it to supplement a class offered in your community that fits the requirements for what a childbirth class should be.

Labor Support. You may want to hire a labor support person to be with you during the birth. She should be a woman with experience in childbirth, perhaps a childbirth educator or a midwife. She is someone who has given birth herself and who has educated herself about assisting women in birth. She can aid you in interpreting your body's signals, finding ways of coping with labor, and making decisions about using medical intervention wisely. Studies have shown that a labor support person can increase your chances of having the birth you planned.

RESOURCES FOR CHRISTIAN CHILDBIRTH EDUCATION

1. Sears, W., and Sears M. *The Birth Book.* New York: Little, Brown, 1994. Everything you need to know to have a safe and satisfying birth.
2. Wessel, H. *Under the Apple Tree.* Fresno, Calif.: BookMates International, 1981.
3. Wessel, H. *Natural Childbirth and the Christian Family.* Fresno, Calif.: BookMates International, 1981.
4. Apple Tree Family Ministries, Childbirth Educator Guide, P.O. Box 2083, Artesia, CA 90702-2083; 310-925-0149.
5. Holy Prepared, A Christian childbirth course, offered through

Reproductive Program Specialists, Inc., P.O. Box 1462, Huntsville, Alabama 35802; 205-830-0882.

6. Fellowship of Christian Midwives and Childbirth Educators, International. P.O. Box 642 Parker, CO 80134 (303) 841-2128, Fax (303) 841-5476

4. Choose Your Birth Attendant Wisely

Part of taking responsibility for your birthing decisions and developing a philosophy of birth is choosing the right birth attendant for you. Birth attendants do just that—attend the birth, but some are more attentive than others. Before you begin your search, decide just what you want in a birth attendant; in choosing a birth attendant, you may learn a lot about yourself.

List the qualities of a birth attendant you want and what role this person will have in your birth. _____

_____

_____

_____

_____

_____

For example, here are two types of mind-sets:

Do you want to be in charge of your birth and simply have an obstetrician on call for at your birth in case a complication occurs? After all, that is what the word *obstetrician* means *(ob stare,* "to stand by"). You will want to choose your positions during labor and birth. Keep interventions to an absolute minimum, and have the primary say in technology and medications. If you feel well prepared and confident in your knowledge of how your body works to give birth and are confident in your ability to read and respond to your body's signals during labor, this would be the birth philosophy for you.

At the opposite end of the spectrum is a mother who feels

more comfortable with her doctor completely in charge. She assumes that decisions made for her must be better than decisions she would make for herself, because she lacks experience and perhaps confidence. This mother generally feels more comfortable in the care of someone else and functions better under this umbrella. This mother may be setting herself up for a less than satisfying birth experience; she may not come to learn the wonderful powers of her body to give birth, or even more important how to use them. For her, the experience of giving birth is less likely to be a life-changing event, and less likely to have a positive effect on her overall self-image.

Put God in charge—Isaiah 66:9! We advise mothers to form a *partnership* with their birth attendant. You bring to birth a knowledge of the normal birthing process, a birth plan that helps you get the birth you want, and you use all the self-help relaxation and labor-easing techniques that work for you. Your birth attendant helps you work out a birth plan that is best for you and your baby and is there to help you change course should circumstances arise beyond your control.

The three VIP's as birth attendants. Your three choices of birth attendants are an obstetrician, a midwife, a professional labor assistant, all of the above, or some of the above. Most women today choose an obstetrician as the primary birth attendant. Some women feel comfortable with the medical model of birth and are delighted with the new pain-relieving techniques (especially epidural anesthesia) though there is some risk. However, for many mothers, an obstetrician-attended birth does not give them the full birth experience they want. Obstetricians, because of their training, approach birth as a potential complication ready to happen. They are more oriented toward a birth that may go wrong. For some women, especially those who have obstetrical complications, an obstetrician as primary attendant will be best. Other women find the chances of having a more positive birth experience are better with a midwife as their primary birth attendant. A midwife approaches birth assuming it will go right. A midwife is usually with the mother throughout her labor, giving hands-on, woman-to-woman support that laboring women need. We believe that for women to get the birth they want it is best to have both: a midwife to attend the birth and an obstetrician available should unexpected complications occur or a surgical birth be necessary. We feel that the obstetrician-midwife partnership is the maternity model of the future. In this way parents get both the science of obstetrics and the art of midwifery—a combination that is best for themselves and their baby.

A relative newcomer to the obstetrical scene, but nevertheless a valuable birth attendant to consider is a professional labor assistant (PLA, also called a labor support person). She may be a midwife, childbirth educator, obstetrical nurse, or any qualified person who is trained to support the mother during labor. The PLA meets with the couple at least once before birth to get acquainted and discuss their birth plan. She then attends the mother throughout her labor, helping her with relaxation techniques and giving continuous hands-on emotional and physical support, such as finding positions to ease the discomfort and speed the progress of labor. The professional labor assistant does not displace the father's role at birth, but rather frees him up to do what he does best: love his wife. The PLA makes no medical decisions herself, but often acts to interpret tests and procedures for the couple, helping them participate in decisions. Studies have shown that mothers having continuous labor support (with either a midwife or a PLA) are much more likely to have a satisfying birth experience and much less likely to need a cesarean birth. And be flexible; the birth script you write may not be the one your baby wants to follow. Be prepared to change birth plans, birth attendants, birth places, and any other on-the-spot alterations that may be necessary to give you both a safe and satisfying birth.

Laboring mothers (and fathers) often find great peace in having their birth attendants pray for them. If this is important to you, seek out a Christian obstetrician, midwife, or labor support person, and let them know how important prayer is during your pregnancy and

THE NEW BABY PLANNER

birth, to be able to ask God for wisdom in making birthing decisions. And pray for your birth attendants. I remember how good it felt when a mother once said to me, "I will pray for you. I always pray for my doctors."

Assembling the right birth team for you. Consider these possibilities:

1. Obstetrician as your only birth attendant. List what you believe the advantages and disadvantages of this solo birth attendant would be. _____

_____

_____

_____

_____

_____

_____

2. Obstetrician and professional labor assistant. _____

_____

_____

_____

_____

_____

_____

3. Midwife only (with medical back-up). _____

_____

_____

_____

_____

_____

4. Obstetrician and midwife (seen separately or in joint practice). _____

_____

_____

_____

_____

_____

_____

Assembling the right birth team is one of the most important decisions in taking responsibility for your birth. This birth happens only once. Make it special.

Selecting a birth attendant. Whoever you choose as a birth attendant will have a major influence on your birth experience. Shop around and interview a number of people before making a decision. Even if your choices are limited by your insurance plan, you will still find that there are differences, even among doctors practicing in the same hospital. As with all the major decisions you will make about your baby's welfare, pray for guidance in selecting the right birth attendant.

It is wonderful to find a Christian physician, one who shares your faith and who is willing to pray with you. However, the doctor's training and willingness to accommodate your desires are more important issues here than his or her religious orientation. Finding someone with whom you can communicate may be more important to you than finding a Christian doctor.

When you call to make an appointment with a prospective birth attendant, make it clear that this visit is only for talking. Questions about hospital affiliation, office hours, insurance, back-up, etc., can be answered over the phone by office staff. Your interview should concentrate on birthing philosophy and your own needs. Both parents should attend this first appointment. Prepare a written list of questions about your concerns. This should not be a laundry list of "what ifs" and possible interventions, but it should include the things that are most important to you: Will I be able to move around during labor? May I choose my own position for delivery? What is your feeling about medications for pain relief? You should also ask for some hard facts: What is your cesarean rate? What percentage of mothers in your practice who desire natural (drug-free, low intervention) childbirth actually achieve it? A low cesarean section rate and a good record of success with drug-free childbirth are clues that the doctor's actual practices support natural birth with more than just lip-service. Ask also about hospital policies, suggestions for childbirth education, and father involvement.

Be frank, honest, and open so that both you and the physician can judge whether you are right for each other. Physicians can't make absolute promises about what they will and won't do. They must reserve the right to use their judgment in each individual situation. When you choose a birth attendant you are not looking for someone who can be made to do all your wishes. Instead you are looking for someone with whom you can develop a trusting relationship based on mutual respect. Then, if problems arise, you can participate in the decision making and feel that you can rely on the doctor's judgment.

Make a list of issues you wish to discuss with prospective birth attendants. Arrange the items in order of priority. _____

_____

_____

_____

_____

_____

_____

Together with your partner, rehearse for an interview with an obstetrician. How will you begin the discussion? Use sentences that start with "We feel" or "We believe," rather than "We don't want . . ." or "What would you do if . . . ?" _____

_____

_____

_____

_____

_____

_____

Today, most births are attended by obstetricians and some by family practitioners. Special health problems usually call for the services of the obstetrician in monitoring the pregnancy and the birth. But when the mother is low-risk, another possibility is using a midwife as her birth attendant. Midwives make a specialty of low-risk, healthy births. They can provide prenatal care as well as attend births on their own. Certified Nurse-Midwives (CNM) have an education on the master's level and usually practice under the direction of a physician to whom they can refer patients if problems arise. Some CNMs do home births, but most work in hospitals or freestanding birth centers. Lay, or direct-entry, midwives receive their training in other ways, through a combination of schooling, study, and apprenticeship, and usually attend only home births. If you are considering a home birth with a lay midwife, ask for details about her training, how many births she has attended or assisted with, what kinds of emergencies she is prepared to deal with, and what her physician back-up situation is.

As specialists in normal birth, midwives bring a healthy mindset to the labor and delivery scene. They understand how mind, emotions, and body interact in labor and provide care for the woman as a person, not as just a medical situation. Many midwives are dedicated Christian women who see their profession as a ministry. (See Exodus 1:15–21 for the story of some canny midwives who served the Hebrew people in Egypt.)

Choosing a pediatrician. You will want to have the same sort of prenatal discussion with prospective pediatricians as with birth attendants. Prepare a written list of questions and concerns. These may include information on routine care for newborns in the hospital, support for breastfeeding, schedules for well-baby check-ups, and knowing when and how to call the doctor in an emergency. You may also want to discuss parenting philosophy with the doctor, especially if you are first-time parents and want to be able to rely on your pediatrician for child-rearing advice.

The pediatrician will also rely on you as parents—the people who know your child best. Intuitive parents make good judgments about how their children are feeling, and this helps the doctor provide a high level of medical care to your family. From this first interview you want to build a trusting, collaborative relationship with your pediatrician, so try to be positive in stating your needs and desires, be open-minded, and listen well.

Explain your parenting philosophy in a few sentences that you could share with a prospective pediatrician. _____
_____
_____
_____
_____
_____

What kind of a role do you envision for your pediatrician in the care and rearing of your child? Will you rely on the pediatrician for parenting advice as well as medical opinions? _____
_____
_____
_____
_____

5. Choose Your Birth Place Wisely

There is no right place to give birth to every baby, only the right place to give birth to *your* baby. Your options to consider are whether it is best for you to deliver in a hospital, in a birth center, or at home. Since today's parents want more than just delivering a baby—they want a positive birth experience—one of your decisions is which one of these birth places is most likely to give you the birth experience you want and is safest for you and your baby. Most of today's parents feel more comfortable with a hospital birth. They want the security of a hospital environment should an unanticipated complication occur. In recent years hospitals have become more labor friendly by yielding to consumer pressure and developing LDR (labor, delivery, recovery) rooms. When you do your search of birth places, spend a few minutes in the LDR room of your chosen hospital. Does this room give you a nesting feeling? Is this the room you would like to give birth in? But the attitude of the attending staff is more important than the physical attractiveness of the room. Like the LDR facility, do the staff also convey the attitude that birth is a normal process and that they will do their best to help birth progress that way? Besides being a conducive atmosphere to give birth, a benefit of an LDR room is that the baby stays in the room with the mother after birth. Fortunately, gone are the days when new mothers were treated like surgical patients, laboring in one room, being wheeled into an operating room-like area for delivery, recovering in a room separated from their baby after birth—a scene befitting delivering an appendix rather than birthing a baby. But don't be oversold with the designer appearance of "the room." In addition to your nest, people make the most difference at birth.

Try this exercise.

The five most important aspects you want from your birth.	Write down which facility (home, birth center, or hospital) is most likely to give you this aspect of the birth you want.

For parents who feel they will not be able to relax giving birth in a hospital or who are afraid that the risk of having a surgical birth goes up if they enter a hospital, a licensed birth center may be an option to consider. A birth center is a facility located near a hospital; it provides a high-touch, low-tech environment for women at low risk for obstetrical complications. Parents are encouraged to participate in the birthing decisions and the atmosphere is more homelike. Birth centers are staffed by certified nurse midwives with obstetrical backup. The main benefit of a birth center is not the physical facility itself, but the woman-to-woman support from midwives and the attitude that birth is a normal process. The fact that birth centers are a woman-run show makes this option very attractive. A birth center is a compromise option for parents who would be fearful of birthing their baby at home, but do not feel they need the high-tech facilities of a hospital. Best is to talk to mothers who have delivered their babies at the birth center you are considering. First, visit the birth center and interview the personnel. If you are considering a birth center, ask yourself the following:

- [ ] Is this a place at which you would feel comfortable birthing your baby?
- [ ] Do you have any obstetrical risk factors that might jeopardize the health of you or your baby if you chose an out-of-hospital birth?
- [ ] Is the birth center licensed and a member of the National Association of Childbirth Centers?
- [ ] Are the midwives licensed?
- [ ] Is there adequate obstetrical backup?
- [ ] How accessible is the nearby hospital?
- [ ] What facilities does the birth center have to transfer you to a hospital if needed?

Some women feel that they could be in harmony with their body best during labor by remaining at home. They are intimidated by the high-tech births at a hospital and may feel that a birth center

BIRTH IN THE CHRISTIAN FAMILY 89

offers little advantage over their home. If you are considering a home birth ask yourself the following:

☐ Are you a candidate for home birth? Do you have any potential or actual obstetrical factors that may put you at risk for a complicated delivery?

☐ Why do you want to give birth at home? Is it only because you're afraid of hospitals, or do you truly want to have a home birth?

☐ Are you confident in your body and your ability to give birth without the medical assistance that can be provided in a hospital? If you are at all afraid of a home birth, then you shouldn't try one.

☐ What professionals will attend your home birth? Do you have an experienced, qualified midwife? Does she have obstetrical backup? Do you live within fifteen minutes of a hospital obstetrical unit?

Use prayerful discernment in deciding where to give birth to your baby. Be responsible for your birth decisions, thoroughly exploring the possible choices of what is the best birth place for you and your baby.

6. Explore the Best Positions for Your Labor and Birth

Back birthing is neither comfortable for the mother nor healthy for the baby. The more you can stay off your back during labor, the faster your labor will progress and the less it will hurt. Lying on your back tenses the pelvic muscles, which need to relax as the baby descends. Tense muscles hurt more. Lying on your back allows your heavy uterus to press on the major blood vessels running alongside your spine, lessening the blood supply to the uterus and to the baby. And in this position you would be pushing your baby *uphill*. Scratch the birth scene of mother lying flat on her back, hands restrained, and feet up in stirrups. This is a scene from birthings past. The more time you can spend out of bed and moving around during labor, the better birth you are likely to experience.

There is no one right position for laboring or giving birth, only the ones that work for you. Stand, walk, kneel, squat as you explore what positions ease your discomfort and speed the progress of labor. Women do not have to be in a certain position, but women are so accustomed to being confined to bed during labor and birth that they may not realize what a valuable labor asset moving can be. Moving in response to signals of your body helps the baby to twist and turn to find the path of least resistance through your birth passage. Being upright allows gravity to help bring the baby down. Squatting widens the outlet of your pelvis. Most important is your freedom to move and experiment with whatever labor and birthing positions work for you. Feel free to improvise and be sure your birth attendants and birth place encourage you to do so. Go with the urges of your body during labor and avoid stereotyped positions that you are expected to assume. You are birthing your baby, and you have the right to choose your position. You can stand during labor, embracing your husband, supported by his caring arms. And you can give birth in a vertical, side-lying, or squatting position should this prove to be the most efficient and comfortable, and if your birth attendant is willing and able to accommodate your desired position. Women we have observed to have the most satisfying birth experiences assume many different positions at different stages in their labor. If one position does not work, they try another, and they are more likely to try different positions if they rehearsed them and conditioned for them before birth. The important thing is for you to choose your best birthing position, not someone else.

7. Use Technology Wisely

It is a wise couple who remembers that there are appropriate and inappropriate uses for technology. The laboring woman must be wary of medical interference in God's design for the birthing process. While tests and technology can be lifesaving in some circumstances, and can contribute to a safe and satisfying birth, some hospital routines and interventions can cause problems that kick off a spiral of interventions, each leading to another until finally the obstetrician determines that a cesarean is necessary.

Just entering the hospital and putting on a hospital gown is enough to slow down labor in many women. Being confined to bed or having one's freedom to move around encumbered by an I.V. or a fetal monitor may also slow down contractions. A drug can then be used to get the labor moving again, but the contractions that follow the use of artificial stimulation are usually much more intense, raising fear in the mother and making it more difficult for her to cope. So then she gets pain-killing drugs or epidural anesthesia, which can also depress labor or give the mother less control over her muscles when it's time to push the baby out. This can lead to a forceps delivery or a cesarean, with greater risks for both mother and baby. This out-of-control spiral can also leave a mother feeling like a passive victim rather than a woman who has grown in confidence from mastering the task of giving birth on her own. Taking responsibility for your birth experience is the best way to minimize the inappropriate use of technology. You are not entering labor expecting to "be delivered"; instead you are planning on giving birth. If you need a high-tech birth, educate yourself about the benefits and risks of technology, so that you can be part of the decision in the wise use of modern technology for birth.

8. Learn Self-help Techniques to Ease the Discomforts of Labor.

Women do not have to suffer or be drugged to give birth. It is not safe for a woman or her baby to be so heavily anesthetized that she is disconnected from her sensations during labor. Pain has a purpose, compelling a woman to make changes to do something to relieve it; and in making these adjustments in her body, she often increases her baby's progress and helps her baby's well-being. Unmanageable pain is not normal during labor, but is your body's signal that you need to make a change. Use the following natural techniques to ease the discomfort and speed the progress of labor—think PROGRESS to help you remember.

P PRAYER AND PROPER POSITION—pray for peace and strength during labor. Change positions frequently if, for medical reasons, you must stay in bed. Walk a lot during early labor.

R RELAX AND RELEASE your mind and muscles through massage, mental imagery (as in Psalm 23), breathing, music, etc.

O OUTPUT—urinate every hour; a full bladder creates painful spasms.

G GRAVITY helps; be upright: sit, kneel, squat, stand, walk.

R REST between contractions and let go of any tension from the previous contraction; don't fearfully anticipate the next one.

E ENERGY check—snack when hungry; drink to avoid dehydration.

S SUBMERGE in water if the going gets rough; best is a labor pool, otherwise a tub or shower.

S SUPPORT throughout labor, from partner and professional labor assistant.

By the time a woman reaches adulthood, she may already have heard or overheard plenty of "war stories" about the horrors of childbirth: "The worst pain I've ever experienced in my life"; "I was yelling 'Just give me drugs' "; "What I went through for you!" Consider the way birth is often portrayed in the movies or on television: a mother convulsed with pain, screaming and out of control, while the husband who is supposed to be helping her is frantic and behaving like an idiot. Many women are very afraid of childbirth because all they heard to expect is uncontrollable pain. It is even possible that a previous birth was a difficult one due to lack of knowledge and/or mismanagement by attendants.

The truth about childbirth. Childbirth is an intense experience, and substituting the word *contraction* for *pain* does not hide the fact that it can hurt. But it should be a good pain, one closely connected to pleasure. Allow yourself to experience it, to moan or make other sounds if that helps you, to turn entirely inward and concentrate on your body. Ride along with the emotions of labor as well: happy and excited when it begins, more intent on the work as it continues.

There is a point in many labors where the birthing woman experiences self-doubt or becomes very cranky. One mother we know, during the birth of her third child, told the midwife that if the next contraction didn't bring the baby down where he was supposed to be, she was going to get up, throw on some clothes, and drive away in her little yellow car. Her husband and the midwife thought this was uproarious—how wonderful to have a sense of humor at this point in labor! She, of course, was dead serious.

Feelings like this often come when contractions are most intense, with little time to rest in between. This happens near the end of the first stage of labor, shortly before it is time to actively push the baby out. This is not the time to call for pain relief, but to know that moments of trial and of doubt are all part of the experience. Remember that the authors of the Psalms, who could shout aloud to God with praise, also had dark moments of doubt in difficult times. You may be considering asking for pain relief. Instead, hang on to the Lord and realize that your baby will soon be in your arms.

We encourage expectant couples to search the scriptures and write verses with special meaning to them on index cards. You can use these verses during labor, to remind yourself of the Lord's presence and to aid you as you pray.

Severe pain during labor is a sign that something is not working properly. Natural childbirth does not mean that you passively suffer through it, but that you find ways to cope and to correct problems. Remember, if the pain becomes unmanageable, it is your signal to check your PROGRESS (see page 93). After twenty minutes or so, if the pain continues, *then* there is always the option of medical relief. Ask yourself, "Am I coping, or am I suffering?" If the problem cannot be corrected, medical or surgical intervention may be necessary, and we can be thankful that God has blessed our modern age with technology that has helped to make childbirth safer for both mother and baby.

Look through the book of Psalms and find some chapters in which the writer cries out to God from depths of despair. (Examples: Psalms 31, 38.) How does the psalmist relieve his fears? _____

_____

_____

_____

Are there promises from God here for you as well? _____

_____

_____

_____

Childbirth classes will teach you other ways, besides relaxation, of coping with pain during labor. Changing positions, getting into a tub of water, standing in the shower, having your back rubbed, being lovingly supported and comforted by your spouse—these comforting measures can all help your body do its work more efficiently. The more you can work with your body, instead of fighting it, the easier it is for your baby to be born. If your class is not spending a lot of time on these matters, with lots of individual attention (which means the class size should be no more than six couples), you need to find another class.

Think about your own history of dealing with pain. What have you done in the past to relieve discomfort from injuries, menstrual cramps, dental procedures? _____

_____

_____

_____

(For example, few women know that to relieve menstrual cramps, crawling into bed with a hot water bottle in a darkened room where you can completely rest and relax works wonderfully.)

Will you build on this experience in preparing for labor, or make different choices? _____

_____

_____

_____

What new techniques for dealing with pain would you like to try? _____

_____

_____

_____

Be open to new ideas; you never know what may work for you during labor.

Being responsible in any situation requires gathering information, making decisions, taking action, and assessing the results. How do these steps apply to the process of preparing for childbirth?

_____

_____

_____

To choosing a birth place or physician? _____

_____

_____

_____

To coping with pain in labor? _____

_____

_____

A word to fathers The prospect of being with their wives in labor scares many men. This is unfamiliar territory. Husbands are often given the role of "coach" during labor, only to discover that the experience is not at all like a football game or even a track-and-field event. "Coach" suggests that you are to be the strategy-maker, the one with the knowledge about the sport; but really, this is more than can legitimately be asked of expectant fathers.

In fact, trying to fine-tune the form of your laboring wife the way a coach might work with a long-distance runner may actually be doing her a disservice. She doesn't need you to be an expert on childbirth, critiquing her form or timing. Instead, she needs you to be an expert at loving and supporting her, and for this you have been preparing all the time that you have known her. Hold her, stroke her, encourage her, comfort her, respect her, but don't "coach" her. Here's where hiring a labor support person can be invaluable. The labor support person can supply the expertise that a coach would at a sporting event. You, the father, provide the loving emotional support that can come only from a lifelong partner.

If you can, talk with some other couples who have recently had babies. How did they work together during labor? _____

_____

_____

_____

What did the women most appreciate about their husbands' being there? _____

_____

_____

_____

While many men feel that they have not contributed much to their wives' efforts in childbirth, the women later say, "I couldn't have done it without you there holding my hand."

9. Use Medical Pain Relief Wisely.

If you leave pain relief up to your doctor and don't use all the self-help labor aids at your disposal, you are likely to be disappointed. A pain-free birth without risks is a promise your doctor can't deliver. Be sure you understand the risks and the benefits of using medication during childbirth. By participating in the decision to use medical pain relief and by doing your part to lessen the need for drugs, you increase your chances of having a satisfying birth and a drug-free baby. While medication, such as epidural anesthesia, may decrease the pain of childbirth, it also decreases your participation in one of the high points of your life. Having a completely anesthetized birth some women find to be a blow to their self-esteem and their female sexuality, and they may have long-term memories of a less than satisfying birth experience. There are situations, however, when the wise use of anesthesia and pain relievers can actually help labor progress (for example, if the pain is overwhelming and you are becoming exhausted), and actually contribute to safer and more satisfying birth. Your childbirth class should address the risks and benefits of using drugs during childbirth.

10. You Can Prevent a Surgical Birth—Most of the Time.

In many American hospitals 25 to 30 percent of mothers give birth by cesarean section. Why does the divine design for childbirth go wrong 25 to 30 percent of the time? Does this mean that the Creator made a mistake in how birth was meant to happen, or could it be that our interference with the divine design creates these alarming statistics? We believe that if mothers are given proper prenatal education and preparation, professional support during labor, the freedom to move with their bodies, then cesarean births should be necessary in only about 5 percent of women. There is a harmony to birth, an interconnection between mind and body and birthing systems. Nearly all labors could go according to divine design if mothers would use the PROGRESS tips listed on page 93. While cesarean births are life-saving in some instances, they are preventable in others.

Another surgical intervention that is nearly always preventable is routine episiotomy. By using perineal massage and support, avoiding the rush to push the baby out, and assuming a more vertical birthing position, you can spare yourself the discomfort of episiotomy most of the time. And I (Martha) speak from personal experience when I state that recovering from tear stitches is much easier than recovering from episiotomy stitches.

The reason why we want you to come to your birth armed with a lot of self-help measures is because a satisfying birthing experience gives a woman a head start toward a satisfying mothering experience. Spending the early weeks of motherhood healing physical and emotional wounds is not a good way to begin life with a new baby. Many times in our practice we see the *poor-start syndrome:* Mother has a traumatic birth experience, often an anesthetized surgical birth, and spends the early weeks devoting most of her energy healing physically and emotionally from her birth experience instead of using the energy to get into mothering.

BONDING AT BIRTH

All the effort put into planning your birth climaxes in the moment when you finally get to meet your baby face to face. Unless a compelling medical reason prevents it, a newborn should be placed immediately in mother's arms, against her warm, soft skin, near her comforting breast. Babies spend the first hour after birth in a state of quiet alertness, wide-eyed and receptive to the people who love them. Now is the time to touch and talk to and nurse this baby whom you know so well from the months inside you, and who is yet so new. The efforts of labor are quickly forgotten, and mother and father are both feeling high from the excitement. This special family time is the perfect beginning to your career as a parent, truly a gift from God. It should not be sacrificed to trivial hospital routines.

What happens if complications prevent you from spending this first hour with your child, because of a cesarean or a medical problem with mother or baby? The parent-child relationship will not be permanently affected. Parent-infant attachment is an ongoing process, and one that involves the rational mind as well as all the hormones and physical changes that follow birth. There is scientific evidence to support the idea of a special sensitive period for bonding in the hour following birth, but there is also evidence that suggests that being deprived of this time has no lasting effects. There is much in the first days with your newborn that will make up for being separated from your baby in the hours after birth, if that is what happens. But we do feel that keeping parents and baby together in the hour after birth gets them off on the right foot faster.

Ask your friends and relatives with children to tell you about their first experiences with their babies after birth. How did their preparation for the birth and the birth itself affect their experiences? What details do they most treasure? When did your mother and father first get to hold you? _____

_____

_____

_____

_____

_____

 ## HEALING THE LESS-THAN-PERFECT BIRTH

Sometimes, despite all the planning and preparation, births do not go as the parents hoped. Problems occur that necessitate medical intervention to safeguard the health of the mother and the baby. If you have done your homework and have talked through all the decision-making with your doctor as it occurs, you can have confidence that the choices made are the best ones possible in your situation. Of course, you will also want to pray about medical decisions made during the course of your child's birth. The more you can participate in determining the care you and your baby receive, the more in control you will feel and the better the outcome in terms of your attachment to your baby and your adjustment to parenting.

If your childbirth experience becomes one in which pain turns into suffering and you experience a great deal of fear and anxiety, it may take some time after the birth to put everything back together in your mind. Even if the baby is beautiful and you both are healthy, you may feel a sense of loss at not achieving the birth you hoped for. It is important to acknowledge these very real feelings and talk about them with someone who can be supportive and understanding. This might be a friend, a nurse, a childbirth educator, or perhaps someone in a cesarean support group. If there are things you wish you had done differently, you can ask God for forgiveness, and knowing that God forgives you will help you to ease up on yourself.

Unhappy feelings about the birth can sometimes get in the way of your developing attachment to your baby. The best medicine for this is large, frequent doses of your baby. As you hold her and enjoy the physical sensation of her, nurse her, and look into her face, you will find that your love for her will bubble up and drown out the grieving.

Do you have memories from past births that need healing in order for this birth to go better? What are they? _____
_____
_____
_____

Are there negative experiences in your past that affect how you feel about your body or your sexuality? _____
_____
_____
_____

If you are greatly troubled by something in your past, you certainly should pray about it and perhaps seek professional counseling before your baby is born.

ROOMING-IN

After the delicious first meeting with your baby, do not hand her over to someone else to care for. Do not think that you should let the nurses care for your baby so you can get some rest. God provides for mothers' rest after childbirth by making newborns sleepy as well. An hour or so after the birth, your baby will fall asleep and sleep deeply for two or three hours. This is the perfect time for the two of you (and also Dad) to rest together. And babies stay sleepy for the first few days, waking only to eat and to be held some. Mothers often enjoy just staying in their nest, holding their sleeping beauty, marveling at the miracle and resting in the after-glow.

I feel very strongly that hospital nurseries should be reserved for sick babies and babies of sick mothers. A mother cannot get to know her baby and start honing her motherly intuition when that baby is in a central nursery forty yards down the hall. The mother herself should be discovering when the baby wants to be fed, to nurse for comfort, to be held and in what way. Her body is primed to respond to her baby's signals. She has the breast ready when the baby is turning her head open-mouthed searching for it. Her hormones respond to the baby's cries. The baby is still so closely a part of her that she cannot be completely at rest without her little one at her side. In fact, mothers who room-in have less trouble with post-partum depression.

Even though the nursery staff has cared for hundreds of babies, they do not know this one specifically, nor do they have the biological attachment to this baby that compels a mother to respond quickly and completely when the baby is distressed. A new mother should not have to wait for someone to decide to bring her baby to her. By the time the baby arrives, wheeled into the room in a plastic box, whatever signal the baby was making has long since ended, and the baby has passed into another stage—perhaps totally un-glued and crying or sound asleep, having given up. Either way, it will be very difficult for the mother to try and nurse the baby or talk to her and enjoy her.

The best baby-care option for attachment parenting is full rooming-in, day and night, from birth until hospital discharge. Nurses should serve as consultants, not as primary caregivers. The baby will be more content, since someone is there to respond quickly to his needs. Mother will get more rest, since she is less anxious about her infant. Breastfeeding gets off to a good start, with lots of practice coming from frequent nursings. The baby is healthier, less likely to be jaundiced, and will actually cry less. Coming home will be less of a shock, since Mother is already beginning to feel competent in caring for her baby, and Father may also have had lots of opportunities for soothing and cuddling.

Even mothers who have had cesareans can have rooming-in, sometimes from very soon after birth if their husband or another helper can be there to assist them with lifting and positioning the baby for breastfeeding. The baby's presence may actually help them recover from the surgery.

Put yourself inside the mind of a newborn baby. How does it feel to be out in the world? What sensations are different from being in the womb? _____

_____

_____

_____

What will help you feel comforted and secure? _____

_____

_____

_____

 ## CIRCUMCISION

Until the last decade or so, virtually all male infants in the United States were circumcised. But parents began to question the reasons for the procedure, and many have chosen not to have their sons circumcised. For a while, the American Academy of Pediatrics was even mildly opposed to circumcision, although their current position on the subject is neutral. This is one more issue you need to think about during pregnancy—unless you are absolutely certain that you are having a girl.

Circumcision is the surgical removal of the foreskin, which covers the head of the penis. The baby, who is just a day or two old, is strapped to a board during the operation. Ideally, a local anesthetic is used, although many physicians perform the surgery without it. Yes, it does hurt, and babies often scream during the surgery and eventually may withdraw into a deep sleep to avoid the pain.

A lot of myths exist about circumcision—that it makes hygiene easier, that it prevents cancer, that it improves sex. Studies have shown that these claims are not true.

Some parents go ahead and have their infant son circumcised "so that he will look like his father" or "like his brother" or "like his friends." There may be strong feelings in the family about this, and these need to be discussed. But parents should realize that children (fortunately) are very accepting of individual differences and will not make the same kind of value judgments that adults might. Also, the number of boys who are circumcised is declining, so your intact son will almost certainly have peers who are also intact. Many fathers who at first are convinced that their sons should be circumcised change their minds as they become more informed.

Does the Bible command circumcision? The Mosaic law of the Old Testament made circumcision on the eighth day of life a sign of God's covenant with the Jewish people. Jesus' parents had him circumcised in accordance with the law (Luke 2:21). However, circumcision became a matter of controversy in the early church, with some Jewish Christians insisting that non-Jews should be circumcised in order to be saved. Paul, a circumcised Jew himself, addressed this issue in a number of his epistles, and he came down clearly on the side of a new covenant, sealed with Jesus' blood on the cross, that does away with all kinds of Old Testament rituals, including the blood sacrifice of circumcision. Circumcision is not necessary for Christians.

There is no mystery about caring for an intact penis. For the first one to three years, the foreskin remains tight and cannot be pulled back from the head of the penis. As it loosens and can be retracted, it is simple to pull it back and cleanse beneath it in the bath or shower. It's no more difficult than washing behind your ears, and young boys can easily be taught what to do. Parents should not pull the foreskin back forcefully, but wait until it retracts in its own good time. And be watchful lest some uninformed health-care provider decides to retract the foreskin. The bottom line in the care of the intact foreskin is simple: Leave it alone.

CHAPTER SIX

CARING FOR YOUR NEW BABY

New babies come in small packages, but they are full of big needs. Knowing what those needs are and how to satisfy them can seem like a real challenge at first, but as you get some practice, you will begin to feel more confident. God's design for parenting gives you lots of opportunities to learn from your baby and become sensitive to his needs.

 ## WHAT TO DO WHEN YOUR BABY CRIES

The dilemma. There is more bad advice floating around on the subject of crying babies than on any other parenting topic. I frequently have asked new parents what advice they have been given about letting their baby cry. Typical answers include: "You'll spoil her if you pick her up every time she cries"; "He must learn to be independent"; "You have to show the baby who's boss"; "Sooner or later he has to learn to soothe himself"; and the ever-popular "Let him cry it out."

This advice runs counter to most parents' instincts, but unfortunately, it does leave them feeling a little guilty, or at least confused. Their voices take on a confessional tone as they tell me, "I just can't let my baby cry like that. It ties me into knots. I have to go pick him up." They wonder if they really are doing the right thing for their baby by responding to his cries.

Identify some sources of "let the baby cry" advice in your life. How do these people make you feel? _____

_____

_____

_____

What are your feelings about living with crying babies? _____

_____

_____

_____

The Crying Communication Network. A mother once said to me, "I wish my baby could talk so that I could know what he wants." What she didn't realize is that her baby could talk, but that she needed to learn how to listen. With babies, crying is a way of talking.

Crying is how a baby communicates, and the more you heed your baby's cries and respond to them, the better you will understand the language. When you are learning a foreign language you have to get away from your book or your audiotape and converse with people who really speak that language. Learning how to communicate with babies also requires on-the-spot, person-to-person practice. The two of you won't always understand each other right off the bat, but if you stick with it and practice, soon you will feel more comfortable "talking" to each other.

Babies' ability to cry is God-given. Crying is not "bad." It is not a sin. It is not the baby trying to take control of his parents. Crying is how babies tell caregivers that something is not right with them and that they need someone to take care of their needs. The cry is actually designed to irritate adults. If it were a pleasant sound, Mom and Dad might not come running to do what they can to help. When a mother tells me, "Oh, her cries don't bother me anymore," I put a red flag on her chart; this mother and baby could be headed for trouble.

Parents, make no mistake about it: Babies' needs are genuine. They deserve the same respect you would offer an adult who was asking for your help. Babies need milk and warmth, comfort, love, clean diapers, a change of scene, security, freedom from pain, help with getting their bodies under control. Try this exercise to get an idea of the needs of the newborn.

Imagine yourself as a tiny baby in the womb. You are fed continuously through the umbilical cord, so you don't know hunger. You are always warm, afloat in water that caresses your skin. You are snugly held by the muscles of the uterus. You hear the rhythmic sounds within the uterus, but outside sounds are muted and distant. As your mother moves, you are rocked and comforted. Now imagine being born. How do all these sensations change? _____

_____

_____

_____

_____

What do you think this new baby needs? _____

_____

_____

_____

_____

One thing tiny babies don't need is to cry. Contrary to medical folklore, crying is not good for the lungs. In fact, it's physiologically stressful. Intense crying causes a surge of stress hormones in a baby's bloodstream and decreases the amount of oxygen in the blood. It is good medical practice to meet a newborn's needs promptly and prevent furious bouts of crying. This is one of the many reasons for having babies room-in with their mothers in the hospital. They will actually be healthier with someone right there to respond immediately to their cries.

What happens when you respond to a baby's cries? A baby cries because something is not right with him. He may be hungry or cold or wet or anxious, or perhaps he does not know what to do with these things called arms that are flailing about on the mattress. His mother, who is nearby, hears his cries and comes quickly to pick him up. He continues to fuss. She is not sure what he wants, but since he seems suitably dressed and his diaper has just been changed, she decides to offer her breast. His stomach has been feeling empty, so the warm milk really hits the spot. Sucking makes him feel good, and being cuddled into his mother's body gives him a sense of security. He nurses for five or ten minutes, falls asleep, and lets go of the nipple.

What has this baby learned? He learns that his distress is followed by comfort, that he can depend on his mother for help, that his own inner feelings are important and he can do something about them. These are all important lessons. As one mother told her husband, who had commented on what a life of ease their baby enjoyed, "He's just learning to be content."

In the long run, prompt responses to a baby's cries will actually help him learn to cry less. As he learns to trust his parents to help him, he discovers that he doesn't have to put out a red alert just to get their attention. They have discovered that a certain sound or action means hungry, or that he prefers being held up over a shoulder, so he doesn't need to cry about these things anymore. And he has gotten so in the habit of feeling right that even when something hurts or disturbs him, he can recover that right feeling very quickly, sometimes even by himself. Research studies show that babies who received prompt attention when they cried spent less time crying as they got older.

Does it seem curious to you that responding to your baby's cries will teach him to cry less? Does this differ from what other

advisers have told you? How do you feel about coming quickly when your baby calls for you? _____
_____
_____
_____

How to respond to your baby's cries. If you accept the fact that your baby's cries are her way of communicating, you will soon be able to figure out what those cries mean. Don't fight it, just respond spontaneously and intuitively to each whimper, complaint, or howl. If one thing does not work, try another. Hold your baby, walk him, nurse him, talk to him, touch him. Knowing exactly what is wrong is not nearly as important as offering some kind of response. If you must analyze, wait until you have calmed your baby; act before you think. Every baby speaks a unique language that parents must discover for themselves.

Eventually you will learn which sounds call for an immediate response and when you can hold off a bit. Sleep sounds may pass as the baby settles into a deeper sleep. Fussing during diaper changes may grow into outrage requiring holding and calming, or it may end once the snaps on the sleeper are all fastened. A cry of pain or any noise that seems to be headed upward on the anxiety scale demands a fast response. It is easier to comfort a baby if you get there before he becomes completely unglued.

Heed your own after-cry feelings. If you feel right about how you responded, then you made the right decision about responding to your baby's cries. If you feel uncomfortable, upset, or guilty, and these feelings are your own—not related to whether you followed the advice of others—then your response was not appropriate. Just as your baby's ability to cry is God-given, so also is your own sensitivity. Christians, after all, are called on to be compassionate and sensitive to others' needs. How often the scriptures tell us that Jesus took pity on those in need and acted to help them. Parents, be sensitive to your children as they try, in their own way, to tell you what they need.

This sensitivity is built right in to a mother's body. When she hears her own baby cry, the blood flow to her breasts increases, her milk may let down, and she will feel the urge to pick up her baby and nurse him. This physical sign is a clue to how God wants mothers to respond to their babies' cries.

As you work on becoming attuned to your baby's needs and cries, remember that it is not your fault that the baby is crying. Babies cry because of their own inner needs, not because their caretaker is learning on the job. Your task is to create an environment for your baby in which her communications are honored. Don't fall into the trap of taking each and every sound as a judgment on your parenting ability. Just offer a quick response and do the best you can. No one, not even one's own child, can be made to be happy 100 percent of the time.

The ultimate in sensitivity. As you get to know your baby better and he trusts you to help him feel right, you will find that you know what he wants without his needing to cry for it. Because you have been responsive, your sensitivity has increased to the point that crying becomes unnecessary. This is the ultimate in baby-parent sensitivity.

It is also a sign that each partner in this relationship trusts the other and trusts self as well. This trust is the foundation for many things to come. A baby who trusts you will grow up to respect your judgment on everything from the dangers of sticking fingers into electrical outlets to the complexities of adolescent friendships. Your trust in your child will show itself in your thorough knowledge of her, which will enable you to guide her better as she matures.

How do you feel about responding promptly to your baby's cries? Do you see it as building trust, or as allowing the baby to manipulate you? How can you increase your inner resources so that you can be more giving in your relationship with your baby?_____

_____

_____

_____

Write a prayer for parents of a crying baby. _____
_____
_____
_____

As your baby gets older, your response to crying need not be as immediate. You don't need to respond to a six-month-old as quickly as you did a six-day-old. The older infant can learn delayed gratification, and you can learn other ways of calming your baby. When a one-year-old cries and you are in the other room, often voice contact such as, "Mama's coming!" is enough to pacify the upset baby. When and how sensitively to respond to your crying baby can only be answered by the parents and not by outside advisers. When in doubt, refer to the original "Baby Book." When we cry out to our Lord for help, he doesn't return our pleas by saying, "Cry it out!" Psalm 3:4, "To the LORD I cry aloud, and he answers me." Parents, listen to this scriptural advice.

Responsive vs. Controlling Parenting. Restraint parenting, in which parents restrain themselves from responding, is very concerned with establishing control from the beginning. This philosophy assumes that responding promptly to a baby's cries allows the baby to manipulate you and, therefore, that it undercuts parental authority. They want to be sure that you are controlling the baby and not the other way around. Tiny babies, even older ones, don't think this way—this is assuming adult thought patterns that simply aren't there. Babies don't cry to "get your goat." They cry to get their needs met.

This philosophy equates control with discipline. However, discipline is something that is connected to a child's inner feeling, his wanting to do right and feel right, as well as his actions. As we discussed above, prompt responses to crying nurture the kind of self-trust and trust in authority that makes discipline possible as the child grows. Ignoring a baby's cries may make a parent feel like he or she is in control at the moment, but the baby learns that he has little control over his fate and develops no inner motivation to go

CARING FOR YOUR NEW BABY 113

along with his parents' leadership. Restraint parenting can seriously damage a baby's emerging sense of self.

But aren't you reinforcing negative behavior when you pick up a baby every time he cries? This is a common argument used by the restraint, controlling school of parenting. The answer is no for a number of reasons. First of all, a baby's cry is not negative behavior. As we said above, it is the baby's way of communicating; it has a worthwhile purpose. Second, if you respond quickly to the cry, you are actually teaching the baby that the early part of a cry, before it becomes desperate and intense, is enough to bring a response. This teaches him to cry "better" in a way that is less ear-splitting, and to develop ways of communicating besides a full-scale scream.

It's all too easy for us as adults to assume that not responding to a baby's cries will simply teach him to stop crying. But is this the lesson he is really learning when he is left to cry it out? After several nights of howling, he may quit crying for Mommy when he needs help, but he has also learned that his actions have no effect on the outside world, that he should expect to feel uncomfortable, and that he should just give up, since no one will listen to him anyway. Are these lessons you want your baby to incorporate into his world view?

Restraint parenting's effect on parents. Advice to "let the baby cry it out" hurts parents as well as infants. It presumes that any thoughts parents might have about why the baby is crying are pointless and that their impulse to comfort the baby is just plain wrong. They end up relying on the advice of outsiders who don't know their child at all. This sets up a poor pattern for dealing with children as they grow, and ultimately, parents do not get the sense of job satisfaction that comes with being encouraged to take responsibility and make their own decisions.

Following restraint advice will eventually desensitize new parents. When you are trying to get your baby to behave "by the book," you miss the signals he himself is giving you. You are more involved with yourself and measuring up to someone else's standards for "good" parents than you are with your unique little baby. There are a lot of mental gymnastics involved when you practice restraint parenting: "Is he crying because of a need or a habit? Is he trying to manipulate me? How can I be sure that I stay in charge?" Trying to answer these questions will tie your brain up in knots every time your baby cries, but all this thinking will not help you get to know your baby the way that simply responding to his needs will.

When babies don't get a response, they sometimes intensify their demands in order to get your attention, but eventually they may shut down, withdraw, and quit signaling altogether. The lines of communication are cut, and the baby loses his only resource for learning trust. And since he is not being responded to as an individual, being instead categorized as a challenger to the lines of authority in the home, he loses much opportunity to develop his sense of who he is as a person. These two losses set him up for major emotional and psychological problems in later life.

The "let your baby cry" advice is counterproductive and damaging to new parents. It sets up a dilemma within the mother and father: Do they follow the words of the experts or listen to their own glimmer of inner wisdom? Because they love their child so deeply and want so much to do what is best, they are very vulnerable and afraid of doing harm. But it is the advisers who wish to tamper with the parent-infant communication system who do the real harm. They should reassess whether their restraining, controling advice about parenting is really in keeping with Jesus' commands and example for us as Christians.

Jesus told us to treat others as we ourselves wish to be treated. He also taught us to pray to our Father in heaven with confidence that our prayers would be answered. How then can we not respond to the cries of our own little ones? Yes, parents must teach their children how to behave and to respect the needs of others, but these lessons are learned more easily and are more deeply incorporated into the child's personality when his own needs and desires are respected from an early age. We love God because he first loved us. Children love their parents because their parents show love to them.

NIGHTTIME PARENTING

Perhaps you think that newborns do nothing but eat and sleep. You'll soon discover that this is a myth. Sleep is a common concern of postpartum parents, but it's not the baby's sleep they are worried about. It's their own. "Lord, please give me one full night's sleep" is a frequent prayer on the lips of new mothers. There is no quick way to get babies to sleep through the night, but it is possible for parents to attend to baby's nighttime needs without becoming sleep-deprived.

You must approach your baby's nighttime cries with the same openness to communication that you have in the daytime. Babies cry at night for good reasons, and although the sound may seem more piercing and more urgent in the darkness, it still represents a baby's way of telling you he needs you. Prompt responses will help him learn to trust. Burying your head under the pillow and hoping that ignoring him will teach him to go back to sleep on his own sets up a cycle of insensitivity and mistrust.

What have you heard from other parents about their babies' sleep habits? What do you think nighttime parenting will be like in your household? _____

_____

_____

_____

Infant sleep patterns. Understanding the how and why of babies' sleep patterns will help you understand what is going on when your baby wakes at night. Babies do sleep differently than adults. God made them that way, and for good reasons. Sleep researchers have divided sleep into two main types: light or active sleep, called REM (for rapid eye movement), and deep sleep. If you watch a sleeping baby you can easily identify which sleep stage she is in. In light sleep, the baby is moving around, her breathing may be irregular, and you may be able to see her eyes moving under the closed lids. Deep sleep is a much sounder sleep, where the body is quiet and even the motion of breathing is almost imperceptible. It is more difficult to awaken from deep sleep than light sleep. The most vulnerable time for babies to awaken is when they are making the transition from deep sleep to light sleep.

Babies experience a greater percentage of light sleep than adults do, and their sleep cycles, the repetitions of light sleep followed by deep sleep, are shorter. This means that they have many more opportunities to wake at night than adults do. In babies, vulnerable periods for night-waking may occur every forty-five to fifty minutes.

Babies also fall asleep differently than adults. Adults can "crash" and fall into a deep sleep rather quickly, but babies must go through a twenty- or thirty-minute period of light sleep first before they are sound asleep. Many a mother can attest to this. The baby nods off to sleep in her arms, she slowly walks to the nursery to put him down in the crib, and just as she turns to walk away, her mind spinning with plans for the coming hour of peace and quiet, the baby wakes up, furious about the cold sheets, the hard mattress, his mother's absence. Back to the drawing board. Next time, she will wait longer, until her baby is utterly still, his body heavy and his arms and legs limp, before trying to put him down. And she'll gradually learn other tricks like using flannel sheets, a nightgown with her scent on it near the baby's nose, and perhaps a firm bolster for the baby to snuggle up to.

The trick to successful nighttime parenting is in gentling a baby through these vulnerable periods for waking. The baby does not yet have the skills it takes to fall back to sleep easily on his own the way an adult would. He needs help from his parents. If you can calm him and prevent him from waking up fully during these vulnerable periods, he will fall back to sleep more quickly, and so will you. Eventually, your baby will get the hang of dropping back into sleep on his own.

When you have the opportunity, watch your spouse sleep. Can you identify the sleep state he or she is in? What signs do you see? _____

_____

_____

_____

How has your sleep changed since becoming pregnant? Do you wake more often to go to the bathroom? Have you found ways to go back to sleep quickly? _____

_____

_____

_____

This is good practice for after the baby is born. If you have trouble getting back to sleep, try using your childbirth relaxation exercises to get comfortable and to clear your mind of daytime worries.

Why babies sleep the way they do. The differences between adult and infant sleep patterns are not just a matter of maturity. There is a grand design at work here. One thing I have learned during my years as a pediatrician is that babies do what they do for good reasons. If I can help parents to appreciate those reasons, they find it easier to accept their baby's nighttime needs. In the case of infant sleep, research suggests that God may have had more in mind than the comfort of new parents.

Night-waking has benefits for survival. A baby who could not easily be aroused by stimuli from within or without would be in danger. He would not get the food he needed when his tummy was empty. He couldn't alert his caregivers when he got cold. If his nose were plugged or he was having trouble breathing, he might not awaken.

Being a light sleeper may even help protect him from Sudden

Infant Death Syndrome (SIDS). One fairly well-accepted explanation for SIDS is that it is a disorder of arousal: SIDS occurs when the baby fails to awake from sleep in response to episodes of apnea, times when a baby momentarily stops breathing. SIDS incidence peaks around two to four months of age, the time when many babies begin to sleep more soundly and for longer stretches. Being a light sleeper may help a baby waken in response to signals from his body and prevent him from running into serious trouble.

Night-waking may also have developmental benefits. During deep sleep, the higher brain centers are inactive, but during periods of light sleep, the entire brain continues to operate. Sleep researchers theorize that this extra brain activity is needed during infancy, a time when the brain continues to develop rapidly. I told this theory to a tired mother in my office one day, and she sighed, "If that's true, this is going to be one smart baby."

COPING WITH INFANT SLEEP

Did God leave parents' needs out of his divine plan for infant sleep? Or is persistent fatigue part of God's plan for breaking in new parents? I don't believe that God would design a baby who was too difficult for parents to care for. Tired parents can neither enjoy their children nor do a good job raising them. How, then, can parents cope?

Here again, the answer lies in being open to a baby's signals. Each baby and family is different, and you must find the sleeping arrangement that works best for all three of you, mother, father, and baby. It should allow all of you to sleep well and leave you with a sense of rightness.

For many families the answer to nighttime parenting dilemmas lies in welcoming the baby into the parents' bed to sleep there from early infancy until he is old enough to sleep alone comfortably. When this happens parents and child share more than just a bed space; they share sleep. Mother's and baby's sleep cycles get synchronized, and the whole family shares an attitude toward sleep that assures everyone enough rest.

Sharing sleep continues the attitude of acceptance and mutual trust that responsive parents seek to build during the day. It accepts the baby's nighttime need for someone to help him through night-waking episodes, and it provides gentle, sensitive support. Parents who share sleep with their babies trust their child's signals and trust their own intuition, and they do this in the face of cultural norms and relentless advisers who insist that babies should sleep in cribs, in nurseries, down the hall and far away from Mom and Dad.

We have come to be advocates for sharing sleep after much prayer, research, and experience. We have practiced sharing sleep in our own family for sixteen years, and I suggest it to families in my practice as well. At this writing we share sleep with eighteen-month-old Lauren. It really works, and it is a beautiful, loving experience. The baby who was conceived in love, carried in mother's womb, and placed in her arms and upon her breasts at birth now sleeps surrounded by the warm, breathing bodies of those who love her. She will not have to leave this secure place until she is ready.

Many a morning I have awakened to gaze on the face of one of our "sleeping beauties." I watch the child stir, almost awake, reaching out for someone. A hand finds my face or Martha's breast and a look of serenity spreads over the chubby face as it settles back into sleep. Moments like this would be missed if our babies slept somewhere else.

Sharing sleep is part of a continuum of parenting philosophy. How is it similar to being responsive to your baby's cries in the daytime? _____

_____

_____

_____

Would letting a baby cry it out at night teach him to sleep better? What would it teach him about sleeping? _____

_____

_____

_____

HOW SHARING SLEEP WORKS

When Mother is close by, babies can go back to sleep easily during sleep cycle changes. Before they are fully awake, they can find the breast or a warm body to snuggle up to. They sense their mother's breathing, and the sound and motion are comforting. They don't have to wake with a sudden cry that disturbs others. And nobody has to get out of a warm bed and walk the floor.

Does this waking bother mothers? Usually not. When you share sleep with your baby, your sleep cycles become attuned to his. You both enter light sleep together, and you sleep deeply at the same time. Thus you are seldom awakened from a deep sleep, which is the kind of waking that is more disturbing and disorienting. As one mother put it: "I find myself waking up in the middle of the night for seemingly no reason, but then I realize that my baby is moving around restlessly, though not quite awake, and certainly not crying. I reach over and pull him close to me. He latches on and nurses, or sometimes just falls back to sleep with his cheek on my breast. I go back to sleep instantly, and in the morning, I can't even tell you if this happened once or four times, because I'm never awake long enough to think about it. I can't imagine getting up out of bed to breastfeed my baby at night."

There are many practical benefits to sharing sleep. Babies learn to sleep well anywhere, as long as Mom and Dad are nearby. This makes traveling and visiting grandparents much easier. It is easier to lie down with a baby, nurse him to sleep, and then slip away than it is to nurse the baby to sleep and then try to lay him in the crib. In the morning, baby is content to nurse and doze while you get to sleep late.

There may even be health benefits to sharing sleep. Certainly the mother gets more of the rest she needs to function well and stay healthy. Sleeping with baby and nursing at night boost breastfeeding benefits. It is our opinion that babies who share sleep grow and develop better, since they feel more secure. We also believe that sharing sleep may lower the risk of SIDS in certain infants. The stimulation that the baby receives from mother's closeness aids in arousal. The mother is a kind of pacesetter for her baby's breathing.

MYTHS ABOUT SLEEP SHARING

"Wait a minute," you say. "Everything I've ever heard about babies at night says don't let them into your bed. It will only cause problems. They'll never want to leave!"

Although cultural norms and plenty of parenting books suggest that there is something wrong with letting your baby into your bed, the practice is more common than you may think. Many parents are reluctant to admit that they frequently sleep with their babies, toddlers, or older children, since they are afraid of disapproval. But wherever parents gather and talk about children together, you'll probably find one mother confiding to another: "Your baby is in bed with you at night? So is ours!" And you'll find frequent magazine articles now written praising this idea, or at least giving it honorable mention as a solution for families to consider. And there are certainly more books giving it "thumbs up" now than there were sixteen years ago when we stumbled onto this solution with our high-need baby.

The objections that advocates of restraint parenting have to sharing sleep fall into three categories: dependency, danger, and interference in the husband-wife relationship.

Does sleeping with parents make a child more dependent? In the short run perhaps, but not in the long run. The fact is that babies are dependent little creatures. When they discover that having someone they love close to them helps them feel good, they will do what they can to continue the situation. What's wrong with that?

You cannot force a child to become emotionally independent. All you can do is trust him and help to create an inner sense of security for him that will become the base for independent operations as he is ready. Your baby will eventually sleep alone, but he does not need to achieve that goal yet. In our experience, when parents freely give the gift of sharing sleep, children ultimately become more secure and independent because they have not been hurried anxiously into a separate sleeping arrangement.

"But isn't sleeping with adults dangerous? What if we roll over on the baby and smother him?" The fear of "overlaying" is at least as old as Solomon. Remember the two mothers who came before him with the argument about who was the real mother of the baby? One of the women's infants had died in the night "because she lay on him" (1 Kings 3:19). This may actually have been a case of SIDS. Because there was no apparent cause for the baby's death, it was attributed to smothering, but we know now that these infant deaths while sleeping have some unknown medical cause. And if it was truly a case of smothering, remember that these women were prostitutes and likely to have been using mind-dulling substances that would render them senseless to the presence of a baby.

Where there are reliable reports of babies being overlaid, there are also extenuating circumstances: the parent is drunk or drugged or there are too many people squeezed into a small space. When mothers share a bed space with tiny babies, they are acutely aware of where the baby is, even while they are sleeping. Fathers may worry about throwing an arm across the baby's face, but this can be prevented by having baby sleep between the mother and a guardrail on the edge of the bed. This arrangement also allows the husband and wife to enjoy cuddling up together.

Perhaps the most loaded objection to sharing sleep is the argument that the baby should never be allowed to come between the husband and the wife. We would agree that a baby should not divide a couple. God, who instituted marriage, did not plan that children should interfere in the marriage relationship; instead, having a family should enrich both husband and wife in their dealing with each other. So what happens to lovemaking when the baby is in the parents' bed? The master bedroom is not the only place to have sex, and the two of you, no matter how devoted you are to your baby, are still smarter than he is. Becoming co-conspirators in search of a time and a place for making love can add a new dimension to your life together. If the two of you want to be alone, the baby can even sleep elsewhere for part of the night, until you are ready for him to join you.

Did you ever sleep with your parents or spend time in their bed when you were young? Did you sleep with a sibling, a cousin, with Grandma? What memories do you have of these occasions? _____

_____

_____

_____

What myths have you heard about babies and parents sharing sleep? Do you have some misgivings yourself? _____

_____

_____

_____

How do you think the parents' attitude toward their baby affects their choices of where the baby should sleep? _____

_____

_____

_____

What does a baby learn from being welcomed into the parents' bed? _____

_____

_____

_____

124   THE NEW BABY PLANNER

WHEN SHARING SLEEP DOES NOT WORK

Sharing sleep works well for most families most of the time, but it does not work for everyone. Mother and father together must make the decision about what is best for everyone. Some couples, and especially fathers, may be reluctant to try this arrangement, because it goes against cultural norms for baby care and the marital bed. We feel that this is an area where fathers should trust their wives' intuition. That biological connection between mother and baby, especially when they are breastfeeding, is a key to God's plan for nurturing.

Sharing sleep works best when parents have positive feelings about the idea. Babies can pick up on the negative vibrations when sharing sleep is tried as a desperate last resort. It is best begun in early infancy. With an older baby there will be a longer adjustment period, during which everyone learns to respect each other's space and avoid (or adjust to) elbows and feet to the ribs.

With some mothers, this nighttime intimacy is simply too much. We sincerely respect and sympathize with the woman who devotes herself to her children all day, but feels that she cannot rest and recharge her energies with her baby in bed with her at night.

LEARNING TO SLEEP ALONE

Most children wean from their parents' bed sometime between two and three years of age. At first they may sleep on a mattress on the floor in your room or with an older sibling, but eventually they will be happy in their own room and in their own big bed.

What variations on sharing sleep are possible in your house? Some parents take off one of the crib rails and push the crib up against their own bed. Some use a mattress on the floor for "overflow" from the big bed—toddlers, teddy bears, nursing babies, or Dad on a restless night. Others invest in a king-sized bed rather than fancy nursery furniture. What do you think will work for you?____

Fun in the family bed. In years to come you'll remember fondly the time when your baby slept in your bed. And you'll have funny stories to share. One mother, a singer, got up early one Sunday morning to prepare her solo for 8:30 church, while baby and Dad slept in. She returned from her shower to find her eight-month-old still half asleep, trying frantically to latch on to Daddy's chest.

GETTING YOUR BABY TO GO TO SLEEP—AND STAY ASLEEP

From our experience of nighttime parenting eight children, here is the Sears family's six-step strategy for getting a baby to go to sleep and stay asleep.

1. **Wear your baby a lot during the day.** Carry your baby in a sling for several hours a day. Babywearing mellows the infant during the day, a behavior that carries over into restfulness at night.

2. **Tank up your baby during the day.** Some babies are so busy playing during the day that they forget to eat and make up for it during the night by frequent wakings to feed. To reverse this habit, feed your baby at least every three hours during the day to cluster the baby's feedings during the waking hours. Upon baby's first night waking, attempt a full feeding (sit up in bed if you need to), otherwise some babies, especially breastfed infants, get in the habit of nibbling all night.

3. **Set up a predictable and consistent nap routine.** Pick out the times of the day that you are the most tired, for example 11:00 A.M. and 4:00 P.M. Lie down with your baby at these times every day for about a week to get your baby

used to a daytime nap routine. This also forces you to get some much needed daytime rest rather than being tempted to "finally get something done."

4. **Honor your husband with his share of nighttime parenting.** It's important for babies to learn to get used to father's way of comforting and being put to bed in father's arms, otherwise mothers burn out. (Remember, burnout occurs more frequently in the most committed mothers. You have to be on fire to burn out.) A father's participation in nighttime parenting is especially important for a breastfeeding infant who assumes the luxury that "mom's diner" is open all night.

5. **Arrive at a sleeping arrangement that works for your whole family.** Some babies sleep better in their own rooms in their own bed, others sleep better in their own bed in their parents' room, and some babies sleep better nestled next to a warm body in their parents' bed. Where all of you sleep best is the right arrangement for you. There is no right or wrong place for baby to sleep. You may find that your older baby sleeps better—and so do you—with him on a mattress next to your bed or in a sidecar arrangement— moving the crib adjacent to your bed.

6. **Remove conditions that cause nightwaking:** food allergies (formula if bottlefeeding or nutrients in your diet if you are breastfeeding), irritating sleepwear (try flame-retardant, 100 percent cotton), squeaky cribs, nasal irritants or allergens in the bedroom (e.g., mildew, dust from feather pillows, down blankets, stuffed animals, chemical fumes from perfumes, cleaners, tobacco, even certain furniture or heavy traffic outside). See also, "Causes of Fussiness," p. 213.

These steps not only help your short-term goal of getting your baby to sleep better but, more important, create a healthy sleep attitude that lasts a lifetime. A baby who enjoys this style of nighttime parenting learns that sleep is a pleasant state to enter, and not a fearful state to remain in. Therein lies the key to nighttime parenting.

BABYWEARING

By now, you have probably figured out that babies prefer to be with their parents, day and night, waking and sleeping. Most don't like to be left alone for long, and they are most content when they are carried or held and can enjoy physical contact with mother or father. If you assume, as we do, that God made babies this way for a reason, you are ready to learn about the art of babywearing.

Babywearing means that for much of the day your baby is carried in a baby carrier, next to your body. Babies who get this kind of treatment cry less, have less colic, and are more content. Babywearing satisfies a number of infant needs and, in doing so, helps them develop better and helps their parents do a better job of caring for them.

Babies prefer to be in motion. This is what they have been accustomed to in the womb. Left on their own in a crib or even in a swing, they cannot get the kind of three-dimensional movement that they enjoy when carried by an adult. This movement stimulates and comforts them, so that when they are carried they are less likely to have missing-the-womb feelings that make them fuss.

Being constantly carried by mother helps a newborn to regulate himself. Newborn infants move in a jerky fashion, and they seem to have little control over their arms and legs. They easily become overstimulated and upset. They don't have a sense of day and night. Being constantly with mother helps to get these problems under control. The rhythm of mother's walk and her breathing, the familiar heartbeat, all help to calm baby. The continued closeness helps to regulate the hormones that influence the rhythm of daytime waking and nighttime sleeping. Hearing mother's voice may help to control limb movements; video analyses of infant movements while mother was talking have shown that babies move their arms and legs in synchrony to the rhythm of mother's speech.

Babywearing also teaches babies to cry "better." When mother is close by, the baby's early crying sounds or even the pre-crying noises get prompt attention. The baby never has to go all the way to "red alert" to get what he needs. Because he feels confident of a response, he soon learns to get what he wants by asking only with the more pleasant early sounds. The mother also learns how to interpret all the baby's non-crying modes of signaling and reinforce them with a nurturing response. Everyone benefits from this sensitive communication network.

Babywearing is especially helpful when babies are going through fussy periods or with high-need babies who would tend to fuss all the time. Wearing the baby helps to calm and mellow the baby. Mother can go about her tasks for the day with the baby attached to her, and her movement and everything she does will help him to calm down. In fact, I have prescribed wearing the baby in a sling for at least four hours a day as a "treatment" for infant crying. When parents come back into the office on a return visit, they tell me that not only is the baby crying less, but when he does cry the sound is less nerve-shattering. This makes a big difference in how parents experience and enjoy their babies. I also prescribe babywearing for infants who have medical problems or who are failing to thrive. Being carried gives these babies a stress-free environment, freeing up their energies for healing and growing.

Carrying also helps babies to learn. Infants who are carried spend more time in the state of quiet alertness, in which they are most receptive to their environment and to people. They get more chances to interact with their parents and learn about the subtleties of facial expression, vocal tone, movement, and other kinds of body language. Parents will also talk more frequently to a baby who is right there under their nose. Traveling around up near adult eye level also exposes infants to more of the world around them. A crib, even if it is well-decorated, has a very limited view of the world, and swings, carriages, and strollers are not really where the excitement is either, at least not for long.

When her baby is right there on her hip, a mother involves her child in what she is doing. This is a real contrast to the thinking that suggests that babies should have lives and schedules separate from mom's, with long stretches spent in a crib, swing, or playpen amusing themselves. Without mother or father there as a guide, the sounds and activities going on around a baby have little or no meaning to her, making them less valuable as learning experiences.

Imagine yourself doing one of your favorite activities or traveling to one of your favorite places. _____

_____

_____

_____

Now redraw the picture in your mind with your baby included. Can you share this experience with your baby? _____

_____

_____

_____

Will babywearing make it possible for you to continue to participate in adult activities? _____

_____

_____

"Shouldn't my baby learn to soothe himself?"

Babywearing is another one of those time-tested infant-care practices that calls forth objections from those who advocate a restraint approach to parenting. They decree that too much carrying spoils children and that babies must become self-soothers in order to be independent and feel good about themselves. God must have had other ideas when he had Isaiah write: "You will nurse and be carried on her arm/and dandled on her knees./As a mother comforts her child,/so will I comfort you" (Isa. 66:12–13 NIV). "He tends his flock like a shepherd:/He gathers the lambs in his arms/and carries them close to his heart" (Isa. 40:11 NIV). And in Isaiah 46:3–4: "Listen to me . . . you whom I have upheld since you were conceived,/and have carried since your birth. . . . I have made you and I will carry you."

"Spoiling" is a strange concept. No one wants to have a spoiled child, one who is bratty and selfish and who talks back to parents. But for fruit to spoil, you have to leave it alone on the shelf for several days. We believe the same is true of children: Leaving them alone is not good. Constant, dependable, loving attention helps them thrive. Yes, babies who are carried a lot come to expect it and will complain when they are left on their own. But this is because they feel good when they are with mom, and they want to go on feeling this way. Give them enough "feel-good" experiences and they will get in the habit of being content.

Self-soothing babies come to depend on pacifiers, blankets, and other inanimate objects for the comfort they seek. They learn at a much-too-early age that they are alone in a cold world and they can't depend on other people, even those who love them. We do not believe that these are healthy psychological lessons. They will not help a child form solid relationships later in life.

Consider how God responds when his people are in need. Does God ever turn his back and say, "You're on your own—it's good for you"? This is not the way God's promises work. "Lo, I am with you always," says Jesus in Matthew 28:20. There are many references in scripture to God carrying and sustaining his children in peace and security. "You whom . . . I have carried since your birth. I have made you and I will carry you" (Isa. 46:3–4). We believe that these images of God have implications for human parents as well.

What are the most effective ways for adults to find comfort? In things or in food or in alcohol? By being left to sulk and stew? Or by talking it over with a spouse or a trusted friend? How does this apply to babies and children? _____

_____

_____

_____

PRACTICAL CONSIDERATIONS FOR BABYWEARERS

Over the years, Martha and I have experimented with a wide variety of baby carriers and have worn our babies in all kinds of situations. We have found that a cloth sling-type carrier is the easiest and most versatile to use. It adapts to infants and toddlers in various stages of development and with different preferences for how they wish to be held. It is easy to use, easy to take along, works for fathers as well as mothers, and comes in a variety of colors and patterns, so it adapts to your wardrobe as well.

At first, a young baby is cradled in the baby sling on the parent's front. He can remain in the sling for breastfeeding, and the mother can pull up the cloth to cover the baby and nurse discreetly. As he gets stronger and can support his head and upper back, he can sit up in the sling, facing forward and looking out—something that can't be done in most front-pack carriers. When he gets big enough, he is shifted to the parent's hip, and the baby sling helps to distribute the weight between hip and shoulder. This keeps arms from tiring and is easier on the mother's lower back.

Some babies take longer than others to get accustomed to being carried in a sling. They may have a tendency to stiffen and arch their backs. Babywearing puts them into a bent position that will counteract these tendencies and help them get their bodies under control. Start wearing your baby as soon as you can after birth and be patient and persistent. The early effort pays off with a peaceful, convenient way of keeping your baby near you. Ask an experienced babywearer for help if your baby can't get comfortable.

We've known mothers who have worn their babies under all

kinds of circumstances—at work, out to formal dinners, while giving lectures or singing in the choir. Baby slings are invaluable for getting work done around the house. You can wear your baby while vacuuming, washing dishes, folding clothes, or playing with older children.

Babywearing works well for getting little ones off to sleep. Put the baby in the sling in the position she finds most comfortable and least stimulating. Then go out for a walk or find something uninteresting to do around the house. Baby will soon settle and sleep. When she is sound asleep, lay her down on the bed, still in the sling, and carefully slip it over your head.

On a trip to the local baby store, investigate different kinds of carriers. How are they used? Which ones can be used with newborns? Which with older babies and toddlers? _____

_____

_____

_____

_____

What kind of carrier would you enjoy wearing? _____

_____

_____

Are baby slings available in your area? If you can't find them easily, contact our babywearing helpline: (800) 541-5711.

As baby gets bigger, the amount of carrying you do will decrease. Your baby will let you know when he wants to be down on the floor to practice his motor skills. But even after he begins to walk, there will be times when he wants to be carried, and toddler-wearing is a peaceful alternative to whining and having an unsteady child clutching at the hem of your skirt.

Babywearing works for dads as well as for moms. Babies enjoy the warm fuzzy of being worn next to dad's chest, skin-to-skin. They also like the neck nestle, when they are carried upright, with their head nestled under dad's chin. If you talk or sing in this posi-

CARING FOR YOUR NEW BABY 133

tion, the baby not only hears the sound but feels the vibrations from your voice box. Since fathers' voices are deeper and the vibrations are slower and stronger, dads have an edge over moms when it comes to using the neck nestle.

Even babysitters can use the baby sling. The familiar feel and style of being held will help the baby feel secure even while mom is away.

Babywearing has been practiced around the world in many cultures. In Bible days, women used their shawls to wrap their babies around themselves and keep them close. As families rediscover how it makes life easier for mother and how good it is for babies, we are certain that babywearing will become the childcare style of the nineties.

THE NEW BABY PLANNER

CHAPTER SEVEN

ADJUSTING TO PARENTHOOD

Parenting calls for a large commitment to your baby, getting to know her needs and responding to her in a way that helps her grow and mature. This commitment to your child needs a nurturing environment in which to flourish. Both mothers and children need fathers to be actively involved with the family, both in child care and in giving the family its spiritual direction. Parents must keep in mind that a stable, fulfilled marriage relationship is the foundation of successful parenting. While children bring challenges to daily living, meeting these demands together helps both husband and wife to improve their sensitivity to each other. As a result, the quality of the marriage relationship improves and matures.

 BECOMING A MOTHER

As the euphoria of birth wears off and the reality of daily baby care sets in, most mothers experience some degree of difficulty adjusting to the changes that have taken place in their lives. *Understanding* and *anticipating* these difficulties, taking steps to alleviate them before they get out of hand, will help to prevent bigger problems from developing.

Postpartum problems are caused by a mother's inability to adjust appropriately to the many changes happening so suddenly. This can show itself as "baby blues" in the first week or two after birth or as a full-blown postpartum depression in the months to follow. Having these feelings is not a sign of weakness, of being a "bad" mother, or of "not really wanting children after all." It is basically an adjustment problem, a reaction to combined stresses. Everyone has a different capacity to cope with change and a different way of doing so.

A woman's body goes through tremendous physical changes in the postpartum period. Hormonal changes affect moods and emotions as well as regulate the body's shift from a pregnant to a non-pregnant, lactating state. Changes in sleep patterns also affect feelings. Even if you are managing to sleep when the baby sleeps, the change from the usual adult, eight-continuous-hours way of sleeping to this more fragmented way of getting your rest can leave you feeling exhausted at first. Being physically and emotionally drained from a difficult birth or having to recover from a cesarean also contributes to postpartum troubles. When the birth did not turn out as you had long planned it, especially if fear and pain predominated, you will need to deal with feelings of loss and anger as well.

List some of the immediate physical changes brought about by the birth of your child. Are some changes for the better? _____

_____

_____

_____

How does attachment parenting help you cope with these changes? _____

_____

_____

_____

136 THE NEW BABY PLANNER

New parenthood also brings changes in identity and even status. The mother's daily life is all wrapped up in the needs of her baby, and she may feel that she is losing sight of herself as a person. If the baby is fussy, isn't sleeping well, or is still trying to master breastfeeding skills, she may not feel very successful as a mother, and her self-esteem is on the line. Her husband or her friends may remind her that she has the beautiful baby she longed for, and she ends up wondering, "What's wrong with me? Why can't I enjoy my baby?" If she worked outside the home before she had children, she may miss the camaraderie of the workplace and the status (and paycheck!) given her as a productive member of the work force.

Babies when they are born do not have a concept of themselves as individuals. They don't have a sense of separateness, but instead feel one with the mother. Mothers, too, often feel that their newborn is still a part of them. How will this affect the way they care for their babies? _____

_____

_____

_____

How will they feel if the baby cries and is difficult to comfort?

_____

_____

_____

How does attachment parenting help to recreate the sense of oneness the mother and baby enjoyed during pregnancy? _____

_____

_____

_____

Even if a woman's feelings about becoming a mother are basically positive, adjusting to change takes time and emotional energy. Having the "blues" or feeling depressed is a sign that some of these social and emotional issues need to be addressed and that steps must be taken to make the adjustment easier. There's a saying, "If Mama ain't happy, ain't nobody happy." This doesn't mean mothers should always put themselves first, but it is a reminder that it is very difficult for a woman to give freely to her children when she herself is feeling stressed out.

 ## EASING THE ADJUSTMENT

As with everything else in life, realistic expectations will make it easier for you to cope with postpartum adjustments. Get rid of your perfect picture of motherhood, and prepare for the reality instead. Be flexible. From the onset of labor, you cannot control everything that will happen to you and your child. You may have an elaborate birth plan for the "ideal" delivery, complete with wardrobe and musical score, but medical necessity may force you to abandon these plans. If you are too rigid about your expectations, you are bound to be disappointed somewhere along the line.

Ask for rooming-in. While it might seem like having the baby with you all the time in the hospital would make you more tired, most mothers find that they get more rest if they can keep their baby with them in the same room. They can begin to get "in sync" right from the start and enjoy their attachment to their baby, even if they are disappointed with other parts of the birth experience. Do limit visitors in the hospital. It's fine for dad to be there most of the time and for grandparents to stop in for a visit, but this should be a time to concentrate on the baby, not on polite chatting with friends and relatives.

Nesting at home. Even after you and your baby return home from the hospital, it is wise to limit visitors and phone calls. But do ask friends and family for help. Delegate household responsibilities. And here's where *anticipation* pays off: You can plan ahead in the month before the birth and cook double amounts for your dinners, freezing half and stockpiling a few weeks' worth of food. When people ask if there's anything they can do for you, say yes! The housework, cooking, and clean-up, even laundry, can be done by someone else. If you can afford it, now is the time to hire help and send out for dinner. This is money well spent, an investment in getting the family off to the right start.

One way to remind everyone that you are concentrating on your baby and on recovering from the birth is to keep your nightgown on for the first week or two at home. (An attractive robe and nursing nightgown make a great baby shower gift. Suggest this when someone asks you, "What do you want for the baby?") As one mother of a large family put it, "I simply sit in my rocking chair, dressed in my nightgown, nurse the baby, and direct traffic."

When helpers (i.e., mother, mother-in-law, aunt, etc.) come to visit, be sure that they help you with household jobs so that you can concentrate on the baby. They should be mothering you, and you should be the only person acting like the baby's mother. Be clear about your needs ahead of time. If it's hard for you to give orders, post a written list on the refrigerator of what has to be done. Let go of any compulsion you have to make sure things are done your way, or that you have to be Superwoman, and enjoy the help. Be sure to tell your helpers that you really appreciate having these jobs done, because it frees you up to do the one job that only you can do: mother your baby.

Make a list of things you would like friends and relatives to do for you in the weeks after the baby is born. _____

_____

_____

_____

_____

Post the list by the phone as a ready reference if anyone offers assistance. Add to it as necessary. Also, start collecting menus from restaurants that offer carry-out food or that deliver, especially ones that offer healthy food along with pizza. Keep these near the phone as well.

Avoid isolation. While too many visitors can be a problem, trying to cope with change all by yourselves is not a good idea either. Seek out friends and family members who can support you in a positive way. Call a La Leche League leader if you have questions about breastfeeding. Talk to experienced Christian couples whose parenting philosophy is similar to yours. Avoid negative advisers, people who want you to care for your baby in a way that goes against your own intuition. Taking their advice sets you up for postpartum depression, since mothers are not designed to function well emotionally in a way outside of God's design. And arguing with negative advisers distracts you from the more important task of getting to know your baby.

What would you say to someone close to you who insists that you should not hold your baby as much as you do or not answer his cries? State your beliefs simply and in a non-threatening way. _____

_____

_____

_____

Think of other ways to deal with criticism without getting into arguments.

Care for yourself. Good nutrition is absolutely essential when you are under stress. Sweets and junk food contribute to blood-sugar swings and emotional ups and downs, filling you up calorically yet adding nothing to the healthy functioning of your body. Lots of fresh fruits and vegetables, along with whole grains, low-fat dairy products, and lean meat and chicken are a healthier diet for new moms and for dads, too. Now is not the time to worry about losing weight. Pounds gained during pregnancy will come off in their own good time, especially if you are nursing. Continue the same balanced diet you ate while pregnant, and let exercise and time take care of the weight loss. Nutritious snacking will help you get all the nutrients you need, even if your meals are interrupted by baby's needs.

THE NEW BABY PLANNER

Make a pre-birth grocery shopping list. Include nutritious, easy-to-fix snacks for both mom and dad. Stock up so that you don't have to do major shopping for several weeks after the birth. _____
_____
_____
_____

We all have what are referred to as "comfort foods" (ice cream, pudding, chocolate, heaps of mashed potatoes and gravy, etc.). If you identify some foods now that can fill the comfort need yet still be somewhat nutritious, you won't feel deprived and depressed about what you "can't" eat. Ask a nutritionist for some help planning this if you get stuck. Make a list. _____
_____
_____
_____

Looking good will help you feel good. Get your hair cut before your due date, and plan what you will wear in the weeks after your baby is born. It can take several months to get your figure back, so it's wise to have attractive elastic-waisted clothes that you can wear in the meantime. Loose, colorful tops that are appropriate for breastfeeding will also help brighten your outlook. Go shopping with your husband or a trusted friend who can hold the baby and help you pick out at least one nice outfit to tide you over until your old clothes fit.

Do something for yourself. Mothers need special time for themselves, to do something relaxing that they enjoy. "But my baby needs me all the time," you may feel, yet unless you take time to replenish your own emotional reserves, your ability to give to your baby is going to wear thin. This is a time for dad to take over, even if for only forty-five minutes, while mom soaks in the bathtub, exercises, or spends time on a hobby. Whatever you do, don't fall into the trap of doing housework during baby's naptime. These precious minutes should be used to do something you enjoy. In the early weeks, sleep is usually the best way to use baby's sleep time.

Think about ways you can take a break after the baby is born. What things do you most enjoy doing? What helps you relax? Do you need to do something that makes you feel productive, or do you prefer to do nothing and let your mind go blank? Which of these activities will give you the greatest return for a relatively short investment of time? _____

_____

_____

_____

_____

Get some exercise. Physical exercise is a tremendous stress reducer and mood enhancer. One of the best exercises is walking, and this is something you can do with your baby. Bundle her up in the baby sling or the stroller and take a brisk forty-five minute walk several times a week. You'll feel better, and some of those extra postpartum pounds will disappear as well.

Involve your husband. Be specific in telling your husband what kind of help you need, both practical and emotional. You may think that he should be able to see this for himself, but many men are unable to sense where a new mother's needs lie. Be nice, but direct. Things that really bug you may not seem like a problem to him, and vice versa.

Make a list: To help me feel loved and cared for, I need my husband to: _____

_____

_____

_____

Dad can make his own list, and then you can exchange them.

POSTPARTUM DEPRESSION

For some women, postpartum difficulties can turn into postpartum depression. Doubt and frustration lead to despair, and all the stress of caring for a new baby and totally changing a lifestyle can overwhelm a woman's ability to cope. Postpartum depression is more than just "baby blues" or a couple of "down" days. It is a serious problem; a woman can't just "snap out of it." Symptoms may include:

- Fatigue, exhaustion
- Inability to sleep, even when the baby is sleeping
- Sleeping all the time
- Crying jags, anxiety attacks (panic)
- Difficulty in concentrating
- Loss of appetite
- Lack of concern for the baby
- Overwhelming feelings of futility and sadness
- Lack of concern for grooming or personal hygiene

All of the previous suggestions can be helpful in overcoming postpartum depression, but if a number of these symptoms are present and persist, despite efforts to alleviate stress, or if symptoms appear suddenly several weeks after the baby's birth, it would be wise to consult your doctor or a mental health professional with experience in women's issues. You don't have to feel like this; support groups and counseling can help. While medication may not be the first choice for treating postpartum depression, there are drugs that can be used even while breastfeeding, if necessary.

RISK FACTORS FOR POSTPARTUM DEPRESSION

Certain characteristics increase a woman's chances of having difficulties adjusting to motherhood or of experiencing postpartum depression:

- A previous history of depression or difficulty coping with combined stresses
- Ambivalent feelings about leaving a high-status job
- An unwanted pregnancy
- Marital discord
- A negative birth experience
- Serious health problems in the baby
- Prolonged separation of mother and baby after the birth

If any of these apply to you, seek counsel during pregnancy so that you can at least start to resolve problems that will make it more difficult for you to mother your baby. Make careful plans for getting enough postpartum help. Make sure you and your husband both have realistic expectations of the challenges ahead. Above all, take it to God and pray for his blessing and aid in the months ahead.

Here's an exercise in preparing for the changes of parenthood.

Things I'm looking forward to about mothering: _____

_____

_____

_____

Things I'm less sure about: _____

_____

_____

_____

Based on what you've read in this book, are these expectations realistic? _____

_____

_____

_____

My usual way of coping with change is: _____

_____

THE NEW BABY PLANNER

_____

_____

Is this usually successful? Do you think it will work postpartum?

_____

_____

_____

_____

Things I will miss about my job: _____

_____

_____

_____

Personal needs that are filled by my job: _____

_____

_____

_____

Ways that I can fulfill these needs during the time I'm home with my baby: _____

_____

_____

_____

MOTHER BURNOUT

Burnout is a state of emotional exhaustion, when a mother feels that she can no longer cope with her baby's needs. But, of course, she has to go on coping, and she feels trapped. Inside her head a voice is screaming, "I can't handle this anymore. I'm not enjoying this. I'm not a good mother." On the outside, her teeth may be clenched, but she goes on trying.

Ironically, women who are highly motivated to do the absolute best for their babies are most likely to burn out. This makes women who are attracted to attachment parenting good candidates for the problem. You have to be on fire with commitment and caring in order to burn out.

Does this mean that there is something wrong with attachment parenting? That it asks too much of mothers? We believe that there is a law of supply and demand in God's plan for parenting. The baby may be demanding, but if the principles of attachment parenting are followed, responding to the baby's needs will help to supply the energy and resources needed for parents to survive and thrive. The experience of loving and connecting with your baby can actually be a source of emotional healing for mothers and fathers who did not have a good attachment with their own parents. Problems arise when attachment parenting is practiced in an unsupportive environment, or in an unbalanced way, or when outside pressures divert energy away from the baby.

The supermom myth is alive and well and continues to exert its influence on women in the 1990s. Shortly after giving birth, a woman is expected to resume being the perfect housekeeper, the fabulous cook, the attentive wife, the eager sexual partner, and a successful wage-earner. With all these demands placed on the circuits, something somewhere is going to frazzle and burn out. New mothers need the luxury of putting the baby first in their priorities and letting other things go by the wayside. Most modern women enter motherhood with confusing or poor role models, little experience with babies, and no prenatal preparation for parenting beyond a hospital class in giving a bath. They need time and patience in order to learn their jobs. It can be a tremendous relief to let go of other obligations, at least for a while.

When mothers burn out it is usually because some part of the plan for attachment parenting is not being followed. There may have been some interference in the bonding relationship at birth. There may be breastfeeding problems, or a bevy of negative advisers are telling the mother to let the baby cry. There may be problems in the marriage, or dad is not involved with the parenting. The baby may have a high need level, but the mother has low tolerance.

Other problems, such as financial pressures, moving, illness, a toddler, or extensive redecorating may complicate the picture.

Think of some ways you can prevent burnout. Which points will be most useful to you? _____
_____
_____
_____

 ## REKINDLING THE FLAME

You can recover from burnout and rekindle your passion for motherhood. A realistic appraisal of what life is like with a new baby is a good first step. Your baby will dominate your life, and adult ideas like schedules and predictability will get tossed to the wind. You also have to realize the limits of your own tolerance. Just as babies' temperaments vary, so also do mothers' abilities to cope. If you are an impatient, hard-driven sort of person who is blessed with a high need baby, it's going to be harder for you to deal with the stress than it might be for a more easy-going woman. Recognize this and adjust your surroundings accordingly. Reduce other sources of stress, so that all your patience can be channeled toward your baby. And find a way to blow off steam, relax, and recharge your sense of self. For example, for you the brisk walks suggested on page 141 can be extended to two-hour walks twice a day every day if this is what it takes for you to stay sane.

Father involvement. I have never seen a case of mother burnout in a family where the father actively cares for his wife and helps create an atmosphere that allows her mothering skills to grow and flourish. This calls for a husband to be sensitive to his wife's needs. Very few mothers readily confess their confusion or ambivalence about motherhood to their husbands, since they have a tremendous emotional investment in maintaining a perfect-mother image in their spouse's eyes. This highlights the need for trust and forgiveness in a Christian marriage.

Father and mother must work together to meet the baby's needs. When they don't, no one flourishes. If there is a high-need baby, mother becomes immersed in childcare and in trying to respond according to God's design. Father may feel a bit shaky about handling the fussy baby, and also feels that his wife is neglecting him. He withdraws and retreats to other interests outside the home where he feels more in control. This hurts the marriage and pushes the mother into burnout, and the father misses the benefits of being involved with his child.

Mothers can do two things to prevent fathers from withdrawing in the face of baby's needs. The first is to state clearly and directly where they need help with the household and with baby care. Don't expect dad to figure it out on his own and then get angry when he doesn't. Second, encourage your husband to find his own ways of relating to and comforting your baby. Do not hover around waiting to "rescue" baby, telling him what to do. This only serves to undermine his confidence.

Stick with attachment parenting. When you are stressed out, parenting advice that promises a well-regulated baby may look very tempting, but the price is high. Strict schedules where the baby has to cry waiting for the clock simply do not work for most mothers and babies. Mothering is not very satisfying when all your effort is directed to making your baby fit the mold of some outside adviser's directions, when this effort goes against your inner sense of what's right and threatens baby's sense of security. With time, attachment parenting will increase your patience and make you a more giving person in the long run. When mothers are burning out, the problem seldom lies with the baby, or even in the mother. It's in all the outside stresses competing for the mother's attention and loyalty.

What kinds of social stresses contribute to mother burnout? Is it easy to be a mother of small children in the 1990s?_____

_____

_____

_____

Establish priorities. Mothers cannot do everything and still have enough energy left for their babies and themselves. Knowing when to say no safeguards a mother from burnout. Make a list of all the things you are expected to do and then assign priority numbers. Things that are low on the list or that don't have to be done by you specifically can be parceled out to other family members—husband or older children. (Neighbors or grandparents can take over carpools; friends can have your preschooler over for some play time.) Some things won't get done, it's true, but the most important work will: the job of mothering your baby. You may not see instant results, but the effects will last a lifetime. Your baby's feelings are far more important than a clean floor, folded bath towels, or three dozen cookies baked for the Cub Scout meeting. Martha unabashedly used "we have a new baby" to get herself off the hook for dozens of requests for her time and energy. We even canceled our weekly radio talk show when baby number eight came into our family by adoption. This was an important part of our ministry, but not as important as keeping the pressures manageable with a new baby in the house.

Save some energy for yourself. It can be difficult for an attached mother to release her baby to the care of someone else, even a loving dad. Still there are times when it is necessary for someone to say, "Let me handle the baby for awhile. You need a break." You'll be no good at all to your baby if you allow yourself to become totally burned out. Do something you enjoy, something relaxing or creative, or just sleep. Both you and your baby will benefit.

FATHERING

It's all too easy for a father to feel like an outsider in relation to the intense mother-baby bond that accompanies breastfeeding and attachment parenting. But fathers have a special role to play with their babies and within God's design for the Christian family. An involved father is an essential part of attachment parenting, and a father who is committed to spiritual leadership is the foundation of the Christian family. Instead of feeling "left out," I encourage dad to become the "left end"—carrying the ball for mom so she has a peaceful nest.

 ## THE FATHER'S POSTPARTUM ROLE

In many cultures, new mothers are given a doula, someone to "mother" and care for them as they care for the baby. Mothers in these cultures are not expected to take care of themselves and their households in the early weeks after birth. Doulas are often older women within the extended family who are experienced in breastfeeding and mothering.

In our culture, the role of doula often falls to the father. As the person who knows the mother best, who lives with her, and who has a strong connection to the baby, he is well suited for the job. He may not know much about baby care, but he can take over household chores, build the mother's confidence, and help her seek answers to any questions or problems she has. Take time off from work—several weeks, if possible—so that you can spend lots of time with your new family.

The best gift a new father can give his wife and his child is the freedom to get to know one another without a lot of outside pressures. He can be the one to control visitors, to ensure that they have a positive effect, and to minimize visits with friends or relatives who are upsetting or who drain energy away from mothering tasks. He is probably better able than the mother to place limits on outside interactions and to say no when necessary.

As a father, you can provide practical help to your wife during these postpartum weeks. If you have older children, their needs become your job. See to it that they are fed and clothed and played with. Spending special time with dad can head off many of the jealous feelings that can arise when a new and needy sibling enters the family. Be aware that toddlers and older children may become more demanding in reaction to the new baby. They need reassurance from both parents.

Take over household tasks, or see to it that someone else does these things for your family. If you can, hire help with the housecleaning. Say yes to any and all offers of help from friends and relatives. If people want to know if they can do anything for you, say yes, and give them specific instructions: "Can you bring supper over one night?" "Can you drive the kids to soccer?" "Do you have time to fold some laundry?"

What essential household tasks can you take over for your wife in the first weeks postpartum? _____
_____
_____
_____

Is there anything you need to learn about in order to do these jobs? _____
_____
_____
_____

Realize that now is not the best time to make major changes in your lives. Respect your wife's nesting instinct, that feeling that makes her want to get everything just so at home, and then stay there. The final month of pregnancy and the first few months with a new baby are not the time to buy a new house or change jobs and move halfway across the country. This kind of disruption goes against your wife's nesting instinct, adding greatly to her stress level.

Above all, be sensitive to your wife's physical and emotional needs. She is putting all of herself into mothering your baby and will be paying little or no attention to her own needs. One father we know, whose wife was spending long hours working with a baby who was having trouble with breastfeeding, took over the responsibility of seeing that she ate well and frequently. Left on her own, this woman skipped meals and neglected her own needs, but dad stepped in and prepared and made sure she ate three meals a day plus healthy snacks. She felt well cared for and better able to cope with the baby's problems.

Be especially alert to emotional needs. Becoming a mother represents a major change in status for women in our society. Without a job to go to and the rewards of promotions and paychecks, she may feel she is slipping down the ladder of personal worth. When she finds she cannot get anything done around home because of the baby's demands, her sense of self-worth drops still farther. Now is not the time to complain about messy surroundings or household tasks left undone. Your wife needs you to respect the work she is doing mothering your baby. Remind her that not only is this the most important job in the world right now, but it is the one you value the most.

New mothers are often reluctant to ask for what they need, because they don't wish to tarnish the image they want to create of being a capable mother. It can be especially difficult to ask a husband because his good opinion matters more than anyone's. Now is the time for sincere, empathic communication between the two of you. Anticipate her needs: "The baby was up a lot last night. What can I do to help you today?" "You've had a busy afternoon. Let's order your favorite Chinese food for supper."

Be sensitive to early warning signs of depression: sleep problems, loss of appetite, lack of attention to grooming, not wanting to leave the house, crying spells, unfounded nagging. If these persist, seek professional help before things get out of hand.

The habits of prayer and relying on the Lord that you practiced during pregnancy should continue after the baby is born. Find time during the day to pray together, perhaps in the morning as you both awaken next to your sleeping baby or for a few moments in the middle of evening fussy spells. Pray for your baby and for your marriage relationship, which is the heart of your growing family.

Think of ways you can encourage your wife to confide in you during pregnancy and the early days of parenting. How can you help her feel safe and secure in her "nest"? _____

_____

_____

_____

FATHERS AND BABIES

While taking care of the new mother is a very important role for fathers in the early weeks, don't think that this means you miss out on all the fun of the new baby. Fathers have a very special role to play in their babies' lives, one that goes well beyond trying to be a substitute for mother. Dads have special ways of relating to babies and comforting them. Try the neck nestle where you hold baby upright against your chest, her head snuggled under your chin. Croon a low, slow song, letting the vibrations of your vocal cords soothe your baby off to sleep. Many babies like the warm fuzzy: falling asleep skin-to-skin on dad's bare chest. The closeness and the breathing motion help them feel secure.

Your baby should learn that dad as well as mom can be relied on for comfort. Find some special time each day to spend with your baby. Take a walk together early in the morning while your wife sleeps. Or take over for a while when you get home from work and mom needs a break. In one home this was like the hand-off in a relay race—mom hands baby off to dad as he comes through the door and she takes a spin around the neighborhood on her bike. It helps to mentally prepare on the drive home—clear your mind of business as you leave your place of work and use the travel time to unwind so you'll be ready for your little baton, eagerly anticipating your reunion. Hopefully, he won't always be unglued when you get the hand-off, but even if he is you'll be glad to know that babies often "settle" for a new face and fresh arms, so you'll get a hero's welcome from your baby's mother as she returns to her nest.

As your baby grows, you will become a unique source of fun

and excitement in her life. Remember, if you want your child to rely on you later in life for advice about boyfriends or school or how to turn a double play, the trusting relationship must be built from the bottom up, starting now.

Imagine yourself soothing or comforting your new baby. What do you think the baby will like? _____

_____

_____

_____

What special things do you want to share with your child right from the start? _____

_____

_____

_____

 ## FATHERS AS FIGURES OF CHRIST

God's plan for Christian marriage is described in Ephesians 5:25–28: "Husbands, love your wives, just as Christ loved the church and gave himself up for her to make her holy, cleansing her by the washing with water through the word, and to present her to himself as a radiant church, without stain or wrinkle or any other blemish, but holy and blameless. In this same way, husbands ought to love their wives as their own bodies. He who loves his wife loves himself" (NIV).

This passage is rich in meaning, and it deserves careful study and meditation. It has special importance for husbands, not only because it makes clear that they are to be the heads of their households, but also because it tells them how they are to exercise their authority.

Marriage is a continuum: Love, submission, and commitment must occur mutually and simultaneously, as part of the whole. A break in one of these elements puts the whole relationship out of balance. Christians are commanded to submit to one another "out of reverence for Christ," and then wives are asked particularly to submit to their husbands. But in order to do this, a wife must know that her husband loves her, in a selfless, non-manipulating kind of way, as Christ loves us. For the husband to love the wife, he must know that he has her respect, and to have this, he must submit himself to Christ and act as a Christian.

Loving your wife requires more than saying, "Yes, honey, I love you." The kind of love that Christ modeled for us, the love for which the Greeks used the word *agape,* is active and giving. A husband must not only have love for his wife, but must also convey his love to her in such a way that she knows she is loved. He does not judge her; he helps her. When she has a problem, he does not preach at her—he shows compassion. He does not sit back and offer advice, he pitches in where he can. He does not undercut her intuition, but instead supports and respects his wife's inner baby wisdom.

In what ways has Christ shown his love for his people?_____

_____

_____

_____

Can you apply this example to a situation in your own family?

_____

_____

_____

The love-and-submission design fosters the growth of mutual esteem in a marriage. Each adult focuses on what he or she can give to the other, and as a result, the relationship prospers, since no one is keeping score of who gets what. However, each partner's self-esteem benefits from the gifts of the other, and the whole marriage operates on a higher level.

ADJUSTING TO PARENTHOOD 155

Think of something you can do for or give to your wife today. Put yourself in her shoes and imagine what she would most like to receive. _____

_____

_____

_____

Authority over children also requires a self-giving love, one whose first concern is the child's needs. Its message is "I will do what is best for you," not "I will make you obey me." The trust that is developed through attachment parenting fits in well with this kind of authority. Based on their own experience, children learn that parents can be trusted. What kind of "experience" does a baby have? The experience of being comforted when in distress, fed when hungry, kept close and held securely when fearful. Parenting that addresses these needs produces children who are obedient and who seek out their parents' wisdom and authority.

REDISCOVERING SEX AFTER BIRTH

New parents, especially fathers, often end up wondering, "Is there sex after childbirth?" Weeks go by after the birth, and even though the doctor has given the go-ahead at the mother's postpartum checkup, couples find it difficult to resume their sexual life together. Fathers frequently begin to feel impatient, and mothers feel pressured. The wife's concerns are all wrapped up in the baby, but the husband feels left out and a bit jealous. Neither gets to enjoy satisfying sex, and soon dad is blaming his wife's attachment to the baby for her lack of interest in him.

All of these feelings, both husband's and wife's, are normal. The key to resolving the conflict lies in the kind of mutual giving discussed above—giving each other the gift of understanding. Here are some clues to what may be going on inside your spouse's head.

Understanding new mothers. The normal hormonal changes that occur postpartum affect a woman's sexual desires. It is

THE NEW BABY PLANNER

important for fathers to understand this. Before birth, the level of hormones that make women want sex are high, even during pregnancy. After birth, the levels of these hormones drop, and the mothering hormones take over. These hormones direct a woman's attention to nurturing and breastfeeding her baby. They are part of God's plan for ensuring that babies get what they need from their mothers. These same hormones can suppress ovulation and menstruation for at least six months of exclusive breastfeeding and prevent another pregnancy from occurring. This guarantees that this baby has a monopoly on mother's attention until the baby is at least eighteen months to two years old.

These biological changes are not the only reasons why women have less interest in sex in the first months postpartum. Fatigue is a big problem. It's hard to feel like making love when you feel drained by the needs of the baby. By the end of the day, many new mothers want nothing more than to go to sleep. With a baby and possibly a toddler or older children making demands on her all day, the woman may feel "all used up" or "all touched out" by nighttime. She may have a strong need to be left alone for a while after the baby is finally asleep. A husband who is waiting and ready to pounce the minute the baby is finally out of her arms may be in for an unpleasant surprise when this woman makes it clear that she needs some time to herself.

When a mother realizes that there are limits to her energies, she must make decisions about how to parcel them out. Dad's wants may end up taking second place behind baby's needs for a while. During the first three or four months after childbirth (sometimes longer), the intensity of a mother's relationship with her baby may not leave much room for intimacy with her mate.

It is normal for dads to feel left out, but this does not mean your wife has lost interest in you. This redirection of a woman's focus from husband to baby is necessary, but temporary. It is only a season of the marriage, not a permanent climate change. Fathers who are sensitive and supportive during this dry spell find that when the sexual season returns, the weather is better than ever.

ADJUSTING TO PARENTHOOD   157

Delaying your own gratification for the sake of your wife and your baby sets a strong spiritual example of selfless giving. You and your family will reap the benefits for many years to come. Realize that this requires a certain level of maturity on the part of the father especially, but also for the mother to realize that she needs to do her part to strike some balance so she'll have some energy for her husband. Remember women, male sex hormones don't drop after birth —pray for your mate to be patient and for yourself to be sensitive to where he is. And remember, love conquers all and God is more than able to help you get through this time and come out closer.

How could a wife prevent her husband from feeling excluded from her relationship with her baby? _____

_____

_____

_____

How could dad himself see to it that he has few chances to feel left out? _____

_____

_____

_____

What kind of physical needs might a tired new mother have at the end of the day? How can her mate help her to relax? _____

_____

_____

_____

 ## HOW TO BE SENSITIVE

Here are some tips from an experienced dad on rekindling your sex life after your baby's birth. While these may seem like the long way around to getting the sex that you really want, the effort is well worth it, both in terms of your overall marriage and within your sexual relationship. Women are most turned on by men who are sensitive to their needs.

- **Go slowly.** Don't put pressure on your wife to resume intercourse before she feels ready. Just because the doctor or the book says it's okay, don't assume that it's okay with your wife. She may need several weeks for her body to feel ready, and even then, her mind may need time to catch up. The mental component is important to good sex, in women more so than men. If your wife has sex with you only because she feels obligated, it won't be very satisfying for either of you.

- **Court your wife all over again.** New mothers enjoy being wooed back into a full sexual relationship. At first your wife may want only to be held or caressed, with no expectation of intercourse to follow. Think of other ways to care for her and show her you love her—a back rub, a foot massage, drawing a bath for her, cuddling. These things will help her to feel sexual again.

- **Share the baby care and the household tasks.** Men may not realize it, but this can be a real turn-on for harried wives. It shows a genuine understanding of your wife's needs if you dry the dishes after supper or take the baby for a walk while she talks to a friend on the phone. Fatigue is an enemy of good sex, and anything you can do to prevent your wife from becoming overtired will be rewarded with positive feelings about you.

- **Remember that baby's needs come first.** Even when you are alone with your wife, you may notice that part of her mind is still with her baby. You have to respect this strong mother-infant bond, because you cannot compete with it and expect to win. If you acknowledge that for now baby must come first, your wife will respect you for your unselfishness, and the relationship will benefit (as will your sex life). Be prepared; sleeping babies have radar that allows them to sense when mom and dad are finally finding time to enjoy each other sexually. When you hear that awakening cry, do not slam your fist into the mattress and cry, "Curses, foiled again!" This reaction is guaranteed to put an end to your wife's sexual receptiveness for the evening. Instead, sigh, smile, and say, "I'll go check." If you help your wife comfort the baby and get her back to sleep, she will love you for it, and there's a good chance the love-making will resume.

Give some thought to how having a baby in the house and in your bed will affect your sexual relationship. Together with your mate, talk about how, when, and where you will manage to make love. _____

_____

_____

_____

Does sneaking around make you feel like a teenager again? The challenges of postpartum sex can prod a couple into creating a more interesting sex life for themselves.

 ## UNDERSTANDING HOW FATHERS FEEL

Men do not have the same physical, hormonal reaction to becoming parents that women do. Their sexual urges are not affected by the arrival of a new baby. Wives need to remember this and make an effort to keep the lines of sexual communication open during the postpartum period. Your husband needs to be reassured that changes in your sexual feelings do not mean your feelings about him have changed. Let him know that you still need him, physically as well as in other ways. Tell him exactly what you want: to be held, to cuddle up on the couch together, to be kissed tenderly.

When you and your husband find time alone together, try to concentrate your attention on him. He can sense when your mind is wandering off to your baby. During lovemaking, the two of you need to focus your energies on each other. It isn't always easy for a new mother to separate herself from her baby in mind as well as body, but with time, you can work these feelings out.

What can you do for your mate that will make him feel special and needed even though your baby is taking up most of your time and energy? _____

_____

_____

_____

Romance is as important to men as it is to women. Plan a romantic dinner at home for you and your husband (and baby makes three, if necessary). How simple can you make it and still have it be romantic and fun for both of you? _____

_____

_____

_____

 ## FACTS ABOUT POSTPARTUM SEX

Women may experience vaginal discomfort during intercourse in the first months postpartum. The hormones responsible for vaginal lubrication are at low levels during lactation, so it may be helpful to use a water-soluble lubricant such as K-Y jelly. If the woman had an episiotomy or a tear during the birth that had to be stitched, this area may be tender for a while. Experiment with different positions to find one that does not put pressure on the scar tissue.

The hormone oxytocin, which controls the milk-ejection reflex, is also released during sexual intercourse. Leaking milk from the breasts is a normal part of a lactating woman's sexual response. Keep a towel handy, if necessary. If the woman's breasts are full, avoid positions that put pressure on them and cause her discomfort. Better yet, nurse the baby down to sleep first. This will minimize leaking and discomfort and with any luck prevent interruptions.

Pregnancy also affects most couples' sex lives in ways that may not be expected. Is/was this true of you and your mate? _____

_____

_____

_____

How have you coped sexually with the changes of pregnancy? _____

_____

_____

Can you take/apply any of these lessons to sex postpartum? _____

_____

_____

 ## NURTURING THE RELATIONSHIP

Your baby needs two parents who love each other and are committed to their marriage. This is as important as your commitment to your baby. Even in the early months after birth, when the baby's demands are powerful and time-consuming, you need to find time to work on being a couple.

Here's the situation you want to avoid: After two or three years of marriage, a young couple, call them Rob and Laura, have a baby. Laura quits her full-time job as a journalist to stay home with the baby, who is rather fussy and demanding. She has always been a perfectionist, and she is committed to doing her best for her baby. She becomes deeply attached to little Sean and struggles to answer his cries and make him happy. Rob, a lawyer, has not had a lot of experience with babies and feels awkward caring for Sean, especially since Laura is always there to correct him or to step in if the baby becomes upset. As the weeks go by, Rob participates less and less in child care and spends more time at his job. Laura becomes more and more involved in being a perfect mother but begins to feel frazzled by the non-stop demands of her high-need baby. Neither Laura nor Rob is happy, and each blames the other for being unsupportive and emotionally distant.

How can they solve their problems? It's time for some mutual giving. Laura needs Rob's support and encouragement and some help with baby care. Rob needs Laura to give him the confidence to get to know their baby on his own, without her criticism. Both need to spend time together as a couple, focusing on each other and the interests and attractions they share.

Finding time together as a couple is a matter of establishing priorities. Schedule and plan for time together, perhaps a special dinner once a week, a long walk on a Saturday afternoon, leisurely Sunday afternoons on the couch, time spent talking while preparing a meal. You may have to include your baby for part of the time, nursing her off to sleep or carrying her in the baby sling as you walk, but your energies should be saved for each other. This is a wise investment in the future of your family.

What first attracted you to your mate? Is this attraction still there today? _____

_____

_____

_____

What did your mate first like about you? Are those qualities still found in your personality? _____

_____

_____

_____

Sometimes mothers feel disconnected from their former selves after pregnancy and the birth of a baby. Think of ways to nurture your unique interests while caring for your baby. What activities that you have always enjoyed together can you and your mate continue to share with your baby along for the ride? _____

_____

_____

_____

 ## YOUR NEEDS VS. BABY'S NEEDS

Throughout your parenting career you will be caught in the juggling act of his needs, her needs, child's needs. And you will come to the realization that everyone's needs cannot be totally met all the time. Perhaps it's part of the divine design for a new mother to sense that baby's needs come first. This is good as long as it is balanced with the realization that what the child also needs is a stable family.

As you grow into a godly and giving mother, it's necessary to develop some balance in your mothering. In the early months, babies are takers and mothers are givers. That's normal. But some babies, especially those with high needs, can overtake the whole family, leaving two sleep-deprived parents and both mother and marital burnout. Try this exercise in keeping balance in your parenting style.

Do you feel, "My baby needs me so much I don't ever have time to take a shower"? _____

_____

_____

Are you beginning to resent your high-giving style of mothering? _____

_____

_____

Is baby thriving, but you are barely surviving? _____

_____

List those high-need interactions that most drain your energy (e.g., nightwaking, feeding frequency, incessant crying, unable to comfort baby). _____

_____

_____

_____

_____

Try these energy and emotion-saving suggestions:

- New moms and dads, be careful of this all-too-common scenario: You have been blessed with a high-need baby, and in your desire to be the "perfect" mother you give constantly to your baby. Every time your baby cries, you respond; every time your baby wakes up, you instantly comfort. Baby is thriving, but you are marginally surviving. Because you are so good at baby comforting, dad becomes less involved during this high-maintenance stage in the early months of baby care. And since you are doing such a good job he feels he is not needed anyway. You become more engrossed in "your" baby, dad in his work. As a couple you drift apart. You are burning out, and dad has not developed his own baby-comforting skills. This family is out of balance. Instead of hovering around ready to rescue upset baby from fumbling daddy, give dad and baby time and space to get acquainted. Leave baby well-fed and take a walk. You will be surprised how fast fathers can develop baby-comforting skills if they have to.

- Be specific in telling your spouse what you need:
  "I need help with the housework."
  "I need you to get up and comfort the baby at night."
  "I need an hour to myself every day."
  "I need you to take the baby for a car ride when she's upset."
  "I need you to wear baby around the house while I get some rest."

Dads, here's what's in it for you. A burned-out mother becomes a burned-out wife. The whole family works better if you and your wife share the baby care. Besides, nothing develops tenderness in a male more than caring for a tiny baby.

Let me share another fathering tip with you. Many times perfectionistic mothers will not ask for help, perhaps for fear it will shake the perfect-mother myth. Be sensitive. Keep your eyes open for specific ways that you can help and initiate the help: "I've made an appointment for you at the spa. I'll drive you there. And I'll pick you up."

Just say no. Parents, it's okay to say no to your kids. This does not mean that you become insensitive and uncaring, but that you develop a balance between giving to your baby and letting your baby overtake the whole family. In the early months, the baby's needs should be met consistently. As the baby gets older, you can teach your baby to delay gratification just a bit. The six-month-old does not to be attended to as promptly as a six-day-old. This high-maintenance stage does not go on forever. A baby is a baby for a very short time. Try to develop a balance between being a nurturing parent and a martyr mother. Nobody benefits from this lack of balance. This can happen in any family, not just attachment-oriented families. If you have the drive to be perfect, recognize this as a red flag, a signal that there is a need inside you that has been unmet and that will have to be addressed. All of us were raised by less than perfect parents—only God is the perfect parent—but some of us were damaged by wrong parenting to a greater degree. If this is interfering with your ability to have peace in your mind and heart, it will interfere with your parenting abilities. You may go way out of balance into either attachment or detachment. If this is you, get prayer and counsel to work toward emotional, mental, and spiritual wholeness.

WORKING AND PARENTING

To work or not to work—that is the question faced by mothers of small children today. While the family's economic needs may play some part in the decision, other factors may have a more significant influence than money alone. First among these is a woman's need for fulfillment; modern women are often afraid that they will go crazy if they stay home full time. Less frequently discussed are the needs of children: How important is full-time mothering to their optimal development?

Our aim in getting you to think about this issue is not to cast blame or to make working mothers feel guilty. The main issue is the strength of mother-infant attachment, not whether or not you work. This is a many-sided dilemma. It is no place for a Christian pediatrician, or any Christian, to make judgments or to start casting stones. Martha worked part-time when our older children were young and I was a student. Although we now feel that there were other alternatives we could have explored, at the time we believed that her paycheck was needed to pay the rent. If combining working and mothering is going to be an issue early in your parenting career, I urge you to give it careful thought and ask the Lord for guidance so that you can make decisions that are good for your baby and workable for you as well.

Some historical perspective. Of course, women have always worked, and full-time mothers will tell you that their workday at home is longer than the one they once put in at the office. But long ago, before the Industrial Revolution, everybody worked at home or close to home. Women produced many of the things their families needed. Men worked close by, in the barn, the fields, or the shop, producing food for their families and something extra to sell or trade for what they could not make themselves. Factories, mass production, cheap goods, and improved agricultural methods changed all this, and fathers left home to work for cash. Families changed from being producers to being consumers, and the economic contribution of mothers at home became less obvious as the role became more service-oriented.

Today, smaller families and more choices available to women have obscured the importance of full-time mothering. Gone are the days when being a homemaker was enough aspiration for a young woman graduating from high school. Women, like men, seek fulfillment in careers, believing that the money, power, and status of a good job will make them happy. The role of mother has lost its glow; being at the beck and call of small children has no status and leaves you lonesome for adult conversation.

This creates a true dilemma for some women, who have worked hard for an education and who love the work they do. They worry about missing their jobs and becoming resentful if they stay home all day with their babies. They want good things for their children, and they know that a happy mother is important to the whole family's smooth functioning. They are also concerned that if they drop out of the work world while their children are young, it will be very difficult to reenter the job force later. Until society catches up with the real needs of women and children (not just more day care), these problems will not have easy answers.

What could be done to raise the status of full-time mothers in American society? Use your imagination. Think public relations, media, finances, role models, slogans—have fun! _____

_____

_____

_____

_____

Can you translate any of these ideas into making the full-time mother in *your* home feel more important? _____

_____

_____

_____

Value of full-time mothering. A strong mother-infant attachment is part of God's design for children to reach their fullest potential. This attachment is not just the product of after-birth bonding or the biological relationship. It takes time and closeness for love and security to develop and for mother and baby to fine-tune their communication system.

The system develops better the more the mother is with the baby. Being constantly in touch assists them in learning about each other. The mother gets to know her baby's cues and discovers how to respond. The baby learns that mother can always be trusted to respond and help her feel better. The baby's responses to the mother's efforts build maternal confidence, and she feels good about her baby and about herself as a mother. Baby feels good about himself as a person. All these good feelings overflow into a loving relationship in which each partner wants very much to be with the other. The child is a joy to parent, and the parent truly enjoys the child. Long-term, the child learns to trust, love, and find joy in relationships, secure in the knowledge of who he is, which will make it possible for him to have intimate, happy relationships with others as he grows. There is true harmony between mother and child.

Mother-baby closeness also has "hormoneous" pay-offs. Frequent nursing stimulates the release of prolactin and oxytocin in the mother, which makes her feel good about being close to her baby. As mother and baby grow closer together, doubts the woman may have had about whether she would enjoy full-time mothering often disappear. Mothers make important discoveries—things like "I never knew I could love someone so much" or "I'm positively addicted to my baby."

What doubts or fears do you have about being home full time with your baby? _____
_____
_____
_____

What do you look forward to (or enjoy already) about the experience? _____
_____
_____
_____

Imagine (or describe) a typical day together: _____

_____

_____

_____

Do your expectations correspond with reality? _____

_____

_____

Effects of separation. Babies must learn about the world through a consistent attachment to one person before they can take it on as independent beings. As they become more mobile, learning to crawl and walk, they experiment with separation, but they are most comfortable when they can set the terms themselves. As one mother said after retrieving her adventurous twelve-month-old from the far side of the empty church gymnasium, "He can crawl forty feet away from me, if he likes, but heaven help us if I try to leave the living room while he's watching!" (See Separation Anxiety, p. 231).

Regular separation of mother and baby, such as happens when women return to outside employment, interferes with the development of a strong attachment. A young baby is not yet ready to experience herself as detached from her mother. She has no concept of an independent self. In her mind, her identity is all mixed up with how her environment responds to her needs and with the person who is doing the responding. When you change the responses or the responder, you shake the very foundation of who she is. You not only make it more difficult for her to trust her environment, but you also make it harder for her to trust herself.

A baby who is juggled between several caregivers does not receive consistent responses to her cues. This makes it much harder for her to learn to communicate, and if it gets too frustrating, she may scale back on her efforts. Substitute caregivers, no matter how loving or how well-trained they are in infant development, do not have your biological attachment to your baby, nor your commitment or utter craziness about her. They cannot respond in the same adoring, sensitive, and dependable way that you can, especially if they are taking care of more than one infant at a time.

Mothers' responses stimulate babies to keep signaling and improving their communication. With a less dependable response, baby's communication skills do not develop to the same high level. Baby is less able to reward his caregivers for attempting to meet his needs. This makes it more difficult for mother to really enjoy being with baby, and she may be more inclined to look for other ways of feeling fulfilled. Although this mother may still love her baby deeply, the two may not enjoy a strong attachment. This is even more likely to happen when there is a mismatch between the baby's temperament and the mother's giving level, or when a woman lacks confidence in her ability to mother and depends heavily on outside advisers or substitute caregivers.

What might a baby be thinking during the time that her mother is away at a job? What goes through her mind? Try to write a monologue from the baby's point of view. Remember to think like a baby.

_____

_____

_____

_____

Several factors influence how separation from mother affects a baby. These include the baby's need level and how sensitive to separation the baby is. Some babies are better able to tolerate the stress of being away from their mothers, especially if they are in the arms of one nurturing caregiver. How much you are away from your baby and what your relationship is like when you are together are also factors.

I must point out, however, that the idea that "quality time" can make up for long absences is a myth. The main problem is that you can't schedule quality time at parental convenience, nor can you concentrate meaningful interactions with a baby into forty-five minutes before bedtime four nights a week. Quality time comes in snatches throughout the day, as situations present themselves to both mother and baby. While it's true that a mother who is with her children all day is not constantly interacting with them on a high level, she is available to point out the airplane flying overhead on the walk to the grocery store, to laugh along with the four-month-old who has just found her toes, or to play peek-a-boo in the sheets while making the bed. Scheduled stimulation cannot make up for the loss of spontaneous interactive moments.

Separation tolerance is also affected by how well the substitute caregiver can respond to the baby's needs. Someone who loves the baby and has spent a lot of time with her—dad, or possibly grandma—would be preferable to an overstressed day-care worker. Choose carefully when you hire a substitute caregiver for your baby. This is someone with whom your baby needs to develop a trusting relationship. Will the caregiver pick up your baby when she cries? Will she hold her frequently, even if she isn't clamoring for attention? Will she talk to your baby and play with her? Is she dependable? Will she be available for many months to come? Babies cannot thrive if they have to adjust to a new caregiver every few months.

More often than not, mothers who really practice the style of attachment parenting decide not to return to outside employment. After a few months at home with their babies, they find that it is inconceivable to think about leaving them. I find that I don't have to discuss separation problems with attached mothers. Their experience with their babies is far more powerful than any lecture that I could put together.

If you are pregnant and are trying to work your way through the returning-to-work dilemma, I would advise you to give full-time mothering a chance, if at all possible. Until your baby is in your arms, you have no idea of the strength of the bond that will develop between the two of you. Your attachment will grow, not lessen, in the months to come, and the desire not to leave your baby is an internal signal that you should respect.

SOLUTIONS TO THE WORKING DILEMMA

If you feel that financially you must work after your baby is born, take some time to evaluate the situation critically. American society has come to take two-income families for granted, but your paycheck may not be as indispensable as it seems. Consider first what will be left from your paycheck after you deduct all the expenses of working: transportation, lunches, child care, taxes, clothing, convenience food and other items purchased to make up for not having enough time to do it yourself. You may be surprised at how little is left—enough to make you reconsider whether it's really worth it.

Are there things you can do without? Your child needs your full-time self more than she needs fancy nursery furniture, the latest in kids' clothing styles, or even high-quality toys. A close look at your own buying habits may reveal that there are a lot of things you can do without during the time your children are small. We live in a materialistic society, and while most of us would be quick to agree that people are more important than possessions, we do not always realize how we are held captive by mere things. If you have trouble coming up with ways to cut corners on your own, look for some books on the subject. You don't have to take every suggestion offered, but an outside perspective can help you think critically about your own values. Your need for the gratification that comes from driving a late-model minivan or purchasing stylish furniture may pale next to your baby's need for full-time maternal care.

If you can, start planning to live on one income from the time you are married. Don't acquire a mortgage so large that mom must work in order to pay it. Build your savings during the time that both husband and wife are working so that you will have a cushion that enables you to survive on one income during your child's first three years. Consider borrowing the money you need to provide your child with full-time nurturing. For example, if grandparents wish to help out financially, make them aware that a stay-at-home mother is a worthwhile investment in their grandchild's future.

Another alternative is earning money at home. There are all kinds of possibilities for home businesses or for working from home. This is a fast-growing area of our economy, thanks both to technology and to an increasing need for services such as childcare and housecleaning. While you may not earn as much as you might leaving home all day for an office, your expenses will be lower and, bottom line, it will make it possible to be with your baby all day.

Even if you must work outside your home, consider working part-time. This is less stressful for both mothers and babies. It can even prove advantageous to employers, since part-time workers are more efficient, yielding more work for less money.

Be aware that you can continue to breastfeed after returning to work and that the effort is well worth it. Your baby gets the advantages of receiving human milk, and you both benefit from the closeness of breastfeeding.

Talk to friends and family members with young children. How have they survived financially? Raise these questions with your own parents, too. What were their lifestyle expectations when their children were young? _____

_____

_____

_____

Page through magazines that you may have around the house. Look at the ads. What means do they employ to make you believe that you must have the product they are promoting in order to be successful, efficient, happy, etc.? Can you feel yourself being sucked in? _____

_____

_____

_____

Working for fulfillment. Some women feel they must return to their jobs in order to avoid going crazy at home. This is a legitimate concern. Contrary to the stereotype of the 1950s TV mom, full-time mothering is not an easy job. Women who have made the transition from career to mother-at-home will tell you that it took most of their baby's first year to make the adjustment. If fulfillment is your main motivation for returning to outside employment, consider whether there are other ways to satisfy this need that won't involve separating yourself from your baby. Part-time freelance or consulting work for their former employers allows many women to keep a hand in their field during the time their children are small. Staying active in a professional organization can also accomplish this goal. Some mothers use this time to explore new interests, take classes, or do useful volunteer work, with their babies along for the ride. Full-time mothering doesn't have to mean that you are cooped up in the house all day long.

It can be difficult to find your own answers to the working and mothering dilemma. While society has found room for women in many jobs and professions, it has not grappled realistically with the needs of these women's children. You may feel all alone as you fight the pressure to go back to work while struggling to maintain an identity for yourself beyond being your husband's wife, your child's mother, and your house's keeper. Many mothers are in this same position. Look around you and talk to other women with young children. You may be surprised at how many have been in your shoes and have found solutions.

Isolation is a big problem for full-time mothers today. You and the elderly lady across the street may be the only ones home during the day in your neighborhood, the ones the delivery man leaves all the packages with. What resources are available to mothers and children in your community? Where do stay-at-home mothers gather? Check in the local paper, on bulletin boards at the grocery store or at church, at the YMCA, La Leche League meetings, the local park, or the library for ways to get in contact with other mothers of young babies. _____

_____

_____

_____

FATHERS AND CAREERS

Everyone is familiar with the term "working mother" and the balancing act that goes along with it. What about the "working father?" The birth of a child may be the first time in a man's life that he has to wrestle with the problem of balancing career and family commitments. The fast track may look like the way to financial security for the family, but it may also make him less available to his wife and children. Even when he is at home, he may be preoccupied with work-related problems, or be too stressed out to enjoy his family. It's a tough world out there, one that offers more lip-service than real support to the idea of family values.

What has helped me to keep my fathering priority is the realization that I am important to my baby's growth and development, and my baby is important to my growth. With a job I can always catch up and try again. With a baby, I can't rewind the tape. Babies go through babyhood only once, and I don't want to miss it. The issue is not who is more important to a baby—mother or father? Each is important in different ways, and babies thrive on that difference. Your baby won't love you more or less than his or her mother; your baby will love you *differently*. With our first few babies, I thought baby rearing was my wife's job and I would get involved once they were old enough to throw a football. Big mistake! I shared the care of the rest of our babies, and we all profited. Nothing develops tenderness and sensitivity in a male like caring for a baby.

Dads, whatever job you have, try your best to incorporate working and fathering. That will be the best investment you'll ever make. Job satisfaction is very important to a man's self-image, but a job is only a means to an end. It is a way of providing for your family and of serving God and others. It is important to keep this in mind as you struggle to adjust your priorities following the birth of a baby. God's will and God's laws must come first.

> Blessed is the man
> who does not walk in the counsel of the wicked

THE NEW BABY PLANNER

> or stand in the way of sinners
>> or sit in the seat of mockers.
> But his delight is in the law of the LORD,
>> and on his law he meditates day and night.
> He is like a tree planted by streams of water,
>> which yields its fruit in season
> and whose leaf does not wither.
>> Whatever he does prospers. (Ps. 1:1–3 NIV)

Prospering does not necessarily mean that you "keep up with the Joneses" down the block or even with other Christian families in your church. But God does promise "fruit in its season" and a rich spiritual life to those who put his ways first on their list of priorities.

Even if your wife is able to be home full time with your baby, you are needed there as well. Stay-at-home attached mothers need the support of their spouses because it is not easy to be alone at home with a baby all day. You may think that the house should be immaculate, because she has so much time on her hands. But she may be working hard all day just meeting the needs of a demanding infant. Many couples fall into more traditional roles following the birth of their first child, as the wife leaves her job for full-time child-care. But don't let this trap each of you in separate worlds, dad spending longer hours at the office and mom taking over all the housework. Your baby needs two parents involved in family life, and the more involved you are at home, the more you will enjoy your children. Just as job satisfaction carries over into your relationship with your family, so also will satisfaction on the homefront carry over into a better relationship with your job.

If your wife is working, your help and support are needed all the more. Nowhere in God's design for marriage does it say that men should not do housework. Everyone must pitch in so that the family can thrive.

Evaluate your relationship with your job. What is good about it? What is stressful? What would you like to change? _____

_____

_____

_____

What are your long-term career goals? _____

_____

_____

_____

How do these fit in with your goals for your family? _____

_____

_____

_____

Do you know someone who seems to do a good job of balancing career and family needs? When you have the opportunity, ask him how he manages to do this.

CHAPTER EIGHT

FEEDING YOUR BABY

God has created a perfect design for the care and feeding of his children. Discovering what that design is and following it is the challenge that we will help new parents meet.

 ## BREASTFEEDING

There can be no doubt that breastfeeding is a wonderful system for the nutrition and nurturing of babies. All the many ways in which breastfeeding benefits you, your baby, and your relationship are a sure sign of God's power and love for us. The interdependence of mother and baby in the breastfeeding relationship is amazingly complex and yet beautifully simple.

 ## BENEFITS OF BREASTFEEDING

Each mother's milk provides the perfect nutrition for her baby. Everything the baby needs to grow and thrive for at least the first six months can be found in human milk. That's why the infant formula industry uses breast milk as a model for its own artificial imitation. Although artificial formula tries to duplicate the nutritional composition of human milk, it is no match for the real thing.

The protein in human milk is very easily digested by tiny babies. Proteins are the building blocks for growth, and human milk has exactly the right kind that babies need to form healthy tissues, grow brain cells, and have bright eyes and beautiful skin. The protein in formulas comes from cow's milk or from soybeans, and even though it's modified somewhat in all the processing, it remains a foreign protein, one that can cause allergic reactions and that is less available for growth.

The fat in human milk is also perfect for infants. Fat provides calories for energy; thus it, too, is important for growth. Human milk contains an enzyme called lipase, which helps the baby digest the fat more thoroughly, so that all of the energy can be used, with none wasted and coming out in the diaper.

All the vitamins and minerals that babies need are perfectly balanced in human milk. This is trickier than it sounds. The presence of one nutrient affects how others are absorbed and used, which is one of the major challenges involved in designing a substitute for human milk. For example, levels of both iron and zinc appear to be low in mother's milk, but the milk also contains substances that assure that these small amounts are very efficiently used. Tinkering with this balance, by giving babies iron or vitamin supplements, can throw the system out of whack. Iron supplements, for example, can compromise the immunological effectiveness of human milk.

Nutritional scientists are constantly discovering new virtues in human milk, and inevitably these discoveries are implemented in redesigning infant formula. Beware of people or things you read that suggest that your milk may not be adequate for your baby or that you may not have enough milk. These advisers simply do not appreciate the grand design of God's plan for feeding infants.

HEALTH BENEFITS OF BREASTFEEDING

Perhaps the most scientifically exciting discoveries about breast milk have come in the field of immunology. In the last twenty years, medical research has learned a lot about how the body protects

THE NEW BABY PLANNER

itself from infection and foreign invaders, and in the case of infants, their mother's milk is an important part of their immunological system.

Babies come into the world not quite ready to deal with all the bacteria and viruses in their environment. They do receive a big dose of immunological factors from their mothers through the placenta, and this protects them from a number of diseases until their own systems are ready to take over or they are old enough not to be seriously affected by such viruses as chickenpox. And breastfeeding provides still more protection.

The immune factors in human milk coat the digestive tract and prevent viruses from taking hold. This is one reason why breastfed babies have fewer problems with tummy aches and diarrhea; if they do happen to get sick, their illness will be less severe and they are less likely to become dehydrated. They have fewer and less severe colds and are less likely to have ear infections. Ear problems are a common nuisance in young children, and chronic ear infections can lead to hearing problems. Children need to hear well during the early years, because this is a crucial time for language development.

Breastfeeding also helps in a very specific way to protect babies from whatever virus or cold bug is going around. When the mother is exposed to a germ, her immune system reacts by making substances that know how to fight this particular invader. These substances make their way into her milk, and thus the baby gets the benefit of the mother's immunological experience. If the whole family comes down with flu, the breastfed baby often escapes the disease or has only a mild case, thanks to the immunities provided by his mother.

Breastfeeding also protects babies from allergies, an important benefit in families with a history of food allergy. Giving babies "foreign" foods like cow's milk or soy can cause reactions, including fussiness and colic, rashes, and stuffy noses. Breast milk is perfectly suited to the baby and will not cause allergic reactions. In fact, breast milk helps babies handle new foods better as they get older.

Some babies do react to foreign proteins from the mother's diet that appear in her milk. These babies are not allergic to their mother's milk, but to some food that she has eaten. Eliminating the offending food, often dairy products or eggs, will clear the baby's symptoms and perhaps leave the mother feeling better as well. If you need help determining what the problem food is, see a lactation consultant. See also, "Causes of Fussiness," p. 213.

Which of the above reasons for breastfeeding are most important to you? _____

_____

_____

_____

How will they make your parenting career easier? _____

_____

_____

_____

 ## MOTHER-INFANT ATTACHMENT AND BREASTFEEDING

All of the scientific advantages of giving human milk to babies would be useless if breastfeeding were terribly difficult or unpleasant. But God planned for that as well. He made breastfeeding enjoyable for both mother and baby. Babies love to nurse at the breast. The feeling of being cuddled next to mother, all the skin-to-skin contact, the sweet taste of the milk, the soothing rhythm of the sucking, and the sense of being full all guarantee that babies will want to breastfeed. Mothers experience a feeling of relaxation when their babies nurse, and, of course, they are rewarded by their baby's contentment. This helps to bond them to their baby, ensuring that the baby will be well taken care of and will receive the love he needs to grow and thrive.

Breastfeeding works best when mothers feed "on demand."

But "demand" is not really the best way to describe how the system works. "Demand" suggests that there is some kind of power play involved; the baby has to state his wants forcefully and make the mother capitulate to his will, like a bank demanding payback of a loan, or terrorists demanding a million dollars and a plane ride to Timbuktu.

I prefer to call the system "cue feeding" or feeding "on cue." This means that the baby gives a signal that he needs to nurse, and the mother takes her cue from her infant and offers the breast. "Cue feeding" acknowledges that there is a more sensitive kind of communication involved here and that the mother is willing and eager to pick up on her baby's cues and reinforce them so that they each learn from the other. This is how breastfeeding helps a mother get to know her baby. She discovers that a certain sort of cry or a turning of the head or an open mouth searching for a nipple means the baby wants to nurse. The baby learns that when he does any of these things, he gets what he needs. This makes him better able to communicate his needs the next time, and it also helps him learn to trust his world and the feelings he has inside. As the psalmist said, "You are He who took Me out of the womb;/You made Me trust while on my Mother's breasts" (Ps. 22:9).

Breastfeeding has been called "the language of love." What does feeding at the breast teach a baby about love? What lessons in love do you think it has for mothers? _____

_____

_____

_____

 ## BENEFITS FOR MOTHER

Breastfeeding is designed to do good things for mothers as well as for babies. There are health benefits, such as a lowered risk for breast cancer and easier postpartum weight loss. Exclusive breastfeeding (meaning few if any bottles, no pacifiers, night feeding, no solids for six months) also postpones the return of fertility, so that babies can naturally be spaced two or more years apart.

Even more important is the effect of the hormones involved in breastfeeding. Prolactin is the hormone that stimulates the breasts to make milk, and animal studies suggest that it also affects mothering behavior. Prolactin levels are very high during the time when a woman is breastfeeding, and this may help mothers feel more motherly. Prolactin is also released during times of stress in human beings, so there is evidence to suggest that it has a calming effect. This idea is well appreciated by experienced nursing mothers who have noticed that during the months (or years) their babies are breastfeeding, irritating details of daily life don't seem to bother them as much. They cope well with older children's needs, household emergencies, and the job of taking care of a baby.

The other hormone that comes into play with breastfeeding is called oxytocin. One of the leading researchers on oxytocin, Niles Newton, who breastfed her own children in the 1940s and 50s, has dubbed it "the hormone of love." Oxytocin is released when the baby nurses at the breast, or when the mother anticipates nursing, or sometimes just when the mother hears her baby (or another baby) cry. It causes the cells far up in the breast to contract and release milk, making it more available to the baby. Some women feel a tingling sensation when this happens or just a feeling of release and relaxation. Oxytocin is also released during childbirth—it stimulates the uterus to contract—and is present in both men and women during lovemaking. It produces a peaceful feeling, one that is conducive to bonding with the other person present during these interpersonal acts of love. It seems to be God's way of making people feel good about becoming a family.

It can be said that breastfeeding mothers enjoy both a harmonious and a "hormoneous" relationship with their babies. The Bible often uses the babe at the breast as a metaphor for the comfort and contentment God offers to those who believe and trust in him.

THE NEW BABY PLANNER

That you may feed and be satisfied
With the consolation of her bosom,
That you may drink deeply and be delighted
With the abundance of her glory. (Isa. 66:11)

How could anything be more right?

Have you already decided to breastfeed your baby? What attracted you to breastfeeding? _____
_____
_____
_____

What rewards and pleasures do you hope to find in breastfeeding? _____
_____
_____
_____

Do you anticipate any problems? _____
_____
_____
_____

OVERCOMING OBSTACLES TO BREASTFEEDING

So why do so many mothers have problems with breastfeeding? If you are like many expectant couples, you have probably heard almost as many horror stories about nursing as you have about childbirth. What goes wrong?

Breastfeeding is a confidence game, and you have to know what you are doing in order to feel confident. This means investing some time and effort in learning about breastfeeding before your baby is born. Breastfeeding is not terribly difficult, but there are some skills involved in putting the baby to breast. You also need to learn about how to tell if the baby is getting enough milk, how often to nurse, how to handle night feedings, how to nurse in public places, and other practical matters.

Centuries ago, this kind of knowledge was probably passed from one generation to the next in an informal way, as girls and young women watched experienced mothers nurse their babies in the course of everyday living. Many modern mothers have no contact with other women who have breastfed successfully and must rely instead on books or health professionals for breastfeeding information. While you can learn a lot from a book, it is no substitute for encouragement and support from your peers.

This is why we feel that La Leche League groups are invaluable for mothers planning to breastfeed. La Leche League's monthly group meetings provide dependable breastfeeding information in an encouraging, supportive setting. They are also a good place to watch and learn from other mothers. Mothers can start attending meetings midway through pregnancy, to get ready for the birth of the baby, and continue afterward for advice and support as the baby grows. Mothers can also call on the group's leaders for telephone help with breastfeeding problems as they occur. To find a La Leche League leader and group near you, call (800) LA-LECHE. The staff at La Leche Headquarters can put you in touch with local leaders and also send you a catalogue and more information about breastfeeding.

Besides breastfeeding assistance, La Leche League is a good source of all-around mothering information. This is because the things you need to do in order to breastfeed your baby are also the things that will make a good mother of you and strengthen your relationship with your baby. Many of the features of attachment parenting, such as early bonding with the baby, responding to baby's cries, keeping baby close, and sharing sleep, contribute to successful breastfeeding and follow naturally from the breastfeeding relationship. Breastfeeding, after all, is God's biological design for the feeding of babies, and it follows that the techniques and attitudes that make breastfeeding work well would thus be part of God's design for parenting infants. Frequent feedings following the baby's cues are essential in breastfeeding, and responsiveness to the baby's signals is the foundation of healthy parenting. Even if, for some reason, you end up bottle-feeding your baby, you will want to do it in a way similar to breastfeeding in order to reap at least some of the benefits for a good parent-child relationship.

How do you see breastfeeding fitting into your lifestyle? Have you given some thought to breastfeeding while you're on the go?

_____

_____

_____

_____

SOME QUESTIONS ABOUT BREASTFEEDING

How many times a day will I have to breastfeed my baby?

There is no set answer to this question. Every baby is different. As a general rule, most newborns nurse eight to twelve times every twenty-four hours, but this may not work out to a predictable every-two-to-three-hour schedule. As with adults, babies' appetites vary throughout the day. There may be times when your baby needs to nurse again only twenty or thirty minutes after the last feeding. At other times, he may sleep longer stretches between breastfeedings. Babies nurse less often as they get older.

How can I be sure that I will make enough milk? My mother tried to breastfeed me, but she says she was too nervous and didn't have enough milk.

Milk production functions on the principle of supply and demand—more accurately, on demand and supply. The more milk the baby takes, the more milk your breasts will continue to make. Milk supply is regulated by how much the baby sucks at the breast and by how much milk is removed from the breasts. The baby's demand tells the system how much milk to supply.

The best way to assure that you have enough milk for your

baby is to nurse your baby on cue. Trying to space feedings further apart or at regular intervals can interfere with this supply-and-demand system. So will giving supplemental bottles. You don't need to wait for your breasts to "fill up" between feedings before you nurse the baby again. The breasts make milk continuously. There will always be at least a small amount of milk there for your baby; there is no such thing as an empty breast.

Some mothers find the baby's frequent requests to nurse unnerving. They're sure that this means that the baby is not satisfied at the breast. This is seldom the case. Breast milk digests very rapidly compared to cow milk and soy formula, so breastfed babies get hungry frequently. Sometimes, too, a baby may want to nurse again soon after a feeding just to get in a little more comfort sucking. Some babies really like and need to suck. Years ago, when breastfeeding mothers were told to feed their babies by a bottle-feeding schedule—at three- or four-hour intervals, many mothers ended up not having enough milk. This was not their fault, or due to any inherited problem with their bodies; it was simply bad advice.

I can't count the ounces with breastfeeding. How will I know that enough milk is getting into my baby?

You will feel more confident about this as time goes on and you see your baby thriving and gaining weight. But even at the beginning of your breastfeeding career, there's a measurable way to be certain that enough milk is going in: pay attention to what comes out. Your breastfed baby will wet at least six to eight cloth diapers daily (four or five disposables) and will have two or more bowel movements daily, at least in the early weeks. It can't come out in the diaper if it hasn't gone in the other end.

I can't feel a let-down reflex. Do I really have one?

Not every mother feels a tingling or releasing sensation when the let-down (milk ejection reflex) occurs, and these sensations may come and go or change over time. But you will notice a difference in the rhythm of your baby's suck when the let-down occurs. The sucks will deepen, and you will hear more frequent swallowing.

Will my baby need formula supplements or bottles?

Babies who are breastfeeding well often do not need formula or water supplements. These should be avoided, because they can make the baby less eager to nurse at the breast. If the baby nurses less, you will make less milk.

Should I get my baby accustomed to taking a bottle, in case I can't be there for a feeding?

Regular bottles interfere with the supply-and-demand system, especially in the early weeks of breastfeeding. Artificial nipples require the baby to use a different sucking action to get milk, and babies under six weeks can become confused, leading to problems with breastfeeding. If you must introduce a bottle because you are returning to work, try to wait until your baby is at least four, and preferably six weeks of age. If baby won't take the bottle from you, it's because he expects the breast when you feed him. You'll have to let dad or the sitter handle this.

What about dad? Won't breastfeeding leave him feeling left out?

There are many things that fathers can appreciate about breastfeeding. It is definitely best for mother and baby, it saves work and money, and dad doesn't have to get up for middle-of-the-night feedings. A Christian father will respect God's plan for different roles for mothers and fathers. Delivering milk is not the only way to show love to a baby. Technically, the word *nurse* means "holding" and "comforting." So dad can nurse his baby to his heart's content and not feel inadequate or left out that God did not equip him with breasts as well. Father love is a part of God's design.

Fathers are *important* when mothers breastfeed. Their support and assistance can make a huge difference to breastfeeding mothers. They can walk babies, burp them, talk to them, give baths, change diapers, and field criticism. A father can also care for his wife in such a way that she knows he feels that her most important work right now is breastfeeding and caring for their baby.

How hard is it to continue breastfeeding after I return to work? Is it worth the bother?

Many women who return to employment outside the home want to continue breastfeeding both to give their babies all the nutritional and immunological advantages and as a way of maintaining a special link with the baby despite regular separations. There is no warmer way to reunite with your baby after an absence than by sitting down and nursing. This is far more relaxing than starting dinner.

You can pump your milk while you are gone, and the baby's caregiver can feed it to the baby in a bottle. When you are with the baby, you can breastfeed frequently to keep up the baby's interest in the breast, as well as your milk supply.

Are sore nipples inevitable?

The main cause of sore nipples is the baby's failing to get enough breast tissue into his mouth during feedings. When the baby is latched on correctly, the nipple is far back in the baby's mouth where it can't be harmed. How to latch the baby on correctly is the single most important thing you need to know in order to get off to a good start with breastfeeding.

Use lots of pillows to position your baby for nursing. One or two pillows should be placed in your lap to bring the baby's mouth up to breast level. Another pillow should support your arm under the baby's head throughout the feeding, and still more pillows should go behind your back to help you sit up comfortably. The baby must be turned on his side, tummy-to-tummy, facing you, with his neck nestled in the crook of your elbow, his back along your forearm, and his buttocks in your hand. His head should be straight, aligned with the rest of his body. He should not have to turn his head or strain to reach the breast. Support your breast with your

 THE NEW BABY PLANNER

hand in the shape of a C, fingers cupped underneath and thumb on top, all well behind the areola, the darker area surrounding the nipple. Gently tickle the baby's lips with your nipple and as he opens his mouth wide, aim the nipple into his mouth, and pull him in quickly. As he takes the breast, he should be held very close to your body. His nose and chin will touch the breast, but you don't have to worry about his being able to breathe. God made babies' faces exactly the right shape for being comfortable at the breast. As the baby sucks, you should notice his jaw muscles working so that his ears actually move a bit.

Most mothers and babies need some practice at learning to latch onto the breast. If you don't get it the first time, take the baby off the breast (be sure to break suction first by slipping a finger into the corner of the baby's mouth or by pressing down on your breast), and try again. You have to be quick, because babies' mouths open and close rapidly. Don't let the baby suck on just the nipple, or you will get sore. It is easy to get frustrated, lose patience, and get more and more tense and anxious if the baby seems determined to want to just suck on your nipple. This will be likely to happen if the baby is given bottles in the hospital.

We find that a session with a lactation consultant in the first few days after birth is invaluable in getting mothers and babies off to a good start with breastfeeding. Or hire a lactation doula to come for a few hours each day. Getting latch-on problems solved early prevents sore nipples from turning breastfeeding into a painful experience.

I'm afraid that I'll have problems with breastfeeding. I'm just not the type. Isn't it easier to give bottles?

There is no one "type" of breastfeeding mother. You don't have to be an "earth mother" or a calm, contented cow sort of person to breastfeed. Breastfeeding fits comfortably into many contemporary lifestyles. In fact, it can be easier to breastfeed than give formula. If you have somewhere to go, just pack a few diapers, pick up the baby, and take off, with no worries about keeping formula cold (then warming it) or bringing enough along. Most problems with breastfeeding can be solved within a day or two. And the pay-off is a happy, healthy baby who is growing and thriving on your milk.

If you are at all interested in breastfeeding, give it a sincere effort. But if you have a lot of inner conflicts about it, or if you're breastfeeding only because your mother-in-law, your husband, or your best friend is pressuring you, then perhaps you should reconsider. You may come to like breastfeeding, but if it is interfering with your relationship with your baby by making you an unhappy person, it may be better for you to bottle-feed. Be realistic, however, about your expectations. Changing from breast to bottle-feeding does not lessen your baby's need for *you*.

We cannot tell you everything there is to know about breastfeeding in the space of one section of one chapter in this book. Get in touch with La Leche League, read some of the books on the list, and talk to experienced nursing mothers. You will get the information you need, and you will also grow more confident in your body's ability to nourish your baby and give love in this wonderful way.

When should I wean my baby?

There is no set age for weaning, although we encourage you to think in terms of years rather than months. Your milk continues to be valuable to your baby, even after he passes the one-year mark. Over time, he will breastfeed less often and give up some feedings in favor of other pursuits. Breastfeeding becomes more important as a source of comfort and security rather than food. Weaning from the breast takes place gradually. There are many weanings in life—from the womb, from the breast, from home to school, from parental authority to independence. Children must be allowed to pass these milestones at their own pace. Wise parents support them along the way, but they do not push. Children who are weaned before their time may feel inwardly frightened or insecure and will show these feelings in aggressive behavior, tantrums, mood swings, and frustration. As a pediatrician I suspect that some of the unpleasant behavior we accept as normal in toddlers may actually be symptoms of premature weaning.

Scripture supports extended nursing, such as found in 1 Samuel 1:21–28: "When the man Elkanah went up with all his family to offer the annual sacrifice to the LORD and to fulfill his vow, Hannah did not go. She said to her husband, 'After the boy is weaned, I will take him and present him before the LORD, and he will live there always.' 'Do what seems best to you,' Elkanah her husband told her. 'Stay here until you have weaned him; only may the LORD make good his word.' So the woman stayed at home and nursed her son until she had weaned him. After he was weaned, she took the boy with her . . . to the house of the LORD. . . . 'So now I give him to the LORD. For his whole life he will be given over to the LORD' " (NIV). In biblical days, nursing was considered in terms of years and not months. Samuel was at least three years of age when he was weaned from his mother to begin instruction in the temple. In 2 Maccabees 7:27 is quoted, "My son, have pity on me that carried thee nine months in my womb, and gave thee suck three years." A discussion of these customs is found in the book *Manners and Customs of Biblical Lands,* by Fred H. Wight (Chicago: Moody Press, 1953). Besides breastfeeding for several years, the biblical concept of weaning implied a readiness and a peaceful transition. By three years of age Samuel was filled with the nurturing of his parents and ready to apply these feelings of rightness (well-being) to other relationships, including one with God. Weaning is not a loss of a relationship, but a time to move on to other things. And we can infer that the relationship the child eventually forms with God depends on the one he has with his parents.

Weaning implies a fulfillment—that a child is securely filled with one relationship and ready to take on another. This is beautifully portrayed in Psalm 131:2: "But I have stilled and quieted my soul;/like a weaned child with his mother,/like a weaned child is my soul within me" (NIV). In this passage, David relates the feeling of peace and security that a weaned child has from its mother to the trust that the child learns with his Lord. Langes' commentary on the

FEEDING YOUR BABY 193

Holy Scripture offers more insight into the meaning of this psalm, "As the weaned child no longer cries, frets, and longs for the breasts, but lies still and is content because it is with its mother, so my soul is weaned from all discontented thoughts, from all fretful desires for earthly good, waiting in stillness upon God, finding its satisfaction in His presence, resting peacefully in His arms."

Weaning also implies a child is ready. The Hebrew word for "wean" is *gamal,* meaning "to ripen." It implies that a child is ready to begin more independence. Genesis 21:8, "The child grew and was weaned, and on the day Isaac was weaned Abraham had a great feast" (NIV), implies that weaning was a festive occasion, as if the child was deemed to be ready to learn from other relationships.

In my long experience as a pediatrician, I have been bewildered over the reason why many mothers wean early. Could it be that they do not in their hearts believe that breastfeeding truly makes a difference? Over the past ten years, volumes of medical research have validated the physical and emotional benefits of extended breastfeeding. Former Surgeon General Dr. Antonia Novello recognized the medical benefits of human milk for human babies and publicly wrote, "Lucky is the infant who is nursed for two years." I use my pediatric practice as my laboratory. In studying the effects of long-term nursing on hundreds of children, I have concluded that some of the most physically and emotionally healthy children that I have ever seen are those that have not been weaned before their time. Breastfeeding does make a difference.

Weaning and independence. The question is inevitable: "Does prolonged nursing make a child too dependent on the mother?" By now you can guess that the answer is no. Children who wean gradually at their own pace and in their own time are actually more secure and more independent. Because their parents trust these babies' inner timetable, these children trust themselves. Their independent behavior is more than just bravado; it is born of solid self-confidence.

Mothers of nursing toddlers will tell you that these little persons are plenty independent. They can't be made to nurse when they

THE NEW BABY PLANNER

don't want to, no matter how much you want them to go to sleep, and they enjoy having breastfeedings their way. They will have their own special word for nursing (thus eliminating every mother's nightmare: the little voice heard during a silent moment of the church service insisting all too clearly, "I want to nurse now"). You'll have priceless stories for your collection as your breastfeeding toddler learns to talk. One of our toddlers announced she was finished with a nursing by saying, "All done, shut the door." One toddler in our practice piped up, "Mommy's moo—no sugar, no caffeine."

If you are feeling restless or ambivalent about continued breastfeeding, pray to God for help in knowing when and how to encourage your child to wean. You may also want to seek the company of other women who are nursing older babies and toddlers. La Leche League meetings are an ideal place to go for this kind of support. The leaders there understand not only your desire to let your child wean at his own pace, but also the challenges this can present to mothers. La Leche's "don't offer, don't refuse" technique for weaning is a good guideline to follow. Don't expect the weaning process to move at a steady rate, in a straight line. There will be times along the way when your child increases his nursing temporarily in response to illness, stress, or the achievements of a new developmental stage.

As your baby weans from the breast, you will substitute other forms of emotional nourishment. Just as solid foods come to substitute for the nutrition of breast milk, other experiences fill in for breastfeeding. Children's needs don't lessen as they grow; they only change. Weaning presents opportunities for more time with dad as well as for mother and child to find new ways of relating and relaxing together. Bedtime and naptime feedings are usually the last to go. Eventually your child will settle for a story and a cuddle instead of nursing.

Mothers of nursing toddlers often face criticism from friends and relatives who find this practice strange or upsetting. What would you say to someone who says, "What! Are you still nursing?"

_____

_____

_____

Why should weaning be gradual? Answer this question from both the baby's and the mother's point of view. _____

_____

_____

_____

If you are struggling with when to wean your infant or there are lifestyle circumstances that necessitate early weaning, try this exercise:

List the Reasons You Want or Need to Wean	List the Benefits You See in Extended Nursing

 ## FORMULA FEEDING YOUR BABY

Even though breast milk is the ideal food for infants, there are lifestyle situations in which the ideal is not possible or not desired. Infant feeding is not only a nutritional exercise, it's a social interaction, and this is the key to bottlefeeding your baby. That means you would always hold your baby closely as he feeds and never give in to the temptation to prop the bottle so you can "get something done" while he feeds. Also, switch sides as in breastfeeding so baby gets the benefit of learning laterality (orienting with both sides of his body).

CHOOSING A FORMULA

Select a formula in consultation with your doctor, not from a magazine advertisement. After your doctor selects a formula for your baby, it is up to you to tell him whether the formula agrees with your baby. If not, in consultation with your doctor, switch formulas until you find one that your baby can take. To tell if your baby is allergic to or intolerant of a formula, watch for these signs:

SIGNS OF FORMULA INTOLERANCE	YOUR BABY SHOWS (List your observations)
• crying as if in pain after feeding • colicky behavior after feeding • constipation or diarrhea • red, rough, sandpaper rash on face • red, ring-like rash around anus • vomiting immediately after each feeding • frequent colds and/or ear infections • irritability and frequent nightwaking	

Rule of thumb for bottlefeeding: Feed your baby 2 to 2½ ounces of formula per pound per day. Divide into feedings every three hours.

For example, if your baby weighs ten pounds he may take 20 to 25 ounces per day, but your baby may not drink this much immediately after birth nor drink this much every day, and on some days may drink more. These are just average amounts.

Reading your baby's feeding cues. You may be tempted to use the bottle as a pacifier, offering it to your baby at every whimper. Not only does this unwise practice contribute to overfeeding, but it deprives you of the opportunity to learn creative ways of comforting your baby. Sometimes baby simply wants to be held or played with and not fed. If your baby fusses shortly after a feeding, he probably wants a nonfeeding type of interaction. If your baby continues to fuss after holding and comforting, then she's probably hungry. By three months of age most babies will show hunger cries that are distinguishable from other need cries. Best is to look for pre-cry cues so the baby does not have to cry for a feeding. The usual signs are lip-smacking, fidgeting, fussing, and the infant's patting your breasts. List the most reliable feeding cues for your baby:

_____

_____

_____

_____

Feeding interactions. Always keep in mind that feeding is a social interaction in addition to delivery of nutrition. Whether by breast or by bottle, *nursing* is comforting and nourishing. Don't prop the bottle, leaving the baby unattended in a crib to feed himself. This practice is not only dangerous because of the risk of choking, but it deprives you and your baby of the joy of relating to each other. During the feeding, touch and caress your baby, make eye-to-eye contact and give your baby the message that you enjoy this special feeding time. As tempting as it may be to detach yourself from the feeding and read a book or engage in other interactions, your baby is a baby for a very short time. Enjoy this special closeness of feeding time together. Try to keep a person attached to both ends of the bottle.

 ## SCHEDULING YOUR BOTTLE-FED BABY

From our twenty-seven years of experience of feeding eight babies we have learned that the key to successful infant feeding is for both parent and infant to be satisfied. You will spend more time feeding your baby than any single interaction during the first year, so you want to enjoy it. And if you approach feeding your baby, either by breast or by bottle, as an enjoyable social time rather than a chore, both you and your baby will get more out of the feeding than just a few ounces of milk. The two terms for infant feeding that you are bound to hear are *demand feeding*—the baby is fed every time her little tummy desires—and *scheduled feeding*—feeding the baby at fixed intervals during the day (usually every three hours) and upon awakening at night. We don't like either one of these terms. Demand feeding implies a tyrant-servant relationship, which is not true. Rigidly scheduled feedings are unhealthy for baby and unwise for parents. We prefer the term *cue feeding:* recognizing when your infant is hungry or thirsty and feeding your baby according to these cues.

Setting a rigid schedule and being inflexible about it often keeps babies from thriving, physically and emotionally. When a newborn experiences hunger, it is a new and frightening sensation. To the newborn, hunger pangs drive his whole being to search for the means to stop this new fear, just as he instinctively seeks out the breast to calm his panic following the trauma of birth. Any threatening sensation, such as hunger and anxiety, means annihilation to this most helpless of beings. So when a tiny baby cries with need (for food or holding), he is screaming for dear life—his *own*. It is very wrong to think these cries can be ignored because the nursery staff is too busy or it's not time for feeding.

In the early months the baby needs only one thing: to know he has the power to survive even though he has to depend on his caretaker to do it for him. This is how he gradually builds a sense of self and trust. Eventually you will hear a difference in his cry—the panic will be gone, and you will know intuitively that he no longer fears death when he's just hungry. There will still be panic cries, but then the causes will be identifiable—pain or the fright of being alone—and these cries will still bring you running. But the usual cries of need will allow for less and less immediacy. It will be up to you as the parent to discern this, not some third-party adviser who thinks babies should be scheduled from the beginning. Some babies do seem to schedule themselves (our first two did), so we have nothing against schedules per se. Hearing a baby cry urgently and fiercely, signaling hunger or other need, and *programming oneself to ignore that cry* is unwise. It is not good enough to hold a screaming newborn, waiting for the correct amount of time to pass, murmuring over and over to yourself and baby, "Mommy's here—you're just fine," when you know all he needs is to suck. When they are hungry and cry for a feeding and don't get it, they eventually learn that their caregivers are unresponsive to their needs, and they quit cueing. Rigid scheduling also creates a distance between the parent and the child. You learn to watch the clock instead of watching your baby. It keeps you from knowing how to read your baby's signals and responding intuitively. It desensitizes your baby to you, and you to your baby, and, as we have said many times, insensitivity is what gets most new parents in trouble.

There is nothing evil in your baby that you are required to purge him of. The sin nature is, of course, present in all of us, parents and baby. But it is not what causes a baby to cry for feeding or holding, even if it's only been twenty minutes since he last sucked. There is no one right way or schedule for any two babies, only a harmony in the divine design that allows the individual mother to know intuitively what her individual baby needs at any particular time. Stop and consider that the whole idea of scheduling developed with the introduction of formula feeding, when it was discovered that babies feed less often because formula takes longer (and is harder) to digest. So bottlefed babies can do well enough on these schedules to not have to cry out of hunger, at least. "How convenient," people must have thought. For the first time, all mothers were free to leave their babies and return at their own convenience, since mother was not even required for feeding time. Our culture bought into this myth that babies could be raised man's way. And now we even have Christian teachers saying that breastfed babies can be put on schedules the same as bottlefed babies, and if they have to cry a little (or a lot) that's just the sin nature in them we have to overcome.

Tiny babies have tiny tummies so that most babies will need formula feeding at least every three hours. During growth spurts—

which occur every three to six weeks during the first six months—your baby is likely to need to be fed more often. Most bottlefeeding veterans and their infants seem to work out a compromise between complete demand feeding and rigid-schedule-feeding: scheduling bottles at two or three set times during the day and interspersing the rest of the feedings according to baby's cues. Most babies—breast and formula fed—will sleep better at night if they are fed more frequently during the day, so you may want to attempt to cluster your baby's feedings during the daytime. If your baby is thriving and you are enjoying the feeding relationship, this is the right "schedule" for you.

If you are wondering whether to try scheduling your infant's feedings, try this exercise.

Why do *you* need to put your baby on a schedule? _____
_____
_____
_____

Is your baby a compliant infant whom you feel will take to scheduled feedings easily? _____
_____
_____
_____

Is your infant a high-need baby who rejects scheduled feedings? _____
_____
_____
_____

Are scheduled feedings working for you? _____ Your infant? _____

INTRODUCING SOLID FOODS

Get ready for those delightful little messes that come with feeding a baby. Most babies begin to need solid foods between four and six months; some want them earlier, some later. Better than watching your calendar, watch your baby for cues of feeding readiness. The usual signs are begging cues: grabbing your spoon, reaching for food on your plate, and looking up at you with an open mouth while you are eating, or cues that mimic you, such as lip-smacking movements while you are eating. Note your baby's individual interest-in-feeding cues: _____

_____

_____

_____

_____

Three favorite starter foods are bananas, rice cereal, and pears. After these favorites, try avocados, apple sauce, carrots, squash, and sweet potatoes. Your fingertip makes the ideal first-feeding spoon. Using bananas as a test-dose, mash up a fingerful of very ripe banana and place it on your baby's tongue. If baby's tongue goes in, the food disappears, and you receive an approving smile, you can then proceed with a larger volume and variety of other solid foods. The amount and scheduling of solid feeding is a negotiation between your baby's needs and your daily schedule. Between nine and twelve months, after baby has mastered fruits, vegetables, and juice, try lamb, veal, poultry, egg yolk, cheese, yogurt, noodles, mashed potatoes, and beans. By a year of age your baby may enjoy eating mashed adult table food. Forget the three square meals a day; that's an adult eating pattern and, for that matter, not all that wise. Most babies *graze* or nibble all day long. The grazing pattern of eating is more physiologic for infants and adults, and is more in keeping with the shorter attention span of a busy baby. Between nine and twelve months your baby may enjoy finger foods. Avoid foods that may choke your baby (nuts, popcorn kernels, seeds, raw carrots and apples, meat chunks, and whole grapes) and stick to those that melt in the mouth, like rice cake pieces and soft-cooked vegetables.

CHAPTER NINE

AS BABY GROWS

Everybody is unique. Each person has his or her own likes, dislikes, needs, and expectations, and each has a distinct way of communicating these things. All together they add up to a personality that makes your baby someone special right from the start. What sort of person he or she turns out to be depends on both these inborn traits and your responses to them.

UNDERSTANDING YOUR BABY'S TEMPERAMENT

Temperament describes the basic wiring of a baby, the personality that comes with the basic package. There is a wide variety of temperaments among babies, with labels including "easy," "demanding," "fussy," "happy," "sleepy," and "colicky." Temperament is inborn; it is the nature part of the "nature versus nurture" debate. It is evident right from the start. A baby with a fussy temperament is not a bad reflection of her parents' caretaking. This is simply the way she is.

While you should not be too quick to label your baby, it is important to understand and accept her fundamental temperament. The kind of responses and stimulation you provide can help to mellow a fussy child or perk up a laid-back one. The temperament concept is especially important if you have a high-need baby, one whose temperament demands a lot from parents. It is much easier to accept and respond to a baby's frequent demands if you can accept that they are part of who she is—and not the fault of your parenting style, your feelings about motherhood.

 ## FIT

When a baby is able to get her needs met and feels comfortable in her environment, we say she "fits." Fit has to do with the relationship between mother and baby. Some pairs fit together more easily, while some mothers and infants have to make a few adjustments along the way in order to improve the fit. The baby's complaints and demands shape the mother's behavior, and the mother can influence her child's development by how she responds.

Just as the baby brings a certain level of needs to the mother-infant relationship, so also the mother brings a capacity for nurturing. Some women (and men), perhaps influenced by the way they themselves were parented, find it easier to nurture than others do. Responsive mothers adapt more easily to their babies' needs than do women who are more restrained in their ways of dealing with infant fussing.

A responsive nurturing mother is a good match for a baby with a high need level; they each bring out the best in the other. The baby challenges the mother's abilities and keeps her interested in her job, while the mother mellows the baby's temperament by helping her to feel right much of the time. But a so-called easy baby may also need a responsive mother, one who recognizes that even though the baby is content to lie in her crib and play by herself, this is not the best thing for her. A nurturing mother brings needed excitement to the life of a baby who is content to just coast along. A highly responsive mother can even compensate for a baby who is slow to warm up or not very cuddly; she will woo the baby into enjoying the close contact needed to develop to her full potential.

Less responsive mothers force babies to work harder at making a good fit. The babies fuss more, and the mother who doesn't know how to respond or who doesn't receive enough emotional nurturing herself may have difficulty giving of herself. She may become very frustrated with her baby's behavior. Advice to be more restrained in her responses may appeal to her, as a way of getting the baby under control, but following this advice only puts greater distance between her and her baby. Because she isn't finding parenthood to be very rewarding, this mother may immerse herself in other activities, leaving less time and energy for baby. Mother and baby drift apart, and neither one develops the capacity for love and happiness that comes from a rewarding mother-child relationship. Even an easy-going baby may have a difficult time with a less responsive mother; she may not fuss much at first, but eventually there will be red flags out signaling that this baby has needs that aren't being met.

Knowing something about your own capacity to respond to your baby's needs will help you recognize if fit is going to be a problem for you. I believe that God has a matching program for parents and babies, and that he will give you the ability to respond to your baby's need level. God will provide the energy you need, along with wisdom, as long as you seek his guidance in practicing a style of parenting that allows your parenting abilities to develop to their fullest. This is where attachment parenting fits so well into God's design. Practicing the attachment parenting concepts will make you a responsive parent, even if you don't naturally feel like one.

Are you a naturally nurturing person? Here are some qualities of an idealized parent. Which ones describe you?

Patient	Empathetic
Self-giving	Understanding
Puts others' needs first	Even-tempered
Calm	Intuitive

Cheerful	Doesn't mind sleep inter-
Mature	ruptions
Well-organized	Emotionally stable

How did you do? None of us is good at all of these things all the time. What parts of parenthood are or will be more difficult for you? _____

_____

_____

_____

Will attachment parenting help you meet these challenges? ___

_____

_____

Mothers and fathers need emotional nourishment themselves in order to be able to give freely to their babies. Where can you get this kind of support in your life? _____

_____

_____

_____

 ## HIGH-NEED BABIES

Some babies are harder to console than others, and some mothers are quicker at learning what their babies need. If your baby continues to cry despite your best efforts, it is hard to feel confident as a parent. What you must understand is that babies cry because of their own sensitive temperaments, not because their parents are incompetent. Some babies cry (sometimes even when they are being held) for several hours each day of their first few months, no matter how experienced their caregivers. Some babies simply can't be put down in a crib and stay happy. They need a higher level of parenting and will work to get it. If you are blessed with this kind of frustrating infant, do not give up and put him down and walk away.

Continue to hold and carry the baby and offer comfort. This is what is needed to mellow the baby's temperament.

It may be difficult to appreciate in the late afternoon or early evening when you have been walking with a crying baby for hours, but you should rejoice that this baby is so insistent on having his needs met. His fussiness assures that he will get the kind of parenting he needs in order to channel his sensitivity into constructive, empathetic behavior.

Some writers on parenting refer to this type of child as strong-willed, or they describe him in a way that makes him sound defiant or difficult. The parent's task becomes "breaking" the child, making him knuckle under to parental authority. We coined the term "high need" to describe these children, because the way to parent them is to respond lovingly and helpfully to their very sensitive "high-need" temperaments. They don't need a firmer hand or harsher methods of discipline; they need a higher level of guidance, tolerance, and ministry from their parents.

How can you increase your acceptance of your child's needs? Write a prayer asking God to help you accept whatever temperament your child has and to give you the strength and wisdom you need to offer this child the best level of parenting. _____

_____

_____

_____

_____

_____

_____

_____

Do you have a high-need baby? List the characteristics of your baby as you perceive them and compare them with what we have found to be the characteristics of most high-need babies. In reality, most babies have many of these high-need characteristics.

Characteristics of High-Need Babies	Your Baby
Super-sensitive—jumps at the normal sudden noises other babies ignore.	
Intense—"I just can't put her down."	
Hyperactive—short cat naps only; needs less sleep than mother; constant motion.	
Hypertonic—holds body rigid, doesn't usually like to snuggle close.	
Draining	
Wants to nurse all the time.	
Unpredictable—what works one time won't work the next.	
Unsatisfied	
Awakens frequently	
Demanding	

The need-level concept. We believe that in accordance with the term *Creator*, God would not give parents a child with whom they could not cope. A baby comes wired with a certain temperament for a reason. We believe every baby has a certain level of need that must be filled if she is to develop to her maximum potential. It also follows that an infant would come wired with a temperament to be able to communicate these needs. For example, an infant with a high level of need is wired with an intense way of communicating those needs. Babies who need a lot of holding in order to thrive to their fullest potential will protest if they are put down. Some babies are labeled "easy" babies. They are content in a variety of caregiving circumstances. They don't cry much because their needs are easily met. They are somewhat predictable in their needs and adapt easily to a variety of schedules and parenting styles (these are the babies everyone else may seem to have!). High-need babies, on the other hand, are super-sensitive to changes in environment. The demanding quality of such babies is a positive character trait that has survival benefits for the baby. If a baby were endowed with high needs yet lacked the ability to communicate those needs, her survival would be threatened. This baby would not develop to her full potential. When the need level of a baby and the giving level of the parents are in harmony, the whole family thrives. It is this relationship that you can pray for. Ask God for wisdom to read and respond to the needs of your baby, and to have the strength to do so.

What happens when a baby's needs remain unfilled? A need that is not filled never completely goes away, but results in an inner stress that sooner or later manifests itself as undesirable behavior—such as anger, aggression, rejection, or withdrawal. This baby does not feel right, and, therefore, does not act right. A baby who does not act right is less of a joy to parent, and baby and parents drift farther apart. The parent becomes less adequate at caregiving, and the baby becomes less motivated to signal her needs. The entire parent-child relationship operates at a lower level and a distance develops between parent and child. A high-need baby and a responsive parent bring out the best in each other. The high-need baby whose needs are listened to develops better communication skills. The parents, because they are open and responsive to the baby, develop a higher level of parenting skills to meet their baby's needs. Parents learn to nurture better, and the baby learns to communicate better, and the entire parent-infant relationship operates at a higher level.

THE CHALLENGE OF A HIGH-NEED BABY

Having a high-need child is a challenge. Martha and I know this from firsthand experience. Our fourth child, Hayden, was in our arms (or very nearby) and in our bed for her entire first year. She asked a lot of us as parents, but we feel that what we gave her in that first year helped her to feel better about her place in the world and has paid off as she has grown older. High-need babies have many positive character traits, including sensitivity, creativity, and the ability to be empathetic, but these must be nurtured along by responsive parenting.

High-need babies are known for their fussiness. They have other characteristics in common as well:

- "She wants to be held all the time." The very existence of toy store aisles full of crib toys and beautiful mobiles suggests that babies should be content to lie in their cribs and gaze passively at these attractions. New parents soon learn the truth behind this illusion. All babies want a lot of hands-on care; high-need babies want it all the time. They are content only in a parent's arms or at mother's breast.
- "Intense." Nothing goes down easily with high-need babies. They express their feelings forcefully, using up a lot of energy. Parental attention can help them redirect all this forcefulness into growth and development.
- "She wants to nurse all the time." The idea of a feeding schedule is as foreign to a high-need baby as afternoon tea would be to a backwoodsman. Remember that babies need to suck for lots of reasons beyond hunger. Nursing is the force that pulls them back together every hour or so.

- "She arches her back and doesn't like to cuddle." Babies who arch their backs and stiffen their limbs benefit from being carried in a baby sling. The sling supports them in a curved, tucked, more relaxed position.
- "She is a light sleeper. She wakes up several times at night, and will not sleep alone." The intensity of daytime needs carries over into nighttime behavior with high-need infants. Often these babies sleep better near a warm and breathing body, which has a regulating effect on their own sleep patterns.
- "She is very demanding and can't wait even a minute." High-need babies see every little problem as an emergency. Their cries go directly to full alert. Learning that their cries receive predictable nurturing responses will help to mellow out their apparent anger and will eventually turn their intensity into regard for others as well as themselves.

To some extent, your perception of your baby's temperament is shaped by your expectations for infant behavior. If you expected your newborn to do nothing but eat and sleep sweetly in her bassinet, even a baby with a moderate need level will seem fussy to you, at least in the early weeks. As you get to know your baby better and make the adjustments that lead to a good fit, you may find that everyone—parents and baby—calms down.

A wise, experienced mother once said, "Don't kid yourself; they're all high-need babies." What do you think? How might the assessment of the baby's needs change with the personality of the parent? _____

_____

_____

_____

How might your parenting philosophy affect your view of your baby's need level? _____

_____

AS BABY GROWS 213

Accepting your baby's need level. A baby who cries and fusses much of the time can try a mother's confidence as well as her nerves. It's hard to enjoy mothering under these conditions. Even if this baby is supposed to be a blessing from God, you may find yourself wishing that God would go bless someone else for a change. Yet your baby needs you to be emotionally healthy and able to care for her. This can take some work.

A baby's anger, desperation, or helplessness can arouse these emotions in his mother as well, opening old wounds, uncovering hidden fears, and shaking self-esteem. If you notice these kinds of reactions in yourself, try to discover where these emotions originate. Ask for God's help in healing past hurts and in forgiving those who hurt you (especially your parents). Pray also for patience and the strength to go on comforting your baby. The Lord will reach out and support you when you need it if you remember to lean on him.

Don't forget to thank God for small daily blessings: naps, calls from good friends, a shower taken without interruption, a smile from your baby. Try to find some ways of spending positive time with your baby, even if it is nothing more than lying beside her and gazing at her once she is finally asleep.

TIPS ON COPING WITH HIGH-NEED BABIES

Don't feel guilty if your baby continues to cry and fuss despite your best efforts. Your job is to be there for your baby. Don't fall into the emotional pit of feeling more and more aggravated or full of self-pity if the baby continues to cry. You have to be the adult here, the one who stays calm and does not get upset. Keep trying to comfort the baby, and don't blame yourself for your child's inner feelings.

Beware of that favorite new mother game: comparing babies. Discussions of how "good" another baby is or how easily he stays with the babysitter can be demoralizing for the parents of a high-need baby. They lead to discouragement and self-doubt because your baby doesn't "measure up." To defend against an attack of baby-comparing, remind yourself that all babies are *different*—not better or worse, just unique. You and the mother of "Baby Perfect" may have very different views on parenting, and her methods may be totally unacceptable to you. Remember, too, that mothers tend to exaggerate their baby's good qualities when they play this game. Rested Rita from Wednesday morning Bible class may claim that her six-week-old sleeps through the night, but that may have been a one-time-only freak accident that happened to have occurred the night before. Or Rita may be willing to accept the idea of her baby crying herself back to sleep without parental assistance.

If you are the parents of a high-need baby, find some ways to relax. Get some outdoor exercise. Take a warm bath with the baby. Lie down when you nurse your baby to sleep. Plan ahead for fussy periods, so that you're not caught trying to prepare an elaborate meal (or any meal) during that 4:00 to 8:00 P.M. hour when your baby needs a calm mother.

GENTLING THE FUSSY BABY

Time-tested methods for soothing crying babies come down to a few basic principles. Babies like motion. They like physical contact. They can be distracted using the principle of competing behavior. When you provide another kind of stimulation that competes with their crying, they may calm down as they shift their attention to the more gentle alternative behavior. Here are some specific suggestions:

- **Skin-to-skin contact.** Babies find touching very stimulating and calming. Hold your baby against your bare chest (wrap a blanket or big shirt around both of you if it's cold), or let her cheek nestle against yours. Stroke her back with your warm hand. Let her sleep with her head nestled against mother's breast.

- **Walking.** Parents of high-need babies log many miles of floor-walking, dancing, stroller-pushing, and babywearing. Experiment with different paces and motions. Walk outside, or do laps around the interior of your house.
- **Wear your baby.** Using a babysling lessens the strain on your muscles when you are walking and holding your baby. It supports the baby in a curved position that discourages tension. The familiarity of being in the sling will calm the baby, as will the familiar closeness.
- **Take a bath together.** The warm water will soothe both mother and baby, as will the skin contact. Many babies like to nurse in the tub.
- **Swaying and bouncing.** Trying to have a conversation with a mother holding a fussy baby is like watching a clock pendulum: Both are always in motion. Unlike the pendulum, however, the mother may be going back and forth and up and down all at once. Try a rhythm of about seventy-five beats per minute (faster than you'd expect), which mimics the mother's heartbeat as heard in the womb.
- **Sound.** Singing or soothing speech calms babies. Use the lower ranges of your voice. Some babies like soft sounds. Others prefer an energy level in the sound that comes close to matching the intensity of their cry. One baby we know never fails to be calmed by an old Lutheran hymn, sung loudly by her mother in exaggerated German diction. Other babies are calmed by Mozart, quiet parental conversation (the "bore-them-to-sleep" method), or the sound of the vacuum cleaner.
- **Infant massage.** Get a book or a video on infant massages and use it just *before* the fussy hour.
- **Offer the breast.** Nursing is the number-one baby-soothing method of all time. And you can put your feet up and read a book while you do it.
- **Go for a ride.** The car provides both motion and sound to soothe a baby to sleep. You can carry the baby back into the house in her car seat to avoid disrupting her once she is finally asleep. This works better in the early weeks; many high-need babies take to hating their car seats by around two to three months.
- **Swings and other mother substitutes.** Mechanical baby swings, audiotapes of womb sounds, cradles, and other things

THE NEW BABY PLANNER

that provide sound or motion may help to calm your baby and give you a few minutes to eat dinner, shower, or get ready to go out with baby. Remember, though, that baby needs you to be his primary comforter, not some man-made device.

You will find your own ways of comforting your baby as time goes on. No one thing will work every time. After all, inconsistency and unpredictability are hallmarks of the high-need baby. But you will master a repertoire you can depend on. With our last baby (and we thought we knew it all by number eight), Martha stumbled onto a trick that calmed Lauren down when nothing else worked: She held her at breast in a vertical position and walked briskly in the room as Lauren finally figured out how to settle down and suck enough to relax off to sleep.

Think of ways to calm yourself while your baby is having a fussy period. Some examples: special music, a familiar prayer, a favorite walk. What will work for you? _____
_____
_____
_____

Who are the most helpful people to talk to about your baby's fussing? Which of your friends and relatives will it be better to avoid? _____
_____
_____
_____

CAUSES OF FUSSINESS

As you learn to cope with your baby's fussiness, you will also want to explore possible causes. Babies fuss primarily because of their own temperaments and not because of physical problems. But they cry because something is hurting them. So it is wise to consider the possibility that there could be a medical problem, an allergy, or an environmental irritant that is contributing to your baby's fussiness. Enlist the help of your pediatrician, especially if it seems that your baby is actually hurting.

Even in an exclusively breastfed baby, fussiness may be the result of an allergy or sensitivity. Although the baby is not allergic to her mother's milk, she may be reacting to something in the mother's diet that is coming through the milk. The most likely candidate is milk or other dairy products; some mothers consume large amounts of milk, cheese, and yogurt during pregnancy or while breastfeeding, and cow's milk proteins can make their way into breast milk, causing a reaction in a sensitive baby. Other possibilities include caffeine-containing substances, tomatoes, apples, and citrus fruits, peanuts, gas-producing raw vegetables such as broccoli, onions, and cabbage, and supplemental vitamins containing iron. If you suspect a sensitivity in your baby, try totally eliminating the suspicious food(s) from your diet for two to three weeks and see if the fussiness improves.

Is fussiness the same thing as colic? Colic is a particular kind of fussiness, one where it often seems to mothers that the baby is hurting. Using the term "the hurting baby" rather than colicky baby compels parents to keep working in partnership with the doctor to find a cause. The typical colicky baby draws up her legs as she cries, her abdomen is tense and seems to be filled with gas, and her fists are clenched and flailing as if in anger. Parents feel helpless in the face of such apparent misery.

Physicians define *colic* as sudden and unexplained outbursts of inconsolable crying that last at least three hours a day, occur three or more days a week, and continue for at least three weeks. Colic begins within the first three weeks of life and seldom lasts longer than three months. Doctors and mothers have speculated about the causes of colic for years, with no definite answer in sight, although suggested reasons include excessive swallowing of air, milk allergy, gastroesophageal reflux, or disturbance of biorhythms.

You can minimize the amount of air your baby swallows with

THE NEW BABY PLANNER

feedings by burping her early and more often. Try feeding her more frequently, before she has a chance to get ravenously hungry. This may cut down on the tendency to gulp the milk down. Some breastfed babies have trouble keeping up with the increased flow of milk that happens with the milk-ejection reflex (MER). It can help to trigger the MER before the feeding by expressing some milk, or taking the baby off the breast for a few moments when the MER occurs and letting the milk gush into a towel. Limiting the baby to one breast per feeding can also help with this problem, as long as you nurse frequently and keep an eye on the number of wet diapers to be sure the baby is getting enough. If you're bottle-feeding, try enlarging the hole in the nipple with a red-hot sewing needle. Or use the collapsible plastic bags to minimize air swallowing.

Try different positions for more effective burping. Get the baby way up on your shoulder, so that her stomach presses on your collar bone to get the air out. Lay her across your thigh or place her on her right side to allow the bubble to rise to the top of her stomach. Then sit her upright, leaning forward against your hand, and pat her back firmly. Some stubborn bubbles come up only after you've gone on to another activity—diaper changing, for example. The change of position will finally bring up the burp. In general, keeping a baby upright will minimize the amount of air trapped in the tummy. Babywearing can provide both the upright position and the motion that will help to expel air swallowed during feedings or crying spells.

If your baby wakes in pain at night, suspect a medical problem such as gastroesophageal reflux, the regurgitation of stomach acids into the esophagus. This causes a heartburn-like pain. Consult your doctor if you think your baby may have reflux.

New theories about colic suggest that it may be a developmental problem, something to do with getting the brain and hormonal system organized. The fact that babies often grow out of colic by three or four months of age, when their sleep patterns become more predictable, supports this idea. The interaction between regulating hormones and behavior is a complex one, and more research is needed before scientists can begin to understand what is going on inside a colicky or fussy baby. But it makes sense that anything parents can do to calm, nurture, and support a baby during fussy spells will help. It is not good for a baby to cry alone, although you may need to walk away momentarily to take a deep breath, calm yourself, or find another pair of arms to take over for a while.

No matter what the cause of your baby's colic, fussiness, or high need level, getting to know your baby better through attachment parenting will help the whole family cope better. Wearing your baby, responding to her cries, keeping her with you during the day and at night will help you become a more responsive parent. If your child continues to be an intense, high-need person as she grows, you will be ready to give her the kind of sensitive parenting she needs. You may actually look back on the days of having a fussy baby and discover that this experience really was a blessing in disguise, one that made everyone in the family more sensitive to each other. It is also an experience that teaches you to rely on God for strength and for a loving example of how to deal with human need.

How can having a high-need baby make a parent less selfish and less self-absorbed? _____

_____

_____

_____

_____

What other admirable qualities can a high-need baby bring out in a parent? _____

_____

_____

_____

_____

GROWING TOGETHER

Babies change enormously during their first year. In just twelve months a helpless newborn becomes a curious, soon-to-be toddler. A lot happens in a short time. One mother told me, "Just when I finally get the hang of one stage, my baby moves on to the next one."

Knowing some basic facts of infant development will enable you to respond to your baby's changing needs, and will also make parenting more fun. One of the joys of being a parent is watching each new ability emerge and grow. Your baby's development may well become your favorite topic of conversation. Fortunately, God created parents in pairs, so that there is always someone to share your obsession, after you've bored friends and even grandparents to death with all the details.

What takes place in the baby's first year truly is a process of growing together. Both baby and parents mature. They develop mutual sensitivity, learning to understand each other's needs and cues. There is mutual shaping of behavior. The parents influence the baby's behavior patterns, and the baby changes the way the parents act as well. For example, the parent may enjoy a particular way of holding an infant, perhaps in a baby sling, and with patience and persistence, she gradually gets the child to like this as well. The baby shapes the parents' behavior, perhaps by fussing until mother feeds her more frequently or by rewarding dad with an especially engaging smile when he holds her up at eye level.

All this mutuality leads to mutual competence. You both feel like you really know what you're doing when you are together. And, since nothing succeeds like success, feelings of competence motivate everyone to continue communicating, teaching, and learning.

Think of other ways in which baby and parents directly shape each other's feeding, comforting, or play behavior. _____

_____

_____

How might restraint parenting practices cause these mutual shaping attempts to lead to frustration and detachment rather than mutual competence? _____

_____

_____

_____

 BUILDING BETTER BABIES

Most parents see the pay-off with attachment parenting from early on. These babies don't just grow; they thrive. They flourish. They delight the people who love them. Research shows that there are also very specific ways in which attachment parenting helps to build better babies. Good things happen when parents and babies are attached.

Babies who are breastfed on cue, whose parents wear them much of the time, who sleep beside their mother at night, and whose cries are immediately responded to have less trouble with organizing their behavior. This does not mean that their naptimes are more predictable or that they will nurse on a regular schedule. It means that they are more able to stay alert, to direct their attention to their environment, and to interact with caregivers. They do not have to spend hours crying or withdrawing into shutdown every day, so they have more quality time left for learning and enjoying life. Even their physiological systems work more efficiently. With fewer stress hormones circulating in their blood, they are able to stay calmer longer.

There is an anatomical explanation for the benefits of attachment parenting. The brain grows rapidly during the first year of life, doubling its volume. Nerve cells, called neurons, proliferate rapidly, looking like miles of tangled electrical wires, but all of the wiring is not hooked up when the baby is born. Interactions with the environment during the first year cause these neurons to form circuits that enable the baby to think and do more things. The more high-quality interaction the baby has with the environment, the more complex the circuit board in her brain. Attachment parenting ensures that the baby gets the necessary stimulation. In studies, sensitively nurtured infants score higher on mental development and IQ tests. Attached styles of parenting are also associated with better development, good social skills, independence, and better growth.

Attachment parenting has other tangible benefits. What do you think the effects might be on infant growth? _____

_____

_____

_____

_____

How could knowing your baby better help you to have a healthier baby or know when to call the doctor? _____

_____

_____

_____

_____

How could it save you money? _____

_____

_____

_____

_____

How might attachment parenting be valuable to a baby with disabilities or chronic health problems? _____

_____

_____

_____

_____

ENJOYING YOUR BABY'S DEVELOPMENT

Infant development is a fascinating subject, and there are many books and resources you can use to learn more about the progression of skills during the first two years of life. This book does not have the space to go into the details of learning to crawl on all fours, to pick up tiny pieces of cereal, or to finally say "Da-da" and mean it. But since the parent-infant relationship changes along with the baby, infant development does play an important role in how attached parents interact with their babies. Here are some highlights of how your attachment to your baby will grow and develop during the first year.

BEGINNING ABILITIES

Scientists and philosophers used to think of a newborn baby as a blank slate, with potential but no actual personality as yet. Wise mothers knew even then what closer scientific observation has confirmed: Babies come into the world with lots of capabilities, many designed specifically to attract parents and other adults so that the babies get the loving care they need.

Eyes are important to attachment. Think of their role in romance! Eye contact is part of falling in love—with your baby as well as your spouse. Newborn eyes are relatively large and round, created by God for parents to gaze into soon after birth. One of a baby's first tasks is to connect with his mother's face, especially her eyes, in that special hour right after birth. Some babies get so engrossed that they put off sucking until later in the hour. Research has shown that babies just a few days old prefer to look at faces rather than abstract patterns. Babies' eyes focus best at a distance of eight to ten inches; compared to adults, they are near-sighted. This eight- to ten-inch focal length is ideal for studying mother's face while nursing at the breast. Fathers should keep this distance in mind when they talk to and play with their newborns.

Researchers have identified various behavioral states common to all babies. When your baby gazes back at you quietly, she is in the state of *quiet alertness,* the state most conducive to interaction and learning. At first these periods are short and infrequent, but as the baby becomes more inwardly organized, she will be able to maintain this state longer. Don't let these periods pass without talking to your baby, smiling at her, and enjoying her. Take advantage of these times to really feel connected to your baby.

When a newborn is in the *active alert* state, legs and arms moving, head turning, she is distracted by her own motion. She will be less able to hold your gaze and appreciate your presence. You can guess what the *crying* state looks like; any meaningful communication with this baby must come through physical contact and soothing behaviors. You can't reason with a baby who is upset, but your comfort measures help her to feel trusting and secure, even if she does not stop crying immediately.

Other behaviors that newborns are born with that are geared toward attachment include the reflexes used in nursing at the breast. A baby searches with her mouth when she feels a touch on her cheek and opens her mouth widely when she feels a touch on her lips. She sucks anything that comes into her mouth. She has a gag reflex to protect her from choking. A baby who acts eager and ready to nurse is more rewarding for the mother to feed, and this helps her to get attached to her infant.

Newborns even smile. Yes, that funny little look that comes over your tiny baby's face from time to time is more than just gas. It is an "inside" smile, one that reflects the baby's inner feelings of rightness. This tiny reward has an enormous effect on parents—and it makes them feel right inside, too.

The language of a newborn is directed toward comfort and satisfaction. As you respond to your baby's cries you are building the foundation for later speech. You are teaching the baby that her sounds have meaning and can produce results. This is yet another reason why a baby's cries should not be ignored.

During the newborn period, you are building the foundation of your relationship with your child. It may seem as if most of the

AS BABY GROWS

225

socializing is going from parents to baby, but if you watch closely you will see all of the ways that your baby is actively attaching herself to you. Keeping your baby with you, breastfeeding frequently, and being responsive to cries ensures that you will be there not only when the baby needs you, but also when she is doing the things that will make you feel good about her.

Can you hold a newborn baby too much? Why or why not? __

_____

_____

_____

Why is it important for babies to have attachment-promoting behaviors? What problems might arise if a baby had poor attachment skills? _____

_____

_____

_____

 ## THE SOCIAL BABY

A baby's portfolio of adult-attracting behaviors increases in size as she grows. Around the age of two months, the social smile appears, the one that spreads over your baby's face in response to people, especially parents. She sees your animated face, recognizes you, and knows that you make her feel good. She breaks out in a smile that lights up her eyes, pulls up the corners of her mouth, shows off her toothless gums, and soon has everyone in the family exclaiming over how precious she is. If you smile back harder, the smile turns into an all-over wiggling grin, which, of course, only makes you want to jazz her up still more. She may even coo or squeal and laugh. These moments make everything else worthwhile. They give parents the feeling that their baby loves them and is happy. While you, the parents, may not be the only people who can elicit a smile from your baby, you are the experts, because the baby associates you with comfort, security, and pleasure.

This growing baby is also better at establishing eye contact with caregivers. She holds your gaze longer and studies the details of faces, not just their general outline. Two-month-old babies can see farther and can follow moving objects by moving their head and eyes. They like to look at patterns with a lot of light/dark contrast, mobiles, ceiling fans, chandeliers, fires in fireplaces, and faces. You can place interesting black-and-white designs so that your baby can see them when she is in her crib, but the best way to prevent boredom in babies is to wear them while you go about your daily tasks. Being up near eye-level in the adult world provides an ever-changing view, with mom's or dad's interesting face close by as backup. The increased visual input that goes along with wearing your baby will help to keep her content, and the stimulation may even make her smarter. If you have been faithful about responding to your baby's cues, by two months of age she will begin to anticipate your response. She knows that when she cries, she will be picked up and comforted. She also has come to associate your actions with nursing—sitting-down, pulling up the shirt, fussing with the bra, tucking pillows, and so forth. (She probably connects the horizontal position with feeding, so warn Grandma that it is best to hold breastfed babies up on your shoulder unless you actually intend to nurse them.) If you pick her up to feed her, but then go off to do one more little thing before settling down, she will get angry because you have violated her expectations. Having just learned that a certain set of actions lead to nursing, she expects the familiar taste and comfort to follow, not more delays.

It may seem as if this baby is spoiled; she must have her way *now*. In reality, this baby has come to trust her parents and to have some understanding of her own needs. Don't let uninformed interpretations of your baby's behavior shake your confidence. Advisers from the restraint school of parenting may warn that you are letting the baby control you and that you should not do this. They may even insist, with biblical certainty, that babies should learn to wait.

This, however, reflects a faulty understanding of infant development (and a biased view of scripture). Babies must learn that they can count on having their needs filled before they can learn to wait. You might think of this "spoiled" stage as the first step in learning to wait, since the concept of waiting implies a certainty that there is something coming. ("Now faith is being sure of what we hope for and certain of what we do not see" [Heb. 11:1 NIV]). Sensitive parents find that as their babies become capable of holding a mental image of the parents' response, they can gradually lengthen their response time without having the baby go to pieces.

Two-month-olds are still mastering the cause-and-effect relationship between their signals and mother's reply, so they are not likely to accept any delays. Trying to make them wait, adhere to a schedule, or cry themselves to sleep can interfere with the learning process and can even lead to shutdown. A baby whose signals are not answered will stop signaling. This baby can become withdrawn, lose sparkle, and even fail to grow. I have seen this happen as a result of parents being pressured into restraint-style tactics by well-meaning friends. Christian parents who are concerned about discipline can easily fall prey to advice that is meant to "teach the baby who's in charge." However, a wise adviser remembers that babies are not always learning exactly what adults think they are teaching. Babies whose cries are ignored do not learn self-control from the experience; they merely learn to give up. Babies do need to understand that their parents are in charge, but feelings of trust must be founded on responsiveness, not on arbitrary expressions of authority.

In what other areas besides feeding will a baby begin to form expectations based on some experience? Think of some examples. _____

_____
_____
_____

How do predictable responses to his signals help a baby learn? _____

_____

_____

_____

Think of some games or toys that will help your baby learn about cause and effect. _____

_____

_____

_____

TALKING TO YOUR BABY

Delightful little sounds are another way that growing babies charm their parents. Responding to these noises will encourage your baby to continue making them. Mothers naturally change their speech when they are talking to babies. Their voices become higher, they slow down what they are saying, and they exaggerate facial expressions. Mothers and babies actually take turns when they are having conversations. Mother says something with a definite beginning and ending and then waits for the baby to process the information. Babies move in synch to their mother's voices. While this is all rather primitive, the baby is learning important skills in listening and keeping an interaction going.

When you talk to your baby, be sure to get her attention first. To have a real conversation, the baby must be looking at you. Use his name, and keep your messages simple and lively. As you carry her around with you, talk about the things you are doing. Talk while you change diapers and get dressed. Use questions; babies like the upward inflection at the end: "Go bye-bye?" You can have a lot of fun mimicking your baby's sounds; this will encourage the baby to keep vocalizing and may cause both of you to dissolve into giggles. Babies also love songs. Music stimulates both sides of the brain, which makes it an excellent learning tool. Besides the usual nursery rhymes, sing simple "Jesus songs" to your baby. They will leave an imprint on your baby's mind even before she can understand the meaning.

Be sensitive to stop signs as well as to your baby's efforts to engage you in conversation. Babies let you know when they have had enough stimulation. They turn their eyes away or stare vacantly. If you honor your baby's own rhythm of interaction, she will learn better how to control herself. Rushing in with more stimulation is not the answer when a baby starts to pull away; changing to a more soothing activity is a better solution.

By four to six months of age, babies begin to use sounds to communicate. An excited "ah-ah-ah" may precede nursing time. A squeal of "eeeee" may bubble out when baby is picked up. "Ah-boo" goes along with a parental game of peek-a-boo. Pay attention and you will find that this new language substitutes for crying. If you respond to these cues, your growing baby may not need to cry at all to have his needs met.

Babies develop best when someone is there to respond joyfully to their efforts to learn. This applies to motor skills, like holding their heads up, rolling over, sitting up, and crawling, as well as to language. A chance to be nose-to-nose with mom's smiling face is a baby's best motivation for learning to lift up her head. Enthusiastic cheers from parents will prod a five-month-old to push just a little harder until she finally rolls over from tummy to back. Sharing these developmental milestones helps parents and baby stay in touch and attached.

You can't always tell what a baby is thinking, but it's fun to try to decipher facial expressions and gestures and match them up with what development books suggest your baby is learning at this stage. The ability to see inside the baby's mind is something I look for at well-baby check-ups. When I ask parents, "What's your baby like?" I'm looking for an empathetic response, not a description of sleep patterns or bowel habits. A mother who is really connected to her baby will tell me something like this: "He's just learned to sit up, but I think what he really wants to do is crawl; he's just frustrated because he can't get around to touch the things he sees." This ability to see the world as your child sees it will help you in all your years as a parent.

Many of the traditional games adults play with babies reinforce the learning of developmental skills. What, for example, can a baby learn from peek-a-boo? _____

_____

_____

From tickling? _____

_____

_____

From a noisy rattle? _____

_____

_____

From looking in a mirror? _____

_____

_____

 ## FEAR OF STRANGERS

Babies under six months of age are often very social. They'll smile for grandmotherly ladies at the supermarket and are often content to be held on Grandpa's lap for long periods of time. But as babies get smarter, some of this social ease disappears. When you meet an old friend whom you haven't seen in a while, baby suddenly gets fearful and buries her face in mother's shoulder.

Don't be embarrassed by your baby's rejection of people she's supposed to like and love. This is a normal stage of infant development. Previously, other people were all pretty much the same in baby's eyes. But babies of six months or more know who is familiar and who is a "stranger." They may eye an unfamiliar face suspiciously, as if to say, "I know who my mama is, and you're not her." This wariness of new people and new situations develops at a time when babies become mobile, able to crawl and explore on their own. God put this newfound caution into their minds to protect them. So what do you do when Grandma or Aunt Isabelle is bearing down on you at the airport, eager to meet your seven-month-old for the first time and shower her with kisses? Remember that your baby will take her cues from you. Head off the attack by engaging Grandma in a lively dialogue, while giving your baby space and time to size her up. Make a proper introduction, in which you remind the other adult that your baby needs some time to get used to her: "Jenny, this is Aunt Isabelle. She's new, but she's nice. You'll see." Since you are holding the baby, you can control the distance and read your baby's body language for when to advance and when to retreat. Encourage her to reach out and touch the new friend, but respect her signals.

It is helpful for you to brief grandparents and others ahead of time about this normal developmental stage in your baby. Let them know that it's important to let the baby approach them rather than the other way around. This avoids hurt feelings and heads off lectures about spoiling. Don't apologize for your baby's behavior; she is only doing what babies do, and for good reasons.

Role-play a stranger situation with your baby. One of you takes the part of baby-loving Aunt Lydia, and the other plays the parent. Can you find a way to keep your baby from bursting into tears and not offend your relative? Whose feelings are more important to you in this situation? _____
_____
_____
_____

Over the next week or so, watch non-related adults interacting with babies at the supermarket, at church, at the park. Observe the different styles of talking to babies. Are some people more sensitive to baby's signals than others? Did you see anyone whose manner you particularly admire? Anyone who makes you cringe? _____

_____

_____

_____

SEPARATION ANXIETY

Picture this: Your nine-month-old baby is playing happily with a few toys in the living room. Dad is close by, so Mom decides to sneak away to the laundry room to throw a load of clothes in the dryer. She has been gone only a minute when Baby looks up and doesn't see her. He looks around the room and begins to worry. Where is Mom? Where could she be? Suddenly he feels scared and panicky. He bursts into tears, and Dad comes over to find out what's wrong. Baby looks him in the face and howls louder. "I don't want you," he seems to say. "I want Mom." Dad knows this look; he has seen it before. He picks up Baby, and they head for the laundry room, with Baby struggling all the way. Finally, they get to the doorway. Baby sees Mom and lunges for her, nearly falling out of Dad's arms. He collapses on Mom's shoulder, stops crying, breathes a sigh of relief. Then, secure once more, he looks over at Dad and smiles.

This is separation anxiety. It compels babies to want to stay close to mother. It begins around six months, with the crawling phase; intensifies around nine months to a year, when baby walks; and may continue until eighteen months or older. As with the fear of strangers, separation anxiety is a safety device that clicks into gear when a baby has developed the ability to move away from you but does not yet have the judgment he needs to keep himself safe.

Watch your baby play on the floor away from you. You'll notice that even though she is moving freely around the room, every few minutes she looks for you, to be sure you are there watching out for her. Who knows? If you leave, a bear might come along and eat her. Or she might have to depend on someone who doesn't understand her signals. These would be serious problems, indeed, so your baby makes every effort to keep you close. She knows she needs a strong attachment figure close by, a parent or a familiar, trusted caregiver, and she will cry, complain, or come looking for you if that's what it takes to ensure her safety.

Has attachment parenting made your baby too dependent on you? Actually, the opposite is true. Separation anxiety is a sign of a healthy mother-baby relationship. Researchers use it as a measure of whether a baby is securely attached to the mother: An attached baby will protest when his mother leaves the room. A baby who does not feel he can count on his mother will not be upset when she is gone, but he may cling to her when she is present, in an effort to hold her attention. Babies who are securely attached are actually more independent than others, as long as mother is present. When they know that mother is nearby, they are not anxious about exploring.

Separation anxiety is probably related to the development of object permanence—realizing that things and people continue to exist even if the baby can't see them. You'll know your baby is experimenting with the concept of object permanence when she looks for an object after you take it away or hide it beneath a cloth. To do this, she must retain a mental image of the object. To be content away from you, she must be able to remember you and feel assured that you will come back.

Acquiring a sense of herself, as a separate individual, is also necessary for feeling secure away from mother. A tiny baby does not know where she ends and other people begin. She feels oneness with mother, and feeling separate or separated will scare her. Awareness of self develops slowly during the first two years of life. A young baby doesn't recognize herself in a mirror, although she may smile at the baby she sees. Eventually she learns that she can act on her own, and when this happens—sometime around eighteen months—look out! This self-assertion stage is what earned two-year-olds the epithet "terrible." (The terrible twos are much

 THE NEW BABY PLANNER

easier to handle if you realize these are your baby's first attempts at individuating.)

Fear of strangers and separation anxiety are two behaviors that have "survival value." This means that they help to assure that the baby thrives and the human race continues. How do you think these behaviors, instilled by God, contribute to infant survival?____

_____

_____

_____

How might they enable a baby to develop to the best of his abilities? _____

_____

_____

_____

How would you measure parenting advice in the light of knowing why babies have certain behaviors, such as separation anxiety? _____

_____

_____

_____

Helping your baby through separation anxiety. Wise and confident parents respect separation anxiety as a normal phase of infant development and will avoid or minimize unnecessary separations during this sensitive time. At home, they will reassure baby vocally of their presence when chores take them out of the room. Calling out "Here I am" or "Mama's coming" can reassure your baby that you are close by even when he can't see you.

The end of the first year, when separation anxiety is at its most intense, is not the best time to go back to work, but if you must, give your baby ample time to get to know and trust the substitute caregiver before you leave him with her for several hours. This may

AS BABY GROWS 235

take several sessions, but it may prevent desperate, unhappy tears later.

Whenever possible, keep your baby with you, if that's what he needs. "Babying" him through this time of dependence will strengthen the mental image of you that he will carry with him as he matures. It will also strengthen his trust in you. At the same time, help your baby know and trust other caregivers. Father involvement really pays off here.

Separation anxiety can be tough on mothers. Not only must they contend with a clingy baby, but they also face a society that understands little about babies' dependency needs in the first and second years. It can be difficult for friends and relatives to understand why your big baby will tolerate no other caretaker besides mom—or maybe dad, on a good day. "He's completely spoiled!" they say. "He's got to learn to be away from you."

Church nurseries are pressure cookers for separation anxiety in Christian families. The message in some churches is especially clear: This is where babies belong. But many attached babies protest strongly when their parents try to leave them in the nursery, no matter how attractive the play area or how capable the caregivers. Parents are caught in a bind. The baby is miserable in the nursery, but too wiggly for the church service (or forbidden for that matter). They don't want to ignore their baby's needs, but they need the spiritual nourishment of Sunday morning worship and Bible study.

There are many possible solutions to this dilemma, and you may try all of them at some time in your family. Take the baby to church, but leave the sanctuary and take a walk when the baby gets restless. Have mom and dad split the time, one taking the baby outside or playing with her in the nursery while the other worships; each attends half the service, or perhaps they go to different services for a few months. Worship at a time that corresponds to baby's naptime; nurse her off to sleep in your arms as the service begins. When our babies went through this stage, Martha volunteered to work in the nursery, baby at her side. She made it her ministry to care for other babies who were anxious while away from their parents. If your church is not baby-friendly, you might consider looking for another that is more accepting of babies and baby noises during worship.

You are the best judge of how much separation your baby will tolerate at any given age. Don't let outside influences pressure you into leaving your baby in a situation that makes you both unhappy. Reassure yourself that this is just a stage your baby is going through and that he is learning important lessons. Research and our own experience with thousands of mother-baby couples show that attachment parenting produces children who are remarkably independent—in their own good time.

Why do you think American society has trouble accepting the dependency needs of infants? _____

_____

_____

_____

_____

Why might Christian parents be especially vulnerable to fears that they are spoiling their baby? _____

_____

_____

_____

What are your own feelings about spoiling? _____

_____

_____

_____

How will respect for your child's feelings prevent him from being spoiled? _____

_____

_____

_____

WATCHING YOUR BABY GROW

An exciting part of being a parent is watching your baby change from month to month. This section will be more than an exercise in baby-watching. We want to help you participate in your baby's changes and, by becoming a keen baby-watcher, learn to read your baby. Just as every book reads differently, so also does every baby. In addition to marveling at God's design for infant development, getting involved in their baby's growth helps parents to develop too. As your baby grows, you grow. This is why we call the first year of infant development *growing together*.

New concepts in infant development. A baby's growth and development used to be viewed as a sort of developmental elevator: Month by month babies ascend a floor, get off, and acquire new capabilities, and then ride to a higher floor. While this simplistic view of infant development is partially true, what is becoming evident is how parental nurturing—or the lack of it—can profoundly affect an infant's social, physical, and intellectual development. The effect of parenting on infant development can be summed up briefly: *The more responsive caregivers are to the cues of the baby, the better the baby will develop.* This is why in chapter 1 we emphasized being responsive to the infant and forgetting the fear of manipulation and spoiling. As part of the divine design, each child comes wired with a certain level of capabilities—what we might call an infant's developmental potential. How closely the baby reaches that potential—we call this *thriving*—depends to a great extent on the nurturing environment. Research is beginning to prove that the attachment style of parenting, as we discussed in chapter 1, enhances infant development in the following ways. Infants who are given attachment parenting:

- Show more advanced developmental skills.
- Eventually become more independent.
- Develop more competent social skills.
- Score higher on mental development and I.Q. tests.

238 THE NEW BABY PLANNER

- Show better physical growth.
- Exhibit more desirable behaviors.

We are now going to take you through a journey of the first year of an average baby's development—and that is all it is, average. The progression of developmental skills is more than the actual timing. If your baby is not doing a certain developmental skill, for example sitting at six months, this does not mean that your baby is developmentally behind. There is a wide range of normal development. Our main goal in this workbook is to help you know your baby, to help you read your baby's capabilities and preferences at each stage of development, and to give you guidelines on how to respond to developmental cues to enhance your baby's development and your own. The ultimate goal in these exercises is to help you enjoy your baby's first year of development.

The following exercise is to help you create your baby's own developmental book. A baby's developmental skills are grouped into five general areas:

- Gross motor skills—how your baby uses the larger muscles of his body.
- Fine motor skills—how your baby uses his hands and fingers.
- Language skills—how your baby communicates using both sounds and body language.
- Social and play skills—the way a baby interacts with caregivers and with toys.
- Cognitive skills—what your baby is thinking and how he is solving problems.

For simplicity, we will combine these into three areas: physical development, language development, and social-intellectual development.

We have done this exercise with all of our babies and in great detail with our last three. It is fun to reopen our babies' first-year development books that we have created. It helps us to appreciate better the person our child is now by reflecting on all the developmental changes he went through to get there. We record only the high points of our babies' development and, so our wisdom doesn't go unrecorded, also make notes on how we grew as parents, how we reacted to a given situation, especially when we reacted in a wise way. We plan to give a copy of each baby book to our children when they become parents themselves. It might help them to understand and appreciate their own baby's development when they read what we recorded.

THE NEW BABY PLANNER

CHARTING YOUR BABY'S DEVELOPMENT

What Babies Usually Do	What Your Baby Does
First Month:	
• Arms and legs drawn tightly toward body.	
• Rotates head barely enough for chin to clear surface.	
• Hands tightly fisted.	
• Bears no weight on legs.	
• Gives demanding, undifferentiated cries.	
• Makes throaty, grunting sounds.	
• Smiles in sleep, but not yet returning your smiles.	
• Sees best 8–12 inches.	
• Sleeps, wakes, feeds erratically.	
• Little day-night distinction.	
• Cries mostly by reflex.	

Second Month:	
• Lifts chin 2–3 inches and head at 45 degree angle.	
• Head wobbly while sitting.	
• Relaxes fists, unfolds fingers.	
• May briefly hold toy placed in hand.	
• Takes aimless swipes at dangling toy.	
• Coos, squeaks, squeals.	
• Increased saliva causes sputters.	
• Startled by sounds.	
• Engages eye-to-eye contact briefly while feeding.	
• Studies face, mimics facial gestures.	
• Smiles in response to your smile.	
• Briefly tracks moving persons around 3 feet away.	
• Shows excitement, distress, and protests.	
• Cries more purposely, to get held or fed.	

THE NEW BABY PLANNER

Third Month:	
• Lifts head over 45 degrees, turns head side to side to search. Head bobs slightly when held sitting.	
• Briefly bears weight on legs before sagging.	
• Flaps arms.	
• Holds hands open most of the time.	
• Holds and shakes rattle, grabs clothing and hair.	
• Studies toy placed in hand.	
• Plays with hands in front of face.	
• Draws out vowels: "Eeeh," "Eeeee," "Aaah."	
• Cries differently for different needs.	
• Imitates social interaction: facial gestures and arm movements.	
• Learns cause and effect: hit mobile, it moves.	
• Shows more emotions: delight, smiles, total body wiggles, grimaces.	
• Feeding and sleeping patterns more predictable.	
• Clusters feeding during day, sleeps longer at night.	

Fourth Month:	
• Stands supported.	
• Lifts head 90 degrees and scans.	
• Head steady when held sitting.	
• Begins two-handed embracing reach.	
• Explores clothing, pats parents' faces.	
• Sees clearly across room.	
• Shapes mouth to change sounds: "Ah, Oh."	
• Sputters, blows bubbles.	
• Laughs hilariously.	
• Begins social gesturing: flaps arms, "Pick me up."	
• Aware things and persons have names.	
• Fusses when mother is out of sight.	
• Fusses when cue not responded to.	

Fifth Month:	
• Sits propped forward on both hands.	
• Pushes up on extended arms with chest off floor.	
• Bears entire weight on legs, supported only for balance.	
• Reaches precisely for toys within arm length.	
• Transfers toys purposely from hand to hand and hand to mouth.	
• Reaches with one hand.	
• Plays with blocks.	
• Babbles "ba-ba-ba-ba" to attract attention.	
• Turns head to look for speaker.	
• Mimics caregivers' sounds and gestures.	
• Vocalizes different sounds for different needs.	
• Reaches toward caregiver to initiate interaction.	
• Uses hands to show dislikes, such as pushing your arm away when giving medicine.	
• Begins highchair and lap-sitting play.	

• May show interest in or protest beginning solid foods.	
• Begins to show decision-making expressions during hand play.	
• Manipulates toys in hands.	

Sixth Month:	
• Sits erect briefly alone.	
• Lifts chest and tummy off floor; pushes up on extended arms.	
• Rolls over both ways.	
• Reaches precisely one-handed and points.	
• Strings out babbling sounds longer.	
• Makes greater variety of sounds.	
• "Talks" to toys and mirror image.	
• Signifies moods with body language: pleasure and excitement, squeals, belly-laughs, waving arms, grunts and growls.	
• Experiments with various sounds and watches reactions.	
• Begins social directing: uses arms to signal need to be picked up.	
• Imitates facial gestures.	
• Shows interest in feeding self, but makes mess.	

• Shows facial expressions as if "thinking" and making decisions during play.	
• Studies toys and how to use them.	

Six to Nine Months:	
• Lunges toward toy.	
• Pivots and crawls on hands and knees.	
• Stands leaning against furniture.	
• Pulls self up to stand.	
• Picks up tiny objects with thumb and forefinger.	
• Drinks from cup.	
• Babbles randomly using consonants and vowels: "Ah, Ba, Da, Ma," etc.	
• Uses tongue movements to change sounds: "Ah" to "Da."	
• Responds to own name.	
• Gives social cues, raises arms to signal "Pick me up."	
• Shows stranger anxiety.	
• Associates words with objects in environment, e.g., "dog."	

Nine to Twelve Months:	
• Experiments with various crawling styles; cross-crawls.	
• Cruises along furniture.	
• Scales and climbs furniture.	
• Crawls upstairs.	
• Stands alone.	
• Walks with assistance.	
• May take a few solo steps with frequent falls.	
• May attempt to climb out of crib.	
• Shows hand dominance.	
• Points and pokes with index finger.	
• Stacks and drops blocks.	
• Makes two-syllable sounds, "Ma-ma," "Da-da".	
• Understands "no."	
• Understands gestures, waves bye-bye.	
• May imitate familiar noises, "night-night," "woof-woof."	
• Shows memory of recent events.	

THE NEW BABY PLANNER

• Cue words trigger mental images of action to expect: "Go . . ."—looks toward door.	
• Shows separation anxiety.	
• Likes games, pat-a-cake and peek-a-boo. Shows hand skills and decision-making in container play: pouring, filling, and dumping.	
• Flirts with self in mirror.	

INTERACTIONS YOU AND BABY ENJOY
(e.g., games, preferences, baby's cues and your reactions to them, etc.)

CHAPTER TEN

DISCIPLINE AND SPIRITUAL DEVELOPMENT

Before we can talk about how to discipline your growing child, we need to discover what discipline is. Many misconceptions surround this word. Understand first that discipline is not the same thing as punishment. Neither is discipline an external force that is applied to a child to coerce him into behaving properly. Discipline is not made of threats, spankings, and lectures, all administered with tight-lipped parental resolve.

Discipline comes from a Latin word, *disciplina,* which means "instruction" or "knowledge." One definition for it reads "training intended to produce a specified character or pattern of behavior." It is related as well to the Latin root *discere,* "to learn" or "to know."

Actually each chapter in this book has taught you how to discipline your child, but we haven't called our message discipline. Every interaction between you and your baby goes into making a disciplined child and disciplined parents. A Christian needs to be "rooted . . . in love" (Eph. 3:17). By practicing attachment-parenting, you plant attitudes in your child and sensitivity in yourself. That's where discipline begins.

Think of Jesus with his disciples as an example of a disciplinarian. Jesus was clearly in charge of them. They regarded him as an authoritative teacher. He taught them how to live by both his example and his words. He was a servant to them, a role beautifully expressed when he washed their feet at the Last Supper (John 13:5, 12–15). When they went astray, he talked to them. His words were so ingrained upon their hearts that the consciousness of their sin could make them weep bitterly, as Peter did after swearing "I do not know the man" in the courtyard of the High Priest during Jesus' trial (see Matt. 26:69–75).

This is the kind of discipline you are striving to write upon the heart and mind of your child, something that comes from within and is motivated by love and respect for parents, for other people, and for God. This is the kind of discipline suggested by the Bible's master verse for Christian parenting: "Train up a child in the way he should go, and when he is old he will not depart from it" (Prov. 22:6). Your child will carry what he learns from your Christian discipline all through his life, and will use it to solve problems, to minister to others, and to heal relationships.

What are some other uses of the word *discipline?* Think of a disciplined athlete, a discipline as a branch of knowledge or teaching, self-discipline. How do these widen your understanding of disciplining your child? _____

_____

_____

_____

What qualities or values do you want to give your child through your discipline? _____

_____

_____

Can you translate these into actions within the grasp of a toddler? For example, a toddler can show concern for others by giving hugs, not hitting, bringing the newspaper to Daddy. _____

_____

_____

_____

How can you model these values for your toddler? _____

_____

_____

_____

DISCIPLINE BEGINS AT BIRTH

Parents often don't think about discipline until their child reaches an age where he can exert his will and get into power struggles with his parents; this is usually sometime in the second year of life. I find that parents often want to discuss discipline at the fifteen- or eighteen-month check-up: "Should I start discipline now?" My usual reply is "You began disciplining your child at the moment of birth."

If you understand that discipline involves teaching your child and helping him to develop his own inner controls, it naturally follows that discipline begins very early, with how you respond to your infant's cries and cues. A parent's sensitivity to what a child is thinking and feeling begins in those early months of responding to the baby's every need. The mother has to learn to trust the baby's signals and to trust her own intuition about what they mean. As the two of them shape each other's behavior, the mother becomes more adept at understanding what the baby is feeling. She can vary her responses. By the time the baby is three or four months old, she does not respond as quickly to fussing out of boredom as she would to a cry of fear or pain. But as the fussing escalates she arrives to respond to the baby's desire for stimulation with a round of play or a change of scene. This is discipline—helping the baby find positive ways to create an inner sense of rightness. Notice that it does not require a contest of wills or a cry-it-out scene. Instead, this mother is teaching her baby to prefer that inner feeling of rightness and is showing him acceptable ways of achieving it. As this pattern of turning not-right feelings into feelings of rightness is repeated over the months and years, the child learns many lessons that will help him control himself in the years to come. I have noticed in my years as a pediatrician that parents who practice attachment parenting have fewer discipline problems with their children.

What has your child learned from your parenting so far? How will these lessons affect his inner controls? _____

_____

_____

_____

How is he more "disciplined" than he was at birth? _____

_____

_____

_____

Self-worth. Just as a mother's gestures, facial expressions, and voice tones mirror to her baby who he is and that he has value, so also a child's behavior mirrors his inner feelings. With responsive parenting, a child learns to feel right inside. His needs are respected, he is comforted, and he is not forced to soothe himself or handle his own emotions before he is ready. This is the foundation of self-worth, and it is laid in the very first year of life. Mutual trust develops between parent and infant, which later makes it easier for the child to submit his will to the parent's.

Christians must acknowledge their own sinfulness before God and recognize that without God's help they are powerless. How, then, can a Christian have self-worth? _____

_____

 THE NEW BABY PLANNER

Pray to God, asking him to help you build your own self-esteem and that of your child on Jesus' love and forgiveness.

Sensitivity. Attachment parenting enables parents to see inside their children's hearts. They know their children well. This makes it easier for them to understand what behavior their children are capable of and why a child may be misbehaving. They can then anticipate problems and prevent them, getting the child back on track more easily.

So discipline starts with knowing your child. Who is this one-year-old creature living with you? You probably have a pretty good idea of what makes him tick. Stop a moment and take inventory of your baby's personality. Try answering the following questions:

When is your baby most happy? What makes her laugh? _____

_____

_____

_____

When is your baby most content? What comforts her? _____

_____

_____

_____

When is your baby unhappy? What makes her fuss and complain? _____

_____

_____

_____

How does your baby tell you what she needs? Are you confident of your responses? _____

_____

_____

_____

Does your baby feel right most of the time? _____

_____

_____

Do you feel that you know what to do to help your baby feel
right? _____

_____

_____

How would you describe your baby right now? What is her
temperament like? _____

_____

_____

How does your baby respond to new situations? Does he rely
on you for help? _____

_____

_____

How is your baby changing? _____

_____

_____

How have these changes affected your responses? _____

_____

_____

THE NEW BABY PLANNER

Do you enjoy being with your baby most of the time? Do you enjoy being a parent? _____

_____

_____

Do you pray for your child daily? Do you pray and seek counsel when problems arise? _____

_____

_____

_____

Are your statements about your baby mostly positive? Are you in tune with each other, communicating well? If so, you are ready for the challenges of toddlerhood.

If your answers have a mostly negative tone or you feel as if you are struggling with your baby, it would be wise to seek counsel. Talk to an experienced, attached mother of toddlers, attend La Leche League meetings, or seek out a professional. Getting the parent-child relationship on a good footing now will make your discipline more effective in the stages to come. It's never too late to become a sensitive parent so your attachment can grow.

Individual differences. You have to know a child well in order to guide him "in the way he should go." But what is the way for him to go? Does the biblical phrase refer to a general way for all children to go, keeping God's commandments and following his teachings? Or does it imply a more specific plan: "the way he should go," an individual plan for each child, one that suits his temperament and abilities? Scholars suggest that the latter interpretation is the correct one, and it requires great sensitivity on the part of parents to keep a child focused on the individual path God has in store for him. The better you know your child and the more accepting you are of him, the better able you will be to guide him, even if the way that is right for him is not necessarily the one you would have chosen.

What daily events are hardest for your child? Transitions from one activity to another? Overcoming fears? Frustration at not getting what he wants? _____

_____

_____

_____

What tasks is he especially good at? _____

_____

_____

_____

Dream a little. Do you have a budding scientist in your home? A craftsman? A musician? A "people person?" It's fun to speculate about your child's future; pray daily that he or she will be open to following God's best plan (read Jer. 29:11).

Family harmony. Sensitivity also helps you to be a good disciplinarian by putting you in harmony with your child. Mother, father, and baby function as a unit, and the discipline flows from this relationship. The child wants to do what will please the parents, and the parents create an environment for the child in which it is a joy for her to do the right thing. All of you work together; there is no "us versus the kids" mentality, not a struggle for control. This harmonious, free-flowing discipline of the family inner circle is far more effective than any of the vast battery of discipline techniques devised by outside advisers.

 ## DISCIPLINE'S SPIRITUAL FOUNDATION

You cannot impart to your child what you do not have yourself. Your example is a strong lesson, and it is far more influential in shaping your child's behavior than rules, lectures, or punishment. You can be an effective example for your child only if you rely on Christ to help you. A commitment to Jesus Christ must be at the very center of your parenting. If you love and fear God and walk in his ways, you will be better able to commit yourself to sensitive parenting as well. In return, as a bonus, God will give you the faith, the wisdom, and the strength you need to be a better, more giving parent. If you lean on Christ to help you maintain your own inner sense of balance, you will be better able to train your child in inner discipline.

As a Christian parent, you must recognize that sin is a very real force in your child's life. The secular trend is to think of children as innocent, but the Bible says differently: "I was brought forth in iniquity, and in sin my mother conceived me" (Ps. 51:5). All of us, adults and children alike, have a sinful nature and cannot do good without the help of God. This is another reason why a commitment to Christ must be at the heart of your relationship with your offspring. Your responsibility for your child before God is to turn him toward the paths of righteousness, and you cannot do this without seeking God's help in walking there yourself.

Praying for your child daily will help your discipline. Pray also for yourself, that you may have patience and wisdom when the going gets tough.

PARENTS AS AUTHORITY FIGURES

Parents should expect obedience from their children. God commands children to obey: "Children, obey your parents in all things, for this is well pleasing to the Lord" (Col. 3:20). The fourth Commandment puts it a little differently: "Honor your father and your mother." So children are to respect their parents as well as obeying them. But this respect does not flow naturally from a child's heart. As with other moral behavior, parents must teach it to their children. This includes making it possible for the child to develop genuine respect for you. So even though children are commanded to honor their parents, father and mother must still earn their children's respect.

The lesson of respect for authority cannot be beaten into children, figuratively or literally. Overpowering or humiliating a child into minding you produces resentment, not respect. As with many other lessons in life, children learn what they are shown. If they are bullied, they learn to bully back or they learn to cower in a corner, literally or figuratively. If their own worth as children of God is honored by their parents, they will know how to hold respect in their hearts for mother and father.

You lay the early foundation for respect when you practice attachment parenting. Openness to your child's cues conveys your respect for him and enables him to trust you as an authority figure. Responding and helping him feel better lets the baby know that you are a wise person indeed. As you prove this again and again, you will earn your child's respect. You will become a true figure of authority to him.

As an authority figure you are to take charge of your child. This is a point that confuses some parents: If I am responding to my child's cues, doesn't that mean that he is in charge? No, not as long as you both know that you are the adult and he is the child. He needs you to be the strong one. It is true that the first few years of parenting are mostly giving, but it is the giving itself that creates your loving authority over your children. Again, think of the example Jesus set. His giving of himself on the cross both commands our respect and makes us want to love him. This is not an easy idea to grasp, but it is at the heart of successful parenting and of Christianity itself.

Here's a test problem in the field of authoritative parenting. It's bedtime, and you know your eleven-month-old is tired. He took only a short nap in the car early in the afternoon, and now, after supper, he is short-tempered, cranky, and irritable. You know that he needs to sleep, but he has other ideas. You sit down on the couch to watch TV while you nurse him, but he wiggles away after only a few minutes and wants to play on the floor. But everything he tries frustrates him. It's time to be the authority figure and get him to sleep. How can you do this in a way that is responsive to his needs and respectful of him as a person? _____

THE NEW BABY PLANNER

OLDER BABY/TODDLER DISCIPLINE

By now you should have some understanding of the why of discipline, that it rests on a foundation of knowing your child, helping him feel right, and earning his trust. But how do you translate this into action when your baby begins to rove? You have been a dependable caregiver for your baby, but now more is called for. Setting limits with baby probably starts with not letting him hurt you; for example, you don't allow your six-month-old to pull your hair, or your eight-month-old to bite you when he's nursing. He is also not allowed to hurt others; you say no when he grabs a fistful of sister's hair. And as he gets more mobile, limit setting keeps him from hurting himself.

As babies learn to crawl and then walk, their environment expands. No longer are they confined to parents' arms and mother's breasts. The caregiver role certainly continues, but now parents must provide guidance as the baby learns about the wider world. The parents' role expands to include being an authority figure, a guidance counselor, and a designer of the child's environment. The first time you actually say no to your baby you may find that she dissolves in tears. It's not because you yelled at her *(hopefully* you didn't); it's because she is being frustrated. And at the appropriate age, frustration is a very healthy and necessary thing. Once a baby is old enough developmentally to understand the difference between her wants and her needs, it's time to learn she can't have everything she wants. Healthy frustration now becomes an important part of a baby's emotional development. Your twelve-month-old may want to pull the lamp cord, but she certainly doesn't need to pull it. But it's an idea she can't let go of, so you'll have to help her by stopping her and redirecting her. She'll howl in frustration *and* she'll learn she can handle being frustrated.

Realistic expectations. Older babies are like the bunny in the battery commercial: they keep going and going and going. They have an insatiable need to explore. They cut a wide swath through the house, opening cabinets, turning knobs, pulling down papers, emptying shelves, dumping, spreading, and leaving confusion behind them. First-time parents may label this behavior as "bad" and feel a pang of dismay that their perfectly lovely little baby is about to become a holy terror. In reality, however, this is normal toddler behavior.

Babies are driven to learn and master new skills. Watch your one-year-old drop blocks into a pail, dump them out, and repeat the action over and over again. He is intent on understanding this concept of a container and takes great delight in experimenting with it. You don't have to motivate one-year-olds. God has given them an amazing capacity to think things out in advance; to reason or calculate, they have to do a lot of hands-on experimentation.

Toddlers are directed by impulse. If their newest skill is climbing, they will try to climb anything available to them without regard to safety or whether they can get down again. They have few internal controls, and so you cannot expect them to obey rules or even to remember that electrical cords are a "no-no." Your role as the parent is to direct your toddler's boundless energy into acceptable channels. You don't want to restrain or discourage him from exploring, but you do want to guide his activities so that he eventually learns what is safe and what is permitted.

Here's where your role as designer of your child's environment comes into play. Make your house safe *for* your toddler and safe *from* your toddler. Putting away the breakables and the family heirlooms is not a capitulation to toddler power; it is simply a way of avoiding constantly having to say no to your child, causing a build-up of frustration and anger in both of you. This is a much better alternative than having to be constantly watchful and protective, or punitive toward a God-given urge to explore. It means that you, as the adult, have the maturity to put your own things aside (up or away) for a while until your child has the maturity to respect adult valuables.

 THE NEW BABY PLANNER

When your child starts to crawl, take a tour of your house from his perspective to discover what needs child-proofing. Here's a room-to-room guide to start with:

Living room/family room:

- Cover electrical outlets.
- Secure lamp cords so they can't be pulled down.
- Anchor floor lamps, or remove them.
- Cover controls on the television, stereo, VCR.
- Cushion sharp corners on coffee tables, piano benches, hearths.
- Display breakables out of baby's reach, or put them away for a few years.
- Reorganize bookshelves (toddlers love to empty these, tearing covers and dust jackets).

Dining room/eating area:

- Push chairs all the way under the table to prevent climbing.
- Install latches on drawers or cabinets that hold breakable dishes.
- Push items on the tabletop to the center.
- Fold tablecloth corners under, out of grabbing distance

Bathroom:

- Medicines, razors, pins, cosmetics, nail polish and remover, scissors, etc., must be out of reach.
- Medicines should have safety caps.
- Medicine cabinet should be kept latched.
- Tub faucets should be padded.
- Place a non-skid mat in the tub.
- Rugs should have non-skid backings.
- Keep the toilet seat down and latched. (Children can drown in toilets.)
- Use plastic cups and soap dishes, not glass or ceramic.
- Keep the bathroom door shut.

Kitchen:

- Store knives out of reach.
- Unplug small appliances. Don't leave cords dangling.
- Store cleaners, solvents, bleaches, dishwasher detergent, etc., out of baby's reach in a latched cabinet.
- Cook on the back burners, and turn pot handles toward the back.
- Store breakables, things baby can choke on, and other dangerous objects out of reach. Remember that toddlers can climb onto kitchen counters.
- Use unbreakable dishes when baby is around.
- Store plastic bags out of reach.
- Keep hot drinks where baby can't grab at them, and away from the edge of a table or counter.

Windows and doors:

- Keep sliding glass doors closed, or keep the screens locked.
- Place decals at toddler eye level on glass doors.
- Lock windows and be sure the screens are secure.
- Shorten the cords on draperies and blinds to get them up out of children's reach.
- Use netting to enclose the rails on balconies or porches so that the baby can't squeeze through.

Many inexpensive products are available that will help you make your home safe for your child. Effort spent baby-proofing your home now will pay off in less conflict with your toddler and more relaxed parents. Child-proofing is also a way of providing your young explorer with guidance from the controlled environment itself.

Once you have the don't-touch items out of the way, consider positive steps you can take to encourage good behavior in your toddler. Give him his own drawer in the kitchen, filled with items to pull out, sort, and study. Provide child-size furniture and things of his own that he can push, pull, turn, and manipulate. Give him a safe outlet for climbing. Let him experiment with water or sand under your supervision.

THE NEW BABY PLANNER

Toddlerhood is an exciting time in a child's life. It can be great fun just to watch him play. Being observant will also help you know when to step in and help out and when to let him work out a problem on his own.

Shaping your child's environment also means helping him handle high-risk situations, such as the supermarket. How could any child fail to be excited in a place designed to tempt fully grown adults to grab impulsively? It's up to you to channel the impulse to reach out and grab things into acceptable behavior. Have your toddler help you get familiar items off the shelf. Or provide a nutritious snack that keeps him busy. Talk to him and focus his attention on you, rather than the candy bars at the check-out.

Whenever you can, say yes rather than no. Catch your child doing the right thing and praise him for it. A child who is left to himself until he gets into trouble soon learns to provoke the "no-no" just to see mom or dad come running. When you correct a child, speak politely and gently, even if this requires some self-control on your part. This is common courtesy, part of treating your child with respect. Saying no in an irritated or angry voice will encourage your child to talk back to you this way, and emotions on both sides will escalate. Say, "You cannot do that" in a calm, matter-of-fact voice with enough firmness for your baby to know he's being told and not asked or begged. He needs to know that you are the gentle giant in charge. Quick action will often prevent you from having to raise your voice in the almighty no. When you see your child headed for your desk chair, eager to clear away the pile of bills and papers, intervene quickly and redirect his climbing or sorting energy elsewhere, preferably in another room. Disciplining a young child is a hands-on activity. A polite "Mommy doesn't want you to do that, dear" from across the room is no match for a toddler's impulses.

When your child misbehaves, ask yourself why he is doing that, rather than focusing on the behavior itself. Is he bored, hungry, sick, or trying to get your attention? Is this the wild hour before bedtime when he truly cannot control himself? If you can answer why, you will probably be able to find a way to put an end to the misbehavior. A snack, a game, a change of scene, or the beginning of the familiar bedtime routine will help him get back on track.

Don't confuse attachment parenting with permissiveness. Although you are avoiding getting into negative power struggles with your child, you are not letting him do whatever he wants. You are setting limits, which children need in order to learn what is right and wrong and to feel secure; but you are focusing more on helping the child stay within those limits than on waiting to zap him for crossing the line. This takes more creativity on the part of parents, and perhaps more self-control, but the results are a child who is happy to do the right things, not one who is merely wary of avoiding punishment.

Imagine this scenario: Thirteen-month-old Sarah wants to touch the breakable figurines on the table. If she holds on with her fingertips and stretches high on her tiptoes, she can just barely reach them, enough to knock them forward and onto the carpet. Mother comes into the room just in time to see the little statute, precious to her, hit the ground. Fortunately, it didn't break. She picks it up, restores it to its place, and tells Sarah, "No, no, no. Don't touch." But a minute later, Sarah is reaching for it again. "No, no," says mother, but Sarah continues to stretch and reach. This has happened before, and mother is becoming increasingly exasperated. "She has to learn to mind me," she thinks, so her tone becomes sharper: "NO! DON'T TOUCH THAT!" Sarah takes a swipe at the fragile object and it falls to the floor again, this time hitting a chair leg and breaking. Mother slaps Sarah's little fingers, and the little girl dissolves into tears. Mother is sorry to see her child crying, but she reminds herself that she is in charge here, not Sarah.

Were this mother's expectations of toddler behavior realistic?

_____

_____

_____

What could have been done differently? _____

_____

_____

_____

Is this a proper use of authority over a child? Is there a better way to convey that mother is in charge here? _____

_____

_____

_____

Disciplining toddlers requires reserves of both patience and creativity. How could this mother prepare for a better outcome the next time a conflict develops with Sarah? _____

_____

_____

_____

Why is it important for the parents to keep a check on their own sin nature when disciplining their children? _____

_____

_____

_____

TODDLER AMBIVALENCE

Social, emotional, intellectual, and motor development do not proceed in parallel, straight lines in children. Sometimes desires exceed capabilities, or the ability to do something runs ahead of knowing when it is appropriate to use this skill. A child may be very adept at climbing the kitchen stool, but doesn't realize the dangers lurking on the counter. A child who can walk on his own may still cling to mommy and want to be carried in a strange place. Toddlers are fascinated by other children, but are not able to cooperate in give-and-take play.

These are all examples of toddler ambivalence, having mutually conflicting feelings about something. In toddlers, ambivalence centers around wanting to be independent while still needing the baby-like security of mother's arms. Ambivalence flare-ups may be manifested in tears, frustration, and temper tantrums. Here again it is helpful to ask yourself why your child is feeling this way, rather than reacting with impatience. This is a good habit to learn now; it will come in handy throughout your years as a parent. Understanding the feelings and the motivation behind an action can help you give your child the specific kind of assistance he needs to change his behavior. (This is also a useful approach to solving problems with adults.)

When your toddler needs to be a bit of a baby, let him. As with infants, you must satisfy dependency needs in order to encourage a child to become independent. Nursing can play an important role in helping a child to feel connected enough to mommy to be free to explore. It recharges his battery so that he can become "cordless" once more.

What at-odds feelings might be at work in each of the following toddler situations?

You take your eighteen-month-old to the park. She wants to climb the ladder to the slide but panics at the top. How do you get her down? _____

_____

_____

_____

You are playing with your fifteen-month-old in the church nursery. He slides off your lap to get a puzzle, but breaks into tears as his feet hit the ground. Why is he acting this way? _____

_____

_____

_____

THE NEW BABY PLANNER

Your two-year-old wants to look closely at the new baby. She strokes his head gently, holds his hand, and bites his finger. You make it clear to her that she is not allowed to hurt the baby, but what is going on in her head? What does she need from you? _____

_____

_____

_____

ASSERTING INDEPENDENCE

As children near their second birthday, their growing language skills give them more ways to try to control the world around them. Certain words and phrases are very characteristic of this stage: "I do it myself," "No," and "Mine!" This normal developmental milestone should not be interpreted as manipulation or defiance. It is a child's way of informing parents that he considers himself to be an independent person, with a will of his own. Treat these kinds of statements as communication, not as opening shots in a year-long battle of the Terrible Twos. Respond in a way that supports your child's desire for independence: "I'll help you with the buttons, then you take your overalls off by yourself." If he's trying to get you to do something his way, go along with him if possible. Don't sweat the small stuff; save the heavy artillery for issues of life and limb. And if he insists that the cereal has to be in the blue bowl every morning, why not? Don't you have a favorite coffee mug?

Think of some of the ways to support an almost-two-year-old's desire for independence in each of the following situations. How can you steer clear of conflict while helping the child learn what is expected of him?

It's mid-January, and time to get dressed for the day. Your child has unearthed a pair of shorts and a tank top from the bottom of the drawer and wants to wear them. What do you do? _____

_____

_____

It's Thanksgiving at Grandma's. The food is on the table, and your child is sitting in his chair, eyeing everything suspiciously. "That looks like I don't like it," she says. "I want peanut butter!"

_____

_____

_____

"I do it myself," says the master builder, piling one block precariously on another, large on top of small, laying cylinders on their sides. The tower crashes to the ground, and he is crushed. But he starts over, again with no regard for engineering stability. _____

_____

_____

 ## MANIPULATION

The threat of being manipulated hangs over the heads of parents, it seems, from the very first cry. When children learn to talk, they begin to experiment with more sophisticated ways of getting their parents to do what they want. Children of two and three are very egocentric, and they assume that the world revolves around their pleasures. Children with healthy self-esteem who feel confident of their communicative powers will use them in whatever way they can.

This is not all bad. There is such a thing as healthy manipulation. A child should feel right about communicating her needs and desires. After all, you want your child to be able to ask, to seek, and to knock. She also needs a chance to practice persuading and influencing others. However, you are still the one to decide what is good for her to do and receive and what is not. You are also the one who

THE NEW BABY PLANNER

must help her live with your decision: "No, we're not buying candy today. How about an apple or some popcorn instead?"

Parents, don't overreact to your child's efforts to manipulate you. Your resolution "not to let him manipulate me" can quickly turn healthy parent-child communication into a power struggle. Decide each case on its merits, not on the basis of who is allowed to win this time. Unhealthy manipulation occurs when parents either deny all requests or fulfill them, without regard to the child's specific signals or needs. If you listen honestly and openly to your child's communication, and the feelings behind it, you will know when to say yes and how to say no.

Some parents have a hard time saying no. Even more parents have a hard time hearing their toddler say no to them. They think or feel that somehow the little one is being defiant and that they must not tolerate this. Remember, it is healthy and developmentally important for your child to individuate while at the same time getting the message that you are the adult. If hearing no from your toddler gets you all bent out of shape, you probably need to take a hard look at yourself. Problems with setting limits indicate that you probably didn't come through this stage well yourself. Perhaps your mother said no rarely, but when she did she exploded all over you. You can pray for God's healing and seek counseling so that you will be emotionally equipped to parent your toddler in a healthy way.

CHILDREN IN CHURCH

To worship or to parent should not be an either-or decision. How much to incorporate your child into the church service depends on the temperament and developmental stage of your child and how baby-friendly your fellowship is. In the first year or two you will probably be torn between your baby's need to stay with you and your need to worship without the incessant demands of a baby. Consider these suggestions both to be with your baby and to nurture yourself spiritually.

- First, consider the advice of your heavenly Pastor: "Let the children come to me" (Luke 18:15–17). It seems that Christ had no problem ministering when children were around. But this verse did not specify the ages. Did he also mean to include rambunctious toddlers?

- Try wearing your infant in a babysling. This contains the infant during the service. In the early months, babies in slings sleep through most of the service anyway. Babywearing allows you to breastfeed discreetly in church and quiets the baby. As baby gets older, he usually will be quiet and contained while in the sling, at least as long as the singing continues.

- When the nine-month-old is no longer content to be a lap or sling baby and begins to "sing" and grab the Bible pages of the nice lady next to you, a decision is in order. You have three sets of needs to consider: Your own need to worship peacefully, the needs of the fellowship, and the needs of the baby. And you try to juggle these needs.

- Consider compromising. Include your baby in the worship part of the service. It's not quiet then anyway. Besides, your little worshiper is likely to catch the spirit of worship, and you'll be amazed at how much of it sinks in. Before the sermon begins, if the baby is not sleeping or is obviously not in the mood to sit still and listen, take him to the nursery and stay with him there if he needs you. Some nurseries have the message piped in over an intercom, or you can get a tape of it.

- How often, how long, and at what age to leave your baby in the nursery depend on how separation sensitive your infant is. Some babies readily warm up to unfamiliar caregivers; others don't. We've heard of some churches that allow neither parents to stay in the nursery, nor babies in the sanctuary. These churches are sadly out of tune with the needs of their present and future members.

- Try shift worship. If your baby is going through a high-need stage or a period of separation anxiety, rather than peeling off a clingy infant and depositing her, screaming, in the nursery, consider one parent staying in the nursery or baby room during half of the service and then switching with the other parent during the other half. Or try alternating weeks. Best is for both parents to worship together with baby. Occasionally, a familiar substitute caregiver, whom the baby knows and settles with, can be brought along to stay in the nursery during the sermon (e.g. a grandmother).

- Consider the health issue. Babies get sick in church nurseries, where germs congregate too. If your infant is prone to colds and ear infections, keep nursery exposure to a minimum during the first two years.

Best is for families to worship together in a fellowship that follows Christ's model: Let the children come to me. If your church has rules against babies and children in church, even though they are not causing a distraction, we encourage you to look for a more baby-friendly setting in which to worship and introduce your little one to life in the Body of Christ.

TEACHING CHILDREN ABOUT GOD

In the mind of a young child, God is what mommy and daddy are. Children of age two cannot conceive of God in an abstract sense. They must imagine God in terms of what they know, and the authority figures they are most familiar with are mother and father. Their parents' behavior toward them provides their earliest image of God. Children can be intimate with God easily if they have learned about intimacy from their relationship with their parents. Intimacy implies trust, mutual respect, love, and harmony, which helps all the partners in the relationship feel good about themselves.

Early images of God can be a potent force throughout a person's life. Think back to your own childhood. What did you imagine God to be like? Where did this image come from? _____

_____

_____

_____

Who first taught you about God and Jesus? _____

_____

_____

What did you learn? _____

_____

_____

_____

Has this helped or hindered you in your development as a Christian? _____

_____

_____

Modeling God for your child is an awesome responsibility. Of course, we earthly parents are sinful, and we will make mistakes and fall short of God's perfection in our relationship with our child. We can try to be Christ-like examples for our child only with God's help. A realistic appraisal of our own shortcomings before our Lord leaves us feeling humble and in need of forgiveness and support. That is why a commitment to Christ and daily prayer and Bible study are so important to attachment parenting. Without submitting ourselves daily to God's will, attempting to be a godly example is only an act of pride, and one we are bound to fail at.

Teaching faith through parenting

The most important lesson your child will learn in his first few years of spiritual training is to trust in God. Responsive parenting will help him with this. A child must first learn how to trust his earthly parents, whom he can see and feel, before he can learn to trust his heavenly Father, whom he cannot see and feel. Parents who respond readily to their children's cues teach their children to trust them. This habit of trusting will carry over into your child's relationship with God. Without this early experience, it is very difficult for a person to fully trust anyone—a friend, a spouse, or even the Lord. While being strong and in charge is part of winning your child's trust, the lesson is taught best by communicating understanding, comfort, security, and love. Don't forget that God's presence includes these gracious and merciful qualities, along with awesome righteousness and power.

What do you want your child to know and feel about God?

_____

_____

_____

How can you teach him these things through your parenting?

_____

_____

_____

A four-month-old baby wakes in his crib and cries in the middle of the night. His parents hear him but decide that tonight he must learn to go back to sleep on his own. What might the baby learn about God from this experience? _____

_____

_____

_____

Sometimes it is easier to think of God as an all-powerful righteous judge than as a tender, merciful parent. Why do you think it can be difficult to comprehend God's mercy? _____

_____

_____

_____

Responding to children's cues also helps them to learn an inner feeling of rightness, which will become the basis of their Christian conscience. When parents help their children feel right much of the time, they know this feeling well and prefer it. Because they feel inwardly secure and trusted, it is easier for them to act right. It is also easier for you the parent to steer your child away from wrong tendencies before they turn into serious trouble. I have noticed through the years that children who are difficult to discipline are often very angry inside, and their behavior is a way of lashing out at a world that treats them unfairly. Children who have an inner sense of rightness can maintain their balance much better; while they will face problems along the way, they don't lose faith in themselves— or in God.

How can your relationship with Christ help you feel inner rightness as a parent? _____

_____

_____

_____

How will this carry over into your relationship with your children? _____

_____

_____

_____

What facets of your spiritual life need particular attention in order for you to be a better parent? _____

_____

_____

_____

Bringing God into your child's life. "When should I start to talk to my child about God? When can he understand? Should I bring God into my discipline?" Here are some tips for creating a rich spiritual life for your child and your whole family.

- Nourish your own spiritual life. Talking to your child about God will feel awkward unless you are conscious of God's working in your own daily life. Set aside a time for prayer and Bible study each day. Learn more about your faith. The knowledge will come in handy, sooner than you know. Children as young as three or four can pose difficult questions about God. ("Why did God make mosquitos?" "If you kept going higher and higher in the sky, when would you get to heaven?") Prepare for the interesting theological discussions ahead of you.

• Pray for your child daily. From the time you first suspect you are pregnant, ask for God's blessing on your child and your parenting. Acknowledge the Lord as the creator and protector of your unborn baby, and thank him for the gift of children. Laying your hand on the pregnant bulge, or on the downy head of your newborn is a beautiful way to connect with your child during prayer.

• Pray together daily as a family. Daily prayer is a vital part of Christian family discipline. It reminds everyone that God is a trusted and vital part of your household. Family prayer will help your toddler come to know God as someone we talk to readily every day, someone who Mommy and Daddy trust to love and protect us. Even before your child can verbalize his own prayers, he can probably understand something of yours. The Bible tells us that God hears even unspoken prayers of the heart, and surely he hears the prayers of a small child, even if parents cannot yet understand them.

• Establish family worship rituals. Saying grace before meals is probably the most common way for children and parents to join together in praising God. Toddlers enjoy these rituals tremendously. They sense prayer time is special when the mood of reverence descends, and they like to imitate their parents, folding their hands, joining their hands together, or lifting them in praise of God. Before you know it, your toddler will be reminding you to pray before meals, at home and at McDonald's. This is a wonderful witness to God's power in our lives. It's also a reminder that prayer is a joyful duty. One family we know has been known to say grace eight or ten times at the insistence of their toddler. She is especially enthusiastic about thanking God when the menu includes pizza.

• Sing with your children. Even before they can understand the words, children can enjoy "Jesus songs." Along with old standbys, such as "Jesus Loves Me," there are many new songs that you can learn together. Christian bookstores carry songbooks and cassette tapes that will bring music into your child's spiritual life. Children love songs with actions; make up gestures to go along with the words and perform these songs with your toddler.

- Model to your child the importance of the Bible. Even a one-year-old can grasp the important connection that the book Mommy and Daddy are always holding must be special. We noticed that our one-year-olds would start carrying around their little Bibles and even mimic us reading the Bible. *Bible* was among one of the early entries on the list of each baby's words. The infant first concludes this book must be important to Mom and Dad; therefore, the baby wants one too. The next conclusion is if the book is important, the Author is important too.

- Read books about God to your child. Children love to look at books, especially in the coziness of a parent's lap. A Bible storybook with simple, attractive pictures is a good place to start. At first, you might just talk about the pictures, pointing out Jesus and telling your child that Jesus is someone special. Later, the child will be ready to hear the story, either read from the page or told by you in simpler words. Your child may also enjoy books that relate Jesus to his daily life.

- Celebrate Christian festivals with your child. Christmas and Easter and other church festivals provide opportunities for teaching even young children about Christ. Even toddlers understand the idea of Baby Jesus, especially if you have a nativity set that they can handle and rearrange. Two-year-olds can celebrate Jesus' birthday with a cake and candles. Easter customs such as dyeing eggs, forcing flower branches into bloom, or baking hot cross buns may be harder to interpret for a young child, but incorporating them into your family celebration now lays a foundation for talking about Jesus in years to come.

- If your child was dedicated or baptized as an infant, celebrate this anniversary as well as his birthday. Some churches give parents a candle to light every year to help the child commemorate his baptism. On Sundays when there is a dedica-

THE NEW BABY PLANNER

tion or a baptism in church, remind your child of his own special day and show him pictures of this special occasion.

- Teach your child to pray his own prayers. Besides traditional prayers, help your child pray his own original prayers, especially at bedtime. Talk about the things he has done that day, ask him what he'd like to talk to Jesus about, and sum up his concerns in a simple one- or two-sentence prayer. He can pray along with you silently, or try the repeat-after-me technique used by Christian preschool teachers; you say a few words, and the child repeats each phrase after you. For example, "Dear Jesus, thank you for my new truck. Help Grandpa feel better soon. Amen."

- Incorporate Jesus into your discipline. As your child learns more about Jesus, talk about how Jesus wants us to act and what makes Jesus happy or sad. A scripture that we find helpful to paraphrase frequently is Ephesians 4:32: "Be kind to one another." Alternate paraphrasing may be more to the point: "Jesus says, 'Do not hit (kick, push, tease, etc.) one another.' "

- Above all, teach your child that Jesus loves him and will take care of him. When one of our children does get hurt, we pray with him for God's comfort and healing, and we make sure to thank God for his protection in the situation. Some of our children have been a bigger challenge to their guardian angel than others!

Someday, parents, you will be called to answer before God for your child's spiritual upbringing. You must actively teach your child about God in your home; this is not a responsibility that can be left up to pastors or Sunday school teachers. Your child's faith will be shaped by your moral example, by your daily prayer habits, and by your frequent talks with him about Jesus. Remember that your child, in turn, will be a spiritual example to your grandchildren, so the effectiveness of your teaching will be felt through succeeding generations.

The pay-off. Your ministry to your children will bear fruit in your own life. Being conscious of modeling Christ for your children can become the motivation and the model for your own spiritual discipline that will strengthen your faith and increase your reliance on God. The lessons of patience, selfless giving, and understanding that are learned through parenthood will make you a more effective minister to others in the years to come.

Your children will minister to you as they grow, and their child-like trust in God will be an example to you when your own faith becomes bogged down in the distractions of the grown-up world. Children who have learned to know and love God can bring amazing clarity to crisis situations, even though the adults may be fumbling around, unwilling or unable to see the light. In times of grief or fear, your child's witness can return you to the foundation of God's promises: "I know I'll see Grandpa in heaven" or "Jesus will take care of us." These are moments when your heart will leap for joy, knowing that God is truly at work in your parenting.

INDEX

ABOUT THE AUTHORS

William Sears, M.D., is the author of sixteen books on child care and is the father of eight children. He is Assistant Professor of Pediatrics at the University of Southern California School of Medicine. He is a regular contributor to many national magazines such as *Redbook* and *Baby Talk* and has been a guest on over 100 television shows. His previous books include *The Baby Book, Creative Parenting, Nighttime Parenting, The Fussy Baby, 300 Questions New Parents Ask,* and *Parenting and Child Care.*

Martha Sears, R.N. is a registered nurse with twenty years experience working with parents. She and her husband, William, co-authored *The Baby Book* and have appeared on "20/20," "Donahue," "The Home Show," and "The Montel Williams Show." She and her husband have eight children.